BAD KID

HARPER ⚫ PERENNIAL

NEW YORK • LONDON • TORONTO • SYDNEY • NEW DELHI • AUCKLAND

BAD KID

A MEMOIR

DAVID CRABB

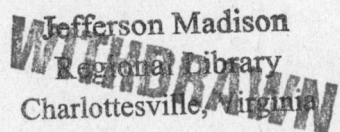

FIRST EDITION

Designed by Michael Correy

Library of Congress Cataloging-in-Publication Data has been applied for.

ISBN 978-0-06-237128-7

15 16 17 18 19   ov/rrd   10 9 8 7 6 5 4 3 2 1

For Teri, Leonard, Greg, Sylvia & Max
You know who you are. I'm glad I do too.

BAD KID

Bigmouth Strikes Again

I want to start by telling you that this is a work of nonfiction. I've written about these kids, clubs, fights and parties the way I've remembered them, to the best of my ability. But I also need to apologize for something.

I'm sorry I did so many drugs. And when I say "drugs" I don't mean little puffs of weed in college dormitories or occasional bumps of coke off a key in a nightclub bathroom. I mean huge, mind-altering, gobs of XTC. I'm talking about sheets . . . no, reams of acid.

As a broke teenager I often had to work with a limited budget. I huffed gasoline, snorted poppers, inhaled Liquid Paper fumes, and ate heaps of over-the-counter speed sold to sleepy, long-haul truckers at gas stations. Sometimes I wonder if I didn't do less drugs than I think I did. Then I realize that not remembering probably means I did a lot, which is part of the reason that some of the names, identities, hair colors, concert t-shirts, and piercing-types in this book have been changed. I've also done this in order to protect the anonymity of the bad kids I've known, most of whom have grown up to raise families, have successful careers, and join PTA groups, which is probably as shocking to them as is it to me.

In some cases, composite characters have been created to further preserve privacy and decrease the number of black-clad kids in combat boots roaming the pages before you. I hope that if you crack the code and recognize yourself in this book, you feel that I've appropriately documented your bad behavior. I would hate to shame people for the *wrong* awful things. You shouldn't have to feel embarrassed for running around a cemetery naked in a pig mask on uppers when you were actually the one on mushrooms who ate a bar of soap during a seance.

Though the conversations in this book come from my keen recollection of them, I am not a robot. There is not a black box recorder installed in my belly. And if there were, the amount of LSD I ingested between the ages of sixteen and eighteen would probably have fried it. These exchanges in nightclubs, locker rooms, and tiny Texas apartments are not written as word-for-word documentation. But I hope I've retold them in a way that evokes the sidesplitting, crush-inducing, heartbreaking essence of the wonderfully colorful people I have known.

Also, several time lines have been altered, mostly to protect privacy and maintain narrative flow. And also because I might not remember how we got from point A to point B, but I remember how we got from point C to point D and made a switch. Maybe we were friends in high school and you're thinking, "Hey! I didn't ride with you to Amarillo in the back of a taco truck with a drag queen. I drove you in my Miata to Waco on LSD! You got it mixed up."

I'm sorry for that, but I also want to congratulate you on your superior memory.

I also need to apologize to my poor, belabored parents.

I'm not sure how far you'll make it through this book before chucking it in the garbage and joining a support group. Well, *another* support group. But as the substance abuse, occult activity, and raw sexual obsession detailed in these pages gets to be too much for you, it might help to tell yourselves that I wrote this simply for the money.

In truth, I wrote *Bad Kid* because I'm a storyteller, and I want to touch people and make them feel understood. I hope this book can be entertaining as a personal narrative but also be universal enough to make readers feel connected to something larger than themselves, regardless of their background and upbringing.

But if you're a member of my family and find these tales psychologically distressing, just go with the "he did it for the money" angle. Remind yourselves that I have an absurd amount of student loans, and although Sallie Mae might sound like an innocent farm girl with pigtails, she's actually a heartless bitch in shoulder-pads who's been trying to ruin my life ever since I graduated. If it were up to her, I'd be rich and dead.

So as you read these harrowing tales, rejoice in knowing that I'll probably be able to buy my own plane ticket home for Christmas this year!

I'm sorry about the wigs. Or lack thereof.

This book is based on my solo show "Bad Kid." We got one negative review from an older, gay writer who was perturbed with the lack of videos, costume changes, and . . . wigs.

Yes. Seriously.

Wigs.

He was also upset that my experience of coming out was so "easy." I found the wig comment so hilarious that I initially glossed over this statement. But then I thought more about it.

As a thirty-nine-year-old man, shouldn't my experience of coming out be different than that of a fifty-five-to-sixty-year-old person? That's around a twenty-year gap. I can't imagine the struggles of gay men in the sixties who had no one to talk to, men who were forced into heterosexual marriages by their terrified mothers and fathers, men with children whose lives were torn apart as their fathers drank, disappeared, or came out of the closet and were forced from their lives.

The only experience I can truly know is my own. And that's what I've written about. I will not justify it or defend its worth based on some generational scale of comparative sadness. It was hard for me and the people I called friends. Just as it was hard for kids forty years ago. And by no means is it over.

It's hard for teenagers now. But I'm happy that many of them live in a world where they can be out, find LGBT resources in their schools, and see gay and lesbian role models in their media. I'm happy that they can fall in love with someone they care about right out in the open and consider a legally recognized marriage. Thinking about all of this in relation to my own teen experience takes my breath away. I can't believe I'm seeing this come to pass in my lifetime.

Of course, there are people who would argue vehemently against this rosy-colored view of things. I can't know what the life of a fifteen-year-old closeted lesbian in the heart of the Bible Belt is like, because that's not part of my experience. And for her, at least for now, it's still a difficult struggle.

All I can know is my own story. And this is it.

Sans wigs.

The pickles.

I'm so very sorry for the pickles. It's too much to get into here. But believe me, when you hit that part of the book, you'll certainly know you're there. Mom. Dad. If you even make it to this part of the book, please remember that whole money-thing I mentioned earlier.

See you at Christmas!

I'm sorry to my friends who are gone. I'm sorry if I wasn't there when you needed me. I'm sorry that we lost touch. I'm sorry if the world hurt you. I'm sorry if the people you loved abandoned you. I'm sorry if the drugs we took together in a spirit of youthful fun became something that damaged your life. I'm sorry for all the pain you never let me know about. But I'm not sorry about forgetting you. Because that will never happen.

I miss you every day.

And to all my dear friends who are still here, thanks for the amazing time. Hating the world would've been a lot less fun without you in it. Thanks for reminding me that shame is bad, fun is good, and that if we believe enough, every day can be like Halloween.

Superheroes

What in God's name is that?" asked my grandma Oggy, tucking a used Kleenex into the cuff of her shirt. It was the summer before eighth grade and my dad had just taken us downtown for a birthday barbecue. At a red light in front of the Alamo she'd seen something shocking.

"Well, I'll be," said my dad, turning down his Merle Haggard cassette as he peered through the windshield.

I peeked around the driver's seat and saw them in the crosswalk: three teenagers wearing layers of black clothes and heavy eyeliner. My grandmother fluffed up her snow-white perm with a hair-pick and leaned forward. "Look at the mop on that poor girl's head!" she said, chomping on a piece of Juicy Fruit. "Looks like she stuck a fork in a light socket."

There's really nothing sadder than goth kids in a warm-weather climate. The day's record-breaking heat made them look like smeared watercolors, a moist wad of painted pleather rolling in slow motion across the pavement. It was the *Abbey Road* cover that time ignored, the one Edvard Munch would have painted.

The girl leading the group wore a heavy velveteen gown marked with sweat circles around her neck and armpits. The hem of it dragged against the cement, collecting bits of garbage and cigarette butts as she morosely Swiffered her way across the street. Manic Panic hair dye dripped from her hairline, turning her forehead violet.

The little guy behind her had a Mohawk that collapsed over the front of his face, making him look like a depressed rooster. His floor-length cape blew out like a sail as it caught a gust of hot wind, lightly noosing him with its drawstring.

In the back of the group was a tall, ghost-white boy with bleached bangs, wearing a purple sateen jacket. He walked regally in blue eye shadow and wore a single shell earring. He was a neon dream in matte finish with shiny peach lips.

My dad lowered his sunglasses, his eyes dancing with wonder. "Well, I'll be," he sighed. "They look like superheroes going to a funeral."

"I guess the circus is in town," drawled my grandma, peering at them suspiciously as she locked the car door. "Hide your children."

I watched them from the back window as we pulled away, black and purple dots getting smaller and smaller against the bright, beige South Texas terrain. As they floated into a sea of cowboy hats and tamale vendors, I felt like I'd seen something exotic and rare, like a unicorn—an extremely sad, very sexy, fishnet-bound unicorn.

They were the most amazing creatures I'd ever seen.

A good boy

CHAPTER 1

That Joke Isn't Funny Anymore

Towards the end of middle school I had what you might call a very "Christian missionary" fashion sense; pressed khaki slacks, a starched blue button-down, and lightly moussed hair parted on the side. I looked like a tiny, chubby cheeked, lesbian employee of Blockbuster Video. This was how I dressed during the last few months of eighth grade, after "the incident." Before "the incident" you would've seen me in a pastel Hypercolor shirt and Vision Street Wear high-tops. I'd be wearing neon-green, knee-length shorts, and my long, Sun-In'd bangs would hang down to the top of my Panama Jack sunglasses.

That all changed one day near the end of eighth grade. I was spending my lunch the usual way, French braiding my girlfriend Amber's hair. I'd been Amber's boyfriend for almost a month and *loved* spending lunches with her and the other girls from our theater arts class. Amber had beautiful strawberry-blond hair and smelled like SweeTARTS. She loved Taylor Dayne almost as much as I did and made me mixtapes adorned with hearts and stars drawn in hot-pink, watermelon-scented marker. Best of all, when we'd slow-danced at the chaperoned spring dance, she hadn't gotten handsy with me. Amber took it slow, and I appreciated that. What wasn't to love?

"Perfect," I said, tying a small pink ribbon to the end of Amber's hair.

"How is it?" she asked, flopping the ginger braid over her shoulder as she turned to me.

"You look so pretty," I gushed.

"You're the one who braided it," she beamed, popping a cherry jelly bean into my mouth.

"What about my hair?" I grinned.

"It looks so cool," she answered, reaching up to touch my newly bleached bangs. "Like those guys who skate in the parking lot after school."

"Thanks! My mom let me get it done in the mall last weekend. I think they're—"

"Chris Wolfe," she interrupted, grimacing at something over my head. "Don't you even think about it."

I turned to look at Chris, the tall, blond football player who gave me the same funny feeling I got watching Patrick Swayze in *Dirty Dancing*. But before I could lay my eyes on his tall, broad frame, my skull reverberated with a booming thud. Chris's deep voice was the last thing I heard before I blacked out.

I woke up on the tiled cafeteria floor with a pounding headache. As my vision cleared, I could make out Amber and the choir teacher, Ms. Mason, a heavyset woman with a tight black perm wearing a chili-pepper necklace and matching earrings. The room was slowly tilting and I couldn't get the sound of ringing out of my ears. I stood up with the help of my theater arts lunch-mates, a dozen teenage Florence Nightingales with glittering fingernails.

"Oh my gawd!" they cried, immediately swept up in the drama of it all.

"Chris Wolfe bashed your head between two big encyclopedias!" Amber sobbed as we walked to the office with Ms. Mason. "I couldn't stop him in time!" she continued, hugging her hot-pink Trapper Keeper, which bore the image of Pegasus leaping through a crystal heart. The theater arts girls surrounded Amber in a vanilla-scented cloud as she cried. The drama was suddenly all about her. "Chris called you . . . He called you a . . . a . . ."

Amber leaned in and whispered the name of the thing I'd been trying to convince myself I wasn't. For most of eighth grade I'd been telling myself that the warm fuzzies I felt watching *Silver Spoons* were simply about Ricky Schroder's awesome clothes. When Kirk Cameron made a funny joke on *Growing Pains* and my pants suddenly tightened in the crotch, I told myself that it wasn't about kissing him. I just wanted to hug him really, *really* hard. But as I left Amber and walked into the school office, my doubts were stronger than ever.

After getting an aspirin from the nurse, I sat outside the school reception area, waiting to be picked up by my mom. Directly across from me sat Chris Wolfe. He stared at the floor, his body trembling so rapidly that the movement was almost indiscernible, like a flickering fluorescent tube light right before it burns out. He was also waiting to go home, but presumably not to be pampered by his mother with cocoa while watching a four-hour marathon of *Saved by the Bell* like I was.

"Leonard Crabb?" called the boy working office duty.

I'd forgotten my dad was in town. I assumed my mom had called him, unable to leave her job. My small, stocky father charged to the front desk, moving with the force and purpose of a linebacker. He was wearing tight Wrangler jeans, snakeskin cowboy boots, and a trucker hat. Passing by, he noticed me, and all that anger switched to sadness and concern. He didn't say a word, but his eyes said it all.

Are you okay?

Does it hurt?

I love you son.

Now show me where that little fucker is.

I wanted to point across the room and say, *There he is, Dad. He's the one. Go nuts.*

But he would have. And as pleasing as it would have been to watch him eviscerate Chris Wolfe, I preferred visiting with my father at Mexican restaurants, not prisons. As my father's gaze slipped away from me, his face hardened. He leaned on the counter and slammed down his wallet, like a gunslinger saying, "Let's go hand-to-hand, you son of a bitch."

"Who would you like to see, sir?" asked the nervous student attendant.

In a slow, measured baritone, my father growled, "Whoever's in charge."

"Um. Yes, sir," the boy's voice cracked. "Um . . . I'll get you the assistant principal."

"You go ahead and *do that*."

I was happy to have a protective dad, but I felt bad for the administrators who were about to deal with his wrath. I'd seen that face on other occasions: when a bad report card came in, when I forgot to weed-whack the yard, and many times during my regrettable two-month stint playing right field. It wasn't pleasant.

I looked at the bully across from me and hoped he knew how lucky he was that my dad hadn't realized who he was. But as I watched Chris apprehensively wringing his hands, I felt strangely sympathetic toward him. He was right in assuming I was "different," which somehow made him seem less guilty. A part of me wanted to tell him it was okay, that he was just perceptive to my flaws and defects. If I could understand exactly how Chris perceived me, maybe I could change all my suspect behaviors.

"Chris?" I said.

When Chris lifted his head, I saw that he wasn't scared at all. He was angry. I could hear the rhythmic jingling of change in his pocket as his Reebok sneaker maniacally tapped the linoleum tiles. He popped the knuckles of one hand and slid it into a fist in the other. As he stared at me, his lips made the silent shape of that word I'd been emotionally dodging.

"Come on, David," called my dad as he came out of the office.

I looked over my shoulder as we left to see Chris still glaring at me, mouthing that word again and again. I wanted to punch him. I wanted to punch him really, *really* hard.

In the car on the way home my dad asked me twenty questions about my girlfriend, trying to raise my spirits after what had happened. I wasn't sure if he knew what Chris had called me. But I didn't want to know if he did. I didn't want to talk at all. I just wanted the summer to come so the two of us could go on our annual road trip in his Winnebago. For two weeks we'd drive through the country to different sites for my dad's work as a fiber-optic technician. In two months I'd be in new places surrounded by new people who had no idea who I was. I couldn't wait.

That Saturday morning I awoke to my mother knocking at my bedroom door. My mom, Teri, was a tiny, red-haired woman from Newfoundland, Canada. Her bizarre accent, Dolly Parton–like figure, and fire-orange hair made her stick out in San Antonio like a busy, busty leprechaun.

"Honey," she sweetly warned, covering her eyes as the door opened. "Are you decent?"

"Mom," I said, rubbing my eyes, "I was only sleeping. What could I be doing at 7:30 in the morning?"

"Well, sweetie," she sighed, sitting on the edge of the bed, "you're becoming a young man and I want to respect not only your privacy but also your changing body."

"Oh God, Mom. We're not having a 'talk' now, are we? It's so early."

"I just wanted to make sure you felt okay," she said, reaching out to feel the small lump Chris Wolfe had left on my temple. "Do you want to come into work with me today?"

"Which work?" I asked, wondering which of my single mom's three jobs she was going to that day. "The maternity store, the arcade, or the rape crisis center?"

Saying yes would mean spending the day with pregnant women, abused women, or Frogger.

"Where do you think?" she smiled.

Thirty minutes later we were at the mall, opening the giant metal gate of the Genie's Castle arcade with Teri's coworker Annie, a nineteen-year-old heavy-metal chick with a blond buzz cut and purple eye shadow. Annie was tall, thin, and covered in leather, like a young Brigitte Nielsen costumed for a *Blade Runner* sequel. In the half hour before the mall opened, as Annie chain-smoked and wiped down the machines, my mom gave me as many credits as I wanted on the music-video jukebox, which controlled the arcade's sound track. I pulled out the crumpled list of songs I'd heard on the radio that week and proceeded to load up the machine with so many music videos that no one would be hearing their requests until well after lunchtime.

At 10 a.m. the mall rats started pouring in: heavy-metal kids and punk weirdos with dirty mullets and filthy denim vests. As they moped around in their Dokken shirts playing Centipede and Donkey Kong, I could sense their slow-building rage at my music-video selections—Taylor Dayne, Rick Astley, Lisa Lisa, and Cult Jam. This was my music, a brand of song completely free of guitar, piano, or any organic instrumentation whatsoever—dance pop by single-named artists like Madonna, Martika, and Pebbles. Songs with high-energy choruses and backup singers who commanded the listener to "sweat," "dance," and "FEEL IT!" These were the tracks played during mid-'80s movie montages in which a ragtag group of inner-city youths in fingerless gloves completely renovated a roller-skating rink while breakdancing.

In the arcade I felt alive, exuberant, and invincible. I could have stayed there for hours, shuffling my feet to the frenetic beat of Janet Jackson or Bananarama. I had endless lives and endless credits, thanks to my mom, the queen of Genie's Castle. And I was its prince.

By noon I was two hours into a marathon game of Joust when

a zit-covered fifteen-year-old in a Guns N' Roses cap walked up to me. I was in the zone, midreverie to Belinda Carlisle's "Heaven Is a Place on Earth," when he interrupted.

"So . . . you fuckin' LIKE this music?"

"Why?" I asked, wondering how he knew it was my request.

"Fucking look at you," he hissed, eyeing my clothes. I looked down at what I was wearing, wondering what was so wrong with it. My electric-blue cargo shorts were clean and unwrinkled. My sneakers were a bit dirty, but the laces were tied. And my hair was—not to brag—perfect. My lightly bleached bangs fell, slightly obscuring the outside of my left eye, just as I'd requested during my last hair appointment at Fantastic Sams.

"We can all see you wiggling over here like a fairy," he smirked, gesturing to a group of three older boys watching us from across the arcade. "You know what you are?"

"Excuse me?" I asked, swallowing nervously at the thought of what was coming.

"You're a faggot."

I froze.

"You don't even like pussy," he whispered in my face, so close I could smell the Fritos on his breath. He puckered his lips into a wrinkled kissy mouth and made wet slurping sounds as Joust alerted me that my player had died. "Are you gonna say anything, faggot?"

I wanted to defend myself, because I wasn't a faggot. A faggot was a guy who lisped and giggled and walked everywhere with a limp wrist. A faggot was a grown man who acted like a lady and loved flowers and dancing. Faggots were on the news at night—older men with mustaches who lived in New York and San Francisco and were getting sick.

I wasn't a faggot. I was a fourteen-year-old boy who had never kissed anyone, let alone a man. Maybe I'd thought about it, but I didn't *do* anything about it. And if I didn't *do* gay things, how could I *be* a gay person?

I put my head down and slunk away as the kid yelled one last thing.

"Your hair makes you look like a fuckin' gaywad!"

His friends laughed as I stormed into the office and sat down next to Annie, who was complaining about her boyfriend while cleaning one of the dozen tiny hoop earrings in her left ear.

"Honey, what's wrong?" my mother asked.

"Nothing," I snipped, noticing Annie's snacks laid out on the office desk. "I just want some Goldfish."

I started to eat handfuls of the little orange crackers, as if the mass of them in my mouth would help soak up the tears in my eyes. It seemed to work. This was when I realized how hard it is to cry while you're eating.

"Mom, I wanna go home."

"Well, honey, I don't get off for a few hours. Don't you want to play more games?"

My mom reached into her saggy blue uniform vest and pulled out a handful of tokens. They looked so shiny and tempting in her hand. I could listen to so many Kylie Minogue songs with those tokens.

"I feel sick," I pouted, unwilling to share Kylie's "Locomotion" with the jerks out on the arcade floor. "I want to go home."

"I can drop him off," Annie offered. "I get outta here at one o'clock. Right, Teri?"

"Sure," my mom shrugged, pushing back my bleach-blond bangs to kiss my forehead. "I sure wish you'd tell me what's wrong."

An hour later I was on my way home in Annie's dirty brown Camaro. At a red light she lit a cigarette and retouched her maroon lips in the rearview mirror.

"So who was an asshole to you?" she yelled over the Ozzy Osbourne tune blasting from the tape deck.

"No one," I murmured.

"What?!" she screamed, turning down the stereo with her free hand.

"No one," I repeated, staring into the distance with my arms crossed.

"Well, *someone* pissed you off."

"Just some . . . jerk!" I yelled, punching the door.

"There ya go!" she said, flipping up her middle finger and grinning. "Fuck 'em!"

I hadn't yet grasped casual profanity, and the idea of it sent me into a fit of laughter.

"David! I'm serious," she snapped disapprovingly as the light turned green. "The next time someone says shit to you, tell 'em to fuck off. Okay? I want you to say it!"

"Say what?" I asked.

"Say, 'Fuck off!' "

"You want me to say . . . *that?*"

"Oh, lighten up. I'm not gonna tell your mom," she said, lighting a new cigarette off the one that was almost out. "Just fucking say it!"

I gathered my courage as we flew down the highway, taking a long, thoughtful pause in preparation for my first attempt at swearing.

"FUCK OFF!" I howled at the top of my lungs.

"Jesus Christ," said Annie, flinching in the driver's seat. "You can bring the attitude without all the volume. Fuck!"

"Oh. Sorry," I muttered.

"Don't apologize," she said, rolling her eyes. "I just MADE you say it, dummy."

"Sorry," I said again.

"If you apologize one more time you're walking home," she warned, holding out her lit Marlboro to me. "Wanna drag?"

"Um, okay," I mumbled, reaching for the cigarette.

"What are you, stupid?" she said, stamping out the butt in the ashtray. "I'm fuckin' with you. Your mother would kill me."

Five minutes later we pulled up to my apartment complex. I shut the car door with a feeling of accomplishment. My new-found comfort with screaming profanity would surely come in handy when fighting off the mall rats and Chris Wolfes of the world.

As I turned from the car, Annie called me back. I leaned into the passenger window as she applied a thick layer of mascara in the rearview mirror.

"David, you know that two dudes kissing is wrong, right?" she asked, staring at her reflection. "Like, you know that shit's gross and against God, don't you?"

"Um . . ." I paused, watching her mouth make a funny shape as she opened her eyes wider for the lash wand. After a long pause I finally replied, "Yes?" as if my answer was a question.

"Good," she said, winking her gooey, tar-covered eyelash at me. She smiled, her nicotine-stained teeth looking jaundiced in the bright Texas sun. "See ya next weekend, kid."

Annie pulled away, leaving me in a thick gray cloud of exhaust. As the big, wooden Spanish Oaks Apartments sign swung in the breeze behind me, I'd never felt more confused. I shuffled into our apartment and fell back into my favorite Papasan chair.

For just a moment, the familiarity of our living room tricked me into feeling okay. I was protected, surrounded by my mother's country-craft motif: a decoupaged dresser, framed paintings of smiling, personified farm animals, and more bowls of potpourri than you could count.

Then I caught a glimpse of my hair in the mirror above the couch. I didn't look like the boys who skated in the parking lot behind school. And I didn't look like one of the cool inner-city youths who break-danced in the movies I loved.

I looked at myself and saw what everyone else was beginning to see: a faggot.

I ran into my mother's bathroom and pulled out a brown eyeliner pencil from her makeup case. Frantically, I pulled my bangs away from my forehead and began to drag the pencil up and down the blond strands of hair, trying to erase my ridiculous whim. In that panicked moment, I was blind to the absurdity of this temporary "fix." I pulled the fist of hair tighter as I scribbled harder, determined to darken them. I would put this away, just like I had put away so many things before: the Donna Summer records I'd loved when I was five; the Miss Piggy puppet I used to put a full face of makeup on when I was six; the "truth lasso" I'd run around with, pretending to be Wonder Woman, when I was seven; the collection of puffy unicorn stickers I'd had when was eight; all the charcoal sketches of Madonna I'd drawn when I was ten . . .

Slowly, as my platinum hairs became darker, I started to relax. Once the blond eventually disappeared, I felt better.

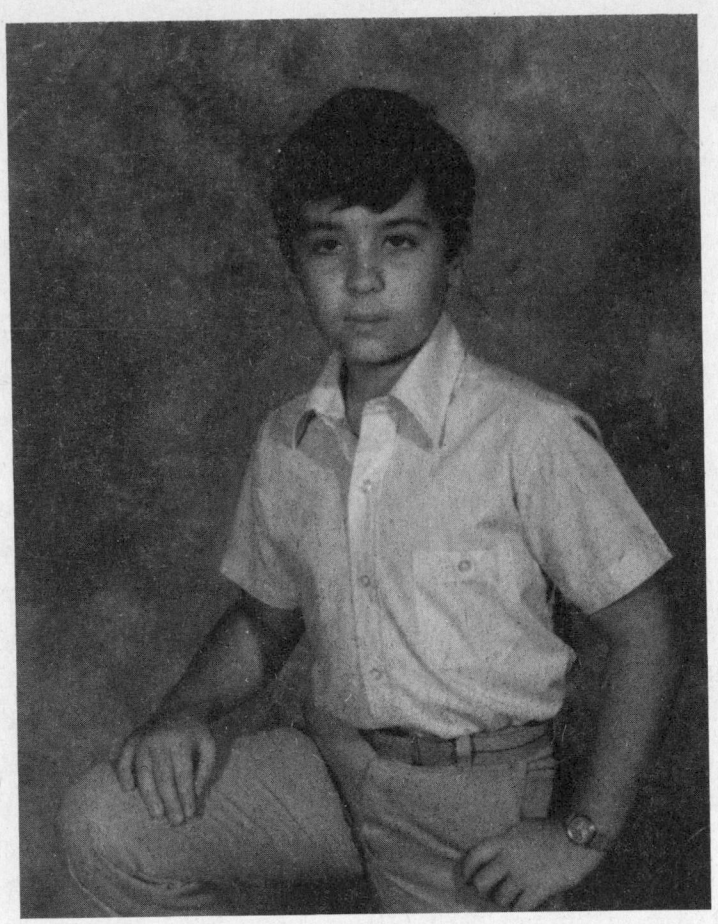

Pop Quiz:

A. A young Mormon missionary

B. Tiny lesbian health inspector

C. Baby Captain Morgan

It's funny how the best attempts at hiding can make you stand out more than anything.

CHAPTER 2

Father Figure

Really, sweetie?" asked my mother, puzzled by the selection of drab clothes resting over my forearm. "*These* are the clothes you want for summer?"

"Yup," I replied, tossing a pile of tan slacks in front of the JCPenney cashier.

"Well," she said, fingering a stack of soft cotton white T-shirts, "everything is just a bit . . . dull. Don't you think?"

"Nope," I answered flatly.

"Do you think Amber will like these outfits?" she cooed with a knowing grin.

"She's not my girlfriend anymore," I huffed.

"Oh no, honey. Why didn't you tell your mother? What happened?"

"She broke up with me," I huffed, grabbing the bag of clothes.

"Oh, sweetie . . ." my mother gushed, her consoling lecture fading behind me as I stomped ahead of her through the mall.

"Time heals all wounds," she comforted me on the drive home. "It's Amber's loss, *not* yours."

But in truth, Amber hadn't dumped me. I'd dumped her. Well, not dumped so much as avoided. In the weeks following the Chris Wolfe incident, Amber had left a dozen strawberry-scented notes in my locker, each one asking where I'd been at lunch. I read her letters each day behind the gym, where I'd taken to eating my bologna sandwich alone by an enormous, humming air-conditioning unit.

"Are you mad at me, David?" she wrote in pastel bubbles, dotting the *I* in my name with a broken pink heart.

What I couldn't tell Amber was that I'd learned an important lesson from Chris Wolfe: stay out of the way. If no one noticed me, then no one could demean my sense of fashion, question my ball-throwing expertise, or bash my head in with encyclopedias. So in the hopes of achieving relative anonymity, I shoved my paint-splattered sneakers and Hypercolor T-shirts to the back of my closet. For the last few weeks of eighth grade I would lie low by wearing flat-front khakis and denim button-downs, no matter how boring my mother thought they were. Feeling safe required disappearing, and disappearing meant being alone.

In the mornings I'd jump the fence and walk to campus the back way, through the empty athletics field. After school I'd linger by my locker for ten extra minutes to avoid kids chatting in the courtyard. I quickly learned how to camouflage, unlike some of my bookish, bespectacled, overweight peers, kids who actually had the audacity to participate in after-school clubs and eat their lunches out in the open. Once I disappeared, I wasn't accosted the way they were. With all my careful planning and covert activity, I thought I was beating bullying. But really, bullying was beating me. It wasn't the confrontation that was isolating me, but the threat of it.

By the end of the school year I'd grown a second brain that constantly monitored my behavior: checking every pronunciation for a lispy *S*, reminding me not to hum Paula Abdul too loudly, and taking note of my posture at all times to ensure I wasn't resting on my hip. When I wasn't monitoring myself, I was monitoring everyone else, especially boys—figuring out what mimicked social cues would keep me safe until 4 p.m., when I was home safe in my bedroom, voguing.

On the last day of school we gathered to hear our principal's "have a nice summer" send-off. In the center of the auditorium I felt stifled, surrounded by five hundred people I'd been trying to avoid for two months. Three rows ahead sat Amber, who slowly turned her head until our eyes met. Across Amber's back stretched the long, muscular arm of her new boyfriend, Chris Wolfe. Amber stared at me with a disappointed, vacant expression. Her eyes seemed to say, *Look what you made me do*, as if the pecking order of middle school had forced her to take Chris's hand. I felt a little guilty about it, knowing I'd made her an eighth-grade widow of sorts. But mainly I felt betrayed. I was so angry at Amber that I even hated her hair, which hung limply in a messy braid that looked terrible.

Look at what you've done to yourself! I wanted to scream. *He'll never treat your hair as well as I did!*

Fifteen minutes later the bell rang, signaling the end of my tenure as a middle-school student. As I left the auditorium, I noticed Chris and his friends. He smirked at me as one of his buddies whispered in his ear. And then I heard that word again, slipping quietly from between Chris's lips.

It was impossible to pretend that it was for anyone but me. I lowered my head and moved on, reminding myself that I was only a few days away from the isolated safety of my summer road trip with my dad. Soon I'd be far away from San Antonio. And the mall. And Chris Wolfe. Soon they would all be out of the picture. And no one would call me that name ever again.

"COCKSUCKER!" my dad screamed at the truck in his rearview mirror.

We were somewhere in northern Alabama, only one day into our two-week road trip. But my dad's temper had already reached a fever pitch.

"Look at this jerk on my ass," he sneered, gripping the steering wheel so tightly that I could see the veins in his fingers throb. Our thirty-two-foot Winnebago rocked back and forth as my father pumped the brakes, thrusting my neck repeatedly against the high-riding seatbelt. "How you like that, you son of a bitch?"

Not at all, I wanted to answer.

The 18-wheeler behind us screeched around us and pulled ahead. As the driver swerved into our lane and began manically pumping his brakes, I noticed the truck's mud flaps, which bore the silhouettes of two giant-breasted women with their legs wrapped around rifles. Leonard laid on his horn and raised his middle finger. "Fuck you!"

Mind you, the window was rolled up the entire time. So my dad was really just screaming at me. And that was the problem with my father's fits of anger: they felt aimed at me even when I knew they weren't. As we jerked around the highway, a pile of books spilled from the dashboard.

"Dammit!" he yelled as they fell into my lap. "Now I'll lose my place!"

"It's okay, Dad," I said, saving the page marks in as many of them as I could. "Wow. How many are you reading now?"

"Too goddamn many!" he barked, his bellowing drawl and massive belt buckle at odds with the titles in my hands: Einstein's *The World As I See It*, *The Complete Essays of Mark Twain*, and Stephen Hawking's *A Brief History of Time*. My dad was a voracious reader of philosophy, astronomy, and theology, equal parts classic and progressive, a mix I'd known was rare and singular ever since I was a little kid. My dad and I could chat for hours about solar systems, dog psychology, and the existence of God, all while listening to Hank Williams and eating Taco Bell. Talking to the secret philosopher in my dad made me feel like it was okay to ask questions that didn't have finite answers. But in this moment, the secret philosopher was losing to the raving psycho. And as the 18-wheeler sped away from us, there *was* a finite answer: punch stuff.

"Asshole!" he sneered, pounding the steering wheel.

"Hey Dad!" I chirped merrily, snapping into damage-control mode. "Let's see what's on the radio."

I casually turned on the stereo, trying to make a big show out of shrugging off the offending big-rig driver. As my dad settled down, so did the speedometer. I cracked the window to let in fresh air as the song on the radio crept into the foreground. I leaned forward and turned up the volume as a rush of funky keyboards, whipping snare drums, and sexy male vocals oozed from the speakers.

What's your definition of dirty, baby?
What do you consider pornography?

"What is this crap?" growled my dad, quickly changing the channel. Rosanne Cash replaced the sexy little earworm, but not before it had lodged itself in my head.

The next day we stopped at a strip mall for supplies. While my dad went into Walmart for underwear and RV-safe toilet paper, I slipped into the music store. I approached a new-wave chick with big hoop earrings and flame-red hair in a Sam Goody apron.

"Welcome to Sam Goody. I'm Susan," she droned with a far-away, bored expression. "What can I help you with?"

"Well, uh . . . I'm looking for a song."

"Okaaaaay," she groaned, smacking her bright-blue bubble-gum, "which one?"

"Well, I don't know what it's called. I just heard it on the radio."

"Sing it to me."

I paused. And then, with all the swanky verve I could muster, I sang:

What's your definition of dirty, baby?
What do you consider porn—

Before I could finish, she gripped my arm with pulverizing force. "Oh my God!" she beamed. "That's George Michael! I LOVE HIM!"

Breathlessly, she dragged me to the front of the shop. There it was: a giant display of George Michael's *Faith* album and assorted paraphernalia: twelve-inch singles, posters, T-shirts, and, towering above it all, a slightly larger-than-life cardboard cutout of George Michael. His distressed denim jeans were torn to shreds, his leather jacket fit like a glove, and his frosted hair defied gravity, tousled on his head like strands of spun gold.

As Susan rang me up, she couldn't stop gushing about the album, describing song-by-song the experience of listening to the record. She bounced, screamed, and giggled, all the while clutching the CD in her hands.

"And you have to get this too!" she yelped, sliding a copy of Andy Warhol's *Interview* magazine across the counter. "There's a tubular photo spread of him in here. He's so cool!"

As we talked, I realized that Susan was the kind of girl whose hair I could brush for hours. As she handed me the receipt, I noticed my dad watching us from the front of the store. I cringed as he flashed me a pearly grin and a big thumbs-up. As I walked out, Susan waved good-bye, genuinely excited that she could bring George Michael into my world. Over his shoulder, my dad tipped his cap to her.

"She's a real beauty," he whispered, patting me on the back. "You love them redheads, huh? A chip off the old block."

In the car I slipped the CD into my Discman, put on my headphones, and skipped to track 3- "I Want Your Sex."

SEX is natural—SEX is good
Not everybody does it
But everybody should

I had never heard the word *sex* so many times in four minutes. But that was only the beginning. Over the next forty-five minutes, *Faith* revealed itself to be an album filled with thrusting grunts, come-hither wails, and a dozen calls to intimacy; its protagonists were teachers, preachers, and uptown boys who were all desperately horny, each one pleading to be "warm and naked at my side."

I listened to *Faith* five times in a row while flipping through *Interview*, the cosmopolitan culture magazine based in New York City. It was full of artists and filmmakers I'd never heard of. There were fashion spreads in which, ironically, the models wore hardly anything at all. The best section was in the back—the party pages, which were full of glamorous people posing with cocktails like sexy mannequins. I read about Calvin Klein's daughter's jungle-themed sweet sixteen on the observation deck of the Empire State Building. David Bowie and Iman were there, laughing with pink champagne. Grace Jones deejayed, wearing yellow contact lenses and a barbed-wire dress. A group of cigarette-smoking women with gaunt faces and blunt bangs were captioned as "gallerists." I wasn't sure who they were. But surely they were important; they were in the party pages!

I scanned the magazine, carefully angling a photo-essay of LA street hustlers modeling thongs away from my dad as he excitedly described a chapter of Carl Sagan's *Cosmos*.

"See, scientists had thought that black holes were just empty space, but it's quite the opposite . . ."

I couldn't pay attention. Outside the window was a wasteland of strip malls and hill country. But in my lap was a secret world—ninety glossy pages full of artists, junkies, fashionistas, club kids, and . . . gay people. Looking at *Interview* while humming "Father Figure" to myself for the umpteenth time, I began to feel the crotch of my pants tighten.

"What Sagan's theory of black holes does is, it reframes the way science . . ."

My dad was droning on about something I really wanted to be interested in, and normally would have been. But as I looked at a muscle-bound European model in wet jeans lying on a bare mattress, it became impossible to hold my focus. There was a supernova in my pants.

"Even light can't escape a black hole because of the gravitational pull of—"

"Um, Dad?" I squeaked, "I gotta go to the bathroom."

"Are you all right, DJ?"

"Yeah," I said over my shoulder, rushing to the bathroom with *Interview* magazine over my crotch. In the minutes that followed, I discovered that spanking the monkey in a three-by-four-foot lavatory traveling seventy miles an hour was no small feat. But for the next forty-eight hours, in spite of the challenging environment, I was a trouper. I spent so much time in the loo over those next two days that my father eventually presented me with a bottle of Pepto-Bismol.

"Life on the road can be sedentary, son," he said with great wisdom. "Sometimes you don't know if you're coming or going. This should help."

"Thanks, Dad," I said, allowing my father to believe I was plagued with intestinal distress. It seemed far less upsetting that the truth: that his son was masturbating ten times a day a few feet away while listening to George Michael and staring at Marky Mark in boxer briefs.

Four days and thirty orgasms later, my father worriedly mentioned taking me to a local emergency room for my "gastro issues." It was time to accept that I was losing control. So I made a concerted effort to curb my chicken-choking by focusing on my summer reading assignment. George Orwell's *1984* is a difficult read for anyone, especially a pubescent, gay fourteen-year-old passing through truck-stop parking lots where shirtless truckers give themselves sponge baths. But abstaining from reading *Interview* and switching out *Faith* for Paula Abdul's far less provocative *Forever Your Girl* seemed to be working. I was going to show my penis who was boss.

But my dominance was short-lived. A week into our trip, I noticed the edge of a magazine under a stack of toilet-paper rolls beneath the bathroom sink. I pulled out the August 1987 issue of *Penthouse* magazine and was flabbergasted. This issue was different from the others I'd seen before at neighbor boys' houses. As opposed to a centerfold of a lone woman, this issue contained a spread of a woman *and* a man getting nasty on the beach. She wore big '80s sunglasses and a big '80s hat, and had big '80s areolas. They were the size of salad plates. The caption referred to her as Candy. Her male companion was swarthy and strapping. Lush locks of black hair hung into his dark, dusky eyes. The only thing covering any part of his muscular, caramel-skinned body was a tiny white G-string that was almost damp enough to see through.

Apparently the editors at *Penthouse* didn't think he deserved a name. But I did.

So I called him . . . Rolando.

I quickly became obsessed with every page of the photo spread, each image burning itself onto my brain like a molten-hot brand.

On page thirty-two Candy was awkwardly bent over a wheelbarrow. Rolando was taking her from behind, gripping her hips with his strong hands; his face was obscured by wet bangs that hung over his eyes. I looked at this image so many times that I started to question its minutiae.

Why there was a wheelbarrow on the beach? Was some beach worker transferring sand around with it? How could someone even operate a wheelbarrow in the sand?

On page thirty-four Candy was spread-eagled on a beach towel as Rolando mounted her missionary-style. Both of this dark stranger's firm, flexed butt cheeks bore the delicate, sandy handprint of his lover in perfect symmetry, a Rorschach butterfly of ass-hands.

Page thirty-seven was my favorite. Candy squatted in front of Rolando in platform heels, her big rump taking up most of the lower part of the page. Just above her head you could see Rolando's sweat-drenched torso, rock-hard abs, defined chest, and square jaw; and then, right above his perfectly shaped lips, the page ended.

Who was this man of mystery?

With no discernible face, he could be anyone: George Michael in reflective aviators and a crucifix earring, telling me "I want your sex" in the back of a London taxi; Ricky Schroder with gelled hair and tapered jeans, saying "I love you" as we rode a mini choo-choo train around his mansion; or Chris Wolfe with his sandy blond hair and Roman nose cornering me in the locker room, telling me he knew exactly how to make up for the encyclopedia incident. Rolando was my dream lover, everyone and no one.

With only a few days left in our two-week road trip, I knew I had to maximize my enjoyment of Rolando, my beautiful Latin (but possibly Italian or maybe even Greek) lover. And unless I wanted my father taking me to the ER for a colonoscopy, I needed to be crafty about it. So while my dad left the RV to work on phone lines, I stayed behind and filled my days with chronic masturbation. It was so epic that my fingers pruned. My forearm ached. My penis felt and looked like it had been resting under a heat lamp, red and throbby like E.T.'s magic finger lighting up to heal Elliott's wound.

Oooooouch.

My dad and I spent the last day of our trip driving for ten straight hours. He was tired and hungry. I was sex-starved and angry. We were both sore, for different reasons. Four spins into George Michael's *Faith*, he poked my arm.

"So, DJ . . . What's the girl situation like?"

It was a question I didn't want to hear and had been hoping to avoid.

"Um, well . . ." I carefully composed my answer, fumbling with my headphones as I paused the Discman. "Um . . . The girl situation is . . . pretty good. There are a lot of girls at my school. And they all . . . really, really like me."

My dad's grin widened. I imagined his eyes beaming with pride behind his sunglasses. "Girls really like me," I exclaimed, getting a little cocky. My dad let out a little chuckle, and I knew it was working. "Yeah! All of them do," I blurted, feeling really proud of myself now. "Actually, all my friends *are* girls!"

I looked at my father's face and knew I'd said too much. His smile went slack as he aggressively readjusted his sunglasses. He cleared his throat and checked the rearview mirror for unwanted rear-enders, a preoccupation that was starting to seem increasingly symbolic. My father spotted a violator and began pumping his breaks. Profanity was screamed. Horns were honked. Birds were flipped. And then silence.

Sitting there beside him at a red light in some tiny town outside Dallas, I could sense my dad's disappointment with my answer. I thought of Amber's sad, sweet-smelling letters and Chris Wolfe's spiteful glare. I remembered my mother's face a few weeks earlier, looking confused and saddened by my stack of khakis and basic white tees. I thought of her repeatedly asking me, "Why are you so quiet lately?" and I wondered what it felt like to see her son fade away from her the way I was. Was it like watching light collapse inside the gravitational pull of a fissure in space?

Maybe, in spite of their credentials and bestselling books, Sagan and Hawking had no idea what they were talking about. Maybe black holes *were* just empty space.

"The girl situation is good," I muttered to my father as he choked the steering wheel in his fists. "It's . . . good."

That day my mom took me and my zits to the mall:
A Family Photo.

CHAPTER 3

Where the Boys Are

I woke up for my first day of high school with a knot in my gut, a gut that had expanded throughout the summer. I'd spent the two months after the road trip eating spray cheese and Ritz crackers while watching Maury Povich with the shades drawn. My lethargic solitude and love of heavily processed foods resulted in my pudgy new back-to-school figure. I grunted and exhaled in the full-length bathroom mirror, laboring to zip up the khakis my mother had bought me only a few months earlier. After gelling down my hair and slipping on my white tennis shoes, I jumped into the car with my mom. The ten-minute drive felt like a walk down the plank. I imagined endless spine-chilling scenarios, most of which ended with wedgies, my head in the toilet, and the F-word. *That* F-word.

"Honey," said my mother as we pulled into the drop-off circle at my new high school. "Are you gay?"

"What?" I shrieked, spitting a sip of orange juice onto the dashboard of the Chevette. "You're asking me this on my first day of high school?"

"I'm not accusing you of anything, sweetheart," she said, turning down our favorite Wham! cassette. "But I worry about you. You used to have friends and date, but all you did this summer was sit in your room alone. If you *were* gay, you could tell your mother!"

Teri always talked about herself in the third person when she addressed me in any serious way.

David, your mother wants you to read this sexuality book for pre-teens.

David, your mother wants you to be open-minded at the metaphysics workshop today.

David, your mother is going to pee her pants if we don't find a gas station.

"David, listen to your mother," she insisted, gripping my hand tightly. "I would understand if you were a homosexual."

Ho-mo-sex-u-al. It's a weirdly clinical word, like something you hear in chemistry class to describe a type of combustion.

"You'll be fifteen soon! You're becoming a man and you'll have needs," she explained. "Your mother wants you to be secure in those desires and . . ."

"I'm NOT gay, Mom!"

"But being gay is perfectly okay! I'd much rather that than a son who was a pervert or schizophrenic like on one of those Lifetime movies your mother watches. Or a pedophile clown! Now *that* would be awful, honey."

My mother had always thought herself an amateur forensics expert. Her bookshelves were packed with a mix of Precious

Moments angels and Charles Manson biographies. It was an odd collision of interests, but that was Teri: a forty-year-old maternity-store manager who'd rather be dusting for fingerprints over the corpse of a partially cannibalized stripper.

"You could be a sex-freak murderer like Ted Bundy," she continued. "Granted, he was handsome, but he *was* a maniac-rapist!"

"MOM! I'm not a rapist!" I huffed as we pulled through the drop-off circle in front of Gunther High.

"But your mother would love you *even* then. Even if you had multiple personalities like Sally Field in *Sybil*! We'd make the best of it," she assured me. "It would almost be like I had *more children*!"

"I don't have a split personality!" I said as I slammed the car door. "And I'm *not* gay!"

By the time fifth-period gym class rolled around, I had never been more sure that I was gay. Eleventh- and twelfth-graders were like fully grown men. They shaved and sweat and layered thick streaks of deodorant onto their hairy armpits. Those ten minutes in the locker room after gym class were the single most nerve-racking part of my first day at Gunther High.

The entire campus was covered in boys who, although they were only a few years older than me, looked like college kids. In the courtyard they roamed in packs, wearing tight jeans and laughing in deep, manly voices. In the cafeteria they gave each other tight, one-armed hugs and threw around the word *pussy* like it was their profession. In the parking lot after school they sat smoking cigarettes while bouncing giggling girlfriends on their laps. As I walked home through the athletic field, I saw them at football practice. A black-haired Mexican boy in a sweat-drenched T-shirt was helping a small, stout blond boy up after a particularly rough tackle. "It's cool, brah," he replied as they slapped each other's asses.

Was this a cruel joke? I thought, watching them grunt and hustle across the field.

I got home at four o'clock feeling like my heart was going to pump out of my chest. My breath was shallow, and my stomach felt like a pincushion full of tacks. *How was I going to do this for four years?*

All the careful planning and structure I'd established for myself in middle school wouldn't work in high school. It was going to be tough, and I needed a new game plan. So I developed a locker-room manifesto.

1. Avoid any boy-on-boy interaction.
2. Keep a towel nearby for coverage at all times.
3. Be the first one in and out of the shower.
4. Monitor the pitch of your voice.
5. Run laps alone to avoid group sports.
6. Don't look anywhere you don't have to.

Number six was my biggest challenge: keeping my latitudinal gaze in check.

The next day, after running laps for forty-five minutes, I found a small corner locker to change by. Just as I sat on the bench, a thickset eighteen-year-old with a husky voice and full, bushy pubes approached me from the shower.

"Hey, dude. Are you using this locker?" he asked, his dewy genitals bouncing mere inches from my face as he towel-dried his hair.

"No," I answered in a low-pitched, testosterone-full croak, like a robot with a vocal modulation disorder.

Don't look down. Don't look down. Don't look down.

I stared as hard as I could into his eyes as he towered over me, which was probably creepier than if I'd just looked down and answered his dick directly.

No, Mr. Penis. I am not using this locker. You and your pendulous, man-size testicles are welcome to use this locker if you wish.

Creepy or not, my little manifesto was working. By carefully following my strict set of guidelines, I avoided all unnecessary human interaction. Sure, there were a few girls I'd chat with in class and a nerdy boy with weird teeth who'd talk to me in the library. But by October, outside of a few blink-and-you'll-miss-them interactions with acquaintances, I hadn't made a single real friend. I was proud of myself.

One day in October I was running laps when I heard Coach Allen blow the whistle. The coach had a head of pale yellow-white hair and a pinched, sunburned face. He looked like a bigger, sloppier John Madden.

"Come on in, ladies!" he bellowed like a human foghorn, his bowling-ball belly hanging over his tight blue shorts. "Time to change out!"

By that point, I had my locker-room process down to a science. After a quick armpit rinse followed by a towel-shielded change-out, I was done. Five minutes later I was walking back to the bleachers to wait for the bell before the other boys were even out of the shower. I felt pretty good about my process over the last few weeks and smiled, happy that I'd reached a whole new level of camouflage and solitude so quickly.

And then I saw him.

Near the top of the bleachers was a new boy. His hair was expertly moussed. His clothes were perfectly unwrinkled. He had clear, tan skin and a strong, square jaw. He wore Ray-Bans and stared down into a notebook. I couldn't tell if he was reading or sleeping, but it was clear that he hadn't broken a sweat in the last hour.

I sat down a few feet away from him in my pale-blue polo shirt and tan slacks, dressed like a used-car dealer or someone's stepfather. In his backpack I noticed the name *Greg Brooks* scrawled across the spine of a textbook. Greg was dressed like someone from television, in stylish acid-washed Guess jeans and a striped Cavaricci pullover. The boy sat as still as a marble sculpture, listening to his Sony Discman. It was the newish pale-gray model with orange control buttons that I'd been wanting for weeks.

Hey, Greg. I'm David.

I could imagine myself saying it, and almost hear the words coming out of my mouth. I cleared my throat and thought I saw his eyebrow flinch, which sent me into an anxiety hole. I had to talk to him. I took a deep breath and parted my lips just as the bell rang. Greg sprang to life and sprinted away with his backpack. He moved so quickly that it took my breath away, like everything he would do over the next few weeks. Every colorblocked ensemble, every slight variation in hairstyle and gelling technique, every pair of patterned socks peeking out beneath his smartly tapered jeans was impeccable.

Each day at 2:20 p.m. I gathered the courage to attempt an introduction. And each day, just as I was about to speak, the damn bell would ring. I failed to see, of course, that the problem wasn't the timing of the bell but my own confidence. The bell could've been late by five minutes or two hours or four weeks, and I still wouldn't have spoken. If the bell never rang again I probably would've spent all of eternity in a panicked silence, unable to simply turn and say, *Hello. I'm David.*

In lieu of speaking to Greg, I spent that fall trying an assortment of nonverbal ways to get his attention. In the bleachers I would cough extraloud to see if I could get him to flinch behind those black-lensed Ray-Bans. *Was he even listening to music?* I thought, straining to hear any sound coming from his headphones as I whooped and gagged. By the end of that week, my persistent hacking had convinced at least one person that I was deathly ill.

"Take a hint, Typhoid Mary," growled Coach Allen as he dumped a handful of Halls cough drops into my palm after gym. "You sound like you're drilling for oil out there."

Every day, as fifty of us walked across the gymnasium floor to run laps outside, Greg stayed behind with a few other boys scattered in the bleachers. As the weather got chillier, the activities moved indoors. Throughout November, as I repeatedly failed to serve a volleyball correctly, Greg sat in the bleachers writing in his wire-bound notebook, somehow exempt from participation. What was wrong with Greg that kept him from physical activity? More important, what was wrong with *me* that I still couldn't speak to him?

The week before Thanksgiving break I tried a new tactic, using the Sony Discman my mom had just gotten me. It was the gray model with orange control buttons, just like Greg's. I sat in front of him and made a point of jamming out extra-hard to my music, practically banging my head to Jody Watley's "Looking for a

New Love." After roll call I made a huge production of putting the Discman away, delicately winding the headphones around it like I was swaddling a preemie.

That's just like my Discman! I imagined Greg thinking when he saw it. *It's a sign. I've gotta talk to this friendless, little typhus-ridden dude who dresses like a Mormon missionary.*

But nothing.

Greg wasn't so expressionless when I saw him in the courtyard with his friends, a group of cool boys who weren't identified with any specific clique. They weren't jocks, but they weren't bookish. They weren't alternative kids, but they weren't quite preps, either. They wore clothes a bit more expensive than the ones my mom could afford: brown leather Bass shoes and fitted Guess jeans cuffed at the ankle, plaid Gap shirts tucked behind woven brown leather belts. My favorite thing about them was their scent, which was strong enough to let you know they were near before you saw them. They didn't smell like all the Eternity-drenched athletes in the locker room. Their more obscure colognes smelled sweeter and spicier. Sitting downwind of Greg every day in the bleachers, I could smell the wondrous, manly musk of him behind me. I had to find that remarkable scent.

In the mall on Black Friday I went to the magazine section of B. Dalton books, where I lingered until the register was so busy that no employees were on the floor. And then I began my research, looking through men's magazines like *GQ* and *Details* for cologne samples. I checked over each shoulder to make sure no one was watching before I began to tear open the glued-down paper strips, quickly smearing my wrists, forearms, and elbow crooks with Escape, Joop!, Cool Water, and Drakkar Noir. I moved quickly from magazine to magazine, trying to remember which scent I had wiped on which part of my body.

"Excuse me, sir," I heard, and turned to see a small brunette wearing a name tag. I froze midsmear, with a copy of *Esquire* magazine pressed against my neck. "You know they'll give you free samples at Dillard's?" she asked with a grin.

"Oh," I stammered. "I didn't mean to . . ."

"It's okay, honey," she said, walking forward and patting my back. "Wanna know which one I love? All the boys are wearing it now."

She looked over either shoulder and pulled down a copy of *Men's Health.* "It's this one," she said, tearing open the sample flap at the center. I lowered my face into the magazine and was suddenly overtaken by the exotic, musky scent of Greg Brooks.

"Thank you," I whispered, genuinely grateful for another retail angel in my life.

That day my mother bought me the fragrance—Fahrenheit. On Monday morning I sprayed loads of it on my neck and wrists, not wanting the scent to fade before fifth period. In gym class I sat in front of Greg and waited for him to say something. I imagined him tapping me on the shoulder to compliment me on my great scent, but nothing happened. Each morning I lathered on more and more Fahrenheit, oblivious to the absurdity of my plan: how would Greg be able to smell *me* over himself when we smelled the exact same way?

By Friday morning the pungent tang of my own body made my eyes water.

"You smell like a French whore," gagged my mom as she rolled down the driver's-seat window on the way to school. "Honey, too much scent is almost worse than none at all!"

In gym class I sat down in front of Greg and waited expectantly for him to say something. After a few moments of silence, I decided to kick it up a notch. I began making big, exaggerated gestures as I took off my coat, hoping to fan my splendiferous odor in his direction. But nothing happened. So I made my movements even bigger, swooping my arms out wider and with more velocity. Within five seconds I was struggling violently with my coat, flapping like some great, crippled bird attempting flight.

"Crabb!" yelled Coach. "What the hell? You got bees in your bonnet?"

"Oh," I stammered over scattered laughter. "My coat's stuck."

"You look like you need the damn Jaws of Life up there!" Coach smiled mockingly as everyone laughed.

"I got it," Greg said as a hand clamped down on my sleeve. With one light tug it was over. Greg had not only talked to me, but touched me. Greg Brooks had . . . touched me.

"Time to change, boys," Coach yelled before focusing his gaze on me. "You think you'll be able to Harry Houdini yourself outta that shirt, Crabb?"

"Um, yes," I whimpered as everyone jogged to the locker room.

I turned to thank Greg but was confronted with his perfectly still, sunglasses-wrapped face, like a contemporary re-creation of *The Thinker* with more stylish hair and headphones. Could he hear me? Was he looking at me? Did he realize how perfect he was? There was no way to know. And, until I grew some balls, no way to tell him.

By December, Greg still hadn't changed out. And I still hadn't really made any friends. As much as my manifesto was working, the isolation was starting to wear on me. Between classes I would look at other groups of kids in their cliques, laughing and whispering in the hallways. To an outsider looking in, their friendship configurations seemed obvious and dull. All the girls with a certain type of purse and blouse ate together in one area, while boys with long hair and rock-band T-shirts smoked cigarettes in another. In the parking lot, clean-shaven guys with big muscles and checkered shirts gathered around one car, while girls in matching school jackets carrying musical instruments rode away in another. There was no special science or deductive method required to figure out why people in high school had the friends they had. Reminding myself of that made it easier to judge them, and judging them made being alone feel easier. Friendships were basic and beneath me.

But on certain days, in certain moods, it all looked so pleasant. I'd watch them cackling hysterically while reading a note by someone's locker or giggling over a foot-long pizza-cheese strand in the cafeteria. Suddenly I'd think that no ill will or cruelty could exist in them. And in that brief instant I would doubt all the careful planning I'd done based on my fear and dread. For a split second I'd feel like a fool. But then I'd remember the dull thud of those heavy, brown leather books on either side of my skull and know that my manifesto was right.

On the last day of school before Christmas break, while the gym class did indoor push-ups and jumping jacks, I watched Greg chat with a few other boys at the edge of the bleachers. The boys looked normal, but I assumed that they, like Greg, harbored some gruesome physical abnormalities that kept them from participating in class.

As I started my set of one hundred push-ups, I considered

each possible secret illness or malady. Perhaps, beneath all those fashionable clothes, Greg's body was horribly deformed. After all, I'd never seen him shirtless or in a tank top. What if he had been in a fire that precisely disfigured his torso but somehow left the smooth, sinewy skin of his arms intact? Realizing I'd never seen him in shorts, I thought that maybe he'd lost his legs in a car accident. Under those perfectly fitted Girbaud jeans might be a complex system of steel rods and hydraulic joints, intricate prostheses that allowed Greg to walk but not run, jog, or jump. I imagined rubbing soothing salve into the burnt cheese pizza–skin of his chest while singing him to sleep at night. In the morning, he'd passionately kiss me good-bye after I WD-40ed the high-tech gears and pulleys of his squeaky RoboCop legs.

Each deformity I imagined was more grotesque than the last, but it didn't matter. I would love him regardless of his scabby foot-long tail, boil-covered penis, or swastika-shaped port-wine birthmark. I would love him for what was on the inside, as he would love me. Greg was gorgeous and effortlessly cool, and he smelled great. And one day he would be mine.

Pushing my body off the ground for the ninety-ninth time, I peered with laser-focused intensity at my intended's face, thinking, *What could be wrong with someone who looks so perfect?*

"One hundred," I groaned before lying flat on the ground. I raised my head up to the bleachers as rivulets of sweat stung my eyeballs, gazing at the length of Greg's body flexing and twitching as he yawned.

"Why are you lying there like a dead frog?" Coach Allen asked, his blinding white sneakers so close to my face I could smell them.

"Just . . . need . . . one . . . minute . . ." I panted, breathing deeply and slowly against the red rubber mat beneath me.

"Well, don't be late, Crabb," he grunted before shuffling away. I lingered on the gymnasium floor and closed my eyes, hoping that the unyielding boner beneath me would dissipate so I could stand up.

Maybe I wasn't quite ready to meet Greg. *After the holidays*, I told myself as the gym emptied. *After the holidays*.

During some of the more painfully anxious years of my life, I would find solace in other peoples' pets. In any situation around family or my parents' friends in which I felt vulnerable to questions about sports and girlfriends, I would find the pet immediately and force every bit of my love and attention onto it. I cannot tell you how many hours I spent in my mom's boyfriends' backyards or my grandparents' garage playing fetch or tug-of-war with a mutt. Parties with other kids my age were the worst, as they weren't easily tricked like adults into thinking I was "normal." Here I am taking solace with Whitney, the poodle of a seventeen-year-old girl named Michelle. I'm also taking solace in the third glass of wine cooler mixed with Sprite that Michelle snuck me at this party. I'm actually quite happy here. Even as an adult, "tipsy while holding a dog" is still one of my favorite states of being.

CHAPTER 4

I Want to Wake Up

If *Why don't I like girls?* was the controlling thought of my life in middle school, my high school brain was consumed by *Why do I like boys?*

I asked myself this repeatedly, my gaze roaming up and down the length of his chiseled physique, his body so spectacular that I didn't know where to focus. The ripples in his abdomen transfixed me. The magnificent striations in his upper thighs were stunning. There was also that beautiful space near the armpit where the muscles of his chest and arm merged, flexed from holding the weight of his body up against the giant wooden cross.

"Benedictum Nomen Sanctum eius," hummed Father Carol, gassing our entire pew with incense fumes from his swinging thurible.

"Oh dear," my mother coughed, overcome by smoke, "it's enough to knock you out. Isn't it, Leonard?" She glanced around me to my father, who was so bored by Christmas Mass that he looked dead, like a pale, bald corpse propped up in his seat as a holiday prank.

"Uh-huh," he groaned as we proceeded to lip-sync another hymn.

Since their divorce when I was two, my parents had held on to the idea that their spending time together in my presence was good for me, regardless of their differences. My mother had grown up deeply embedded in the Catholic Church. She remained devout in an open-minded way that allowed for her other interests: metaphysics, exorcisms, and Shirley MacLaine books. Her esoteric hobbies were at odds with my dad's interests in astronomy and fiber-optics.

After Mass my father took us to Church's Chicken for lunch, a prospect that appalled my mother.

"Church's?" she muttered as we arrived. "Fast food on Christmas Day?"

Half an hour later we were gathered around a sad pile of cardboard and Styrofoam that sat atop a yellow linoleum table. My mother was not happy and, in a passive-aggressive fashion, made a big show of picking greasy bits of napkin off her manicure.

"I guess it's not about where you are but who you're with," she sighed with a Plasticine smile, sounding like she'd rather be anywhere else. I stayed quiet and gorged myself on drumsticks, again trying to soak up the tension in my bones with the food in my mouth.

"You eat up, sweetie," my mother encouraged. "You've gotten so skinny lately. Hasn't he, Leonard?"

My father nodded silently behind the reflective lenses of his sunglasses, which were lightly misted with mashed-potato steam. Mom continued to chatter on the way home, a nervous response to my dad's silence that, ironically, only made things more tense.

By the end of the day I was emotionally exhausted. I went to bed early but couldn't stop thinking about Jesus, in the *bad* way. As I imagined dragging a moist cloth down the length of his torso, it occurred to me that maybe, instead of giving him a sexy sponge bath, I should ask him for help. So I closed my eyes and posed the simple question: *Dear God, why do I like boys?*

I waited for an answer from on high until eventually I fell asleep, but I decided to keep at it. I started the new year praying all the time: in the car on the way to school, in the locker room after gym class, during my lunch break in the library. Sometimes I prayed in sync with my sinful thinking, asking Christ to heal my wayward soul while I watched Greg Brooks's beautiful butt ascend the bleachers ahead of me.

At first, I asked God for his help nicely.

Dear God, please help me get rid of the ideas in my head about boys. Let me meet a nice girl who will marry me one day and have my kids. Thanks and amen.

But as the weeks passed and I sensed no improvement in my condition, I began to daydream about suicide. I imagined an elaborate, cinematic death scored by Sinéad O'Connor's "Nothing Compares 2 U." In my fantasy, a camera descended from an overhead crane as my father found me bled-out in a pink-hued bathtub surrounded by white candles. Trembling, he'd read the epic twelve-page good-bye poem I'd left for him beneath a razor blade. He'd lift my limp body from the tub and gently lay me across his lap before raising his fists to the sky, creating a tableau that was part Pietà, part *Platoon*. As thunder rumbled and a torrent of rain was somehow unleashed inside the bathroom, Leonard would scream skyward, "NOOO!!! If only I'd accepted you for YOU! But it's too LATE! TOO LAAAATE!!!"

Suicide wasn't a way out but a high-drama bartering tool for fair treatment. *My dad would finally understand me*, I thought, glossing over the fact that my being six feet under might get in the way of feeling accepted.

Look, God, I eventually demanded, *I didn't do anything to hurt you or anyone else. I love my parents and I don't steal or cheat. The only sin I commit is lying, which I have to do because of you. And it's all your fault! You are making me a sinner by letting me be this way. So stop being a jerk and make me better already. Amen!*

I talked to God less like he was a deity and more like he was a negligent customer-service operator at Verizon.

I took the whole day off work and it's already 5:30! Where's the damn cable guy?

As nothing changed, I became more fearful. The threat of familial rejection and social isolation of being gay was scary enough. But now there was something else. Something worse—AIDS.

In 1990 you couldn't watch MTV for more than ten minutes without hearing about AIDS.

Stay tuned for Madonna's new PSA about . . . AIDS!

Next on The Real World: *in which someone struggles with . . . AIDS!*

Here's TLC in costumes made of condoms, rapping about . . . AIDS!

At first I thought I could contract it through the air, as if HIV particles floated around, waiting to slip into my pores as soon as I thought about something remotely gay. I became my own thought police during high-risk scenarios involving underwear catalogues or Johnny Depp scenes in *21 Jump Street*. I even trained myself to avoid looking at Greg, whose dapper spring wardrobe and slightly blonder hair were proving hard to ignore.

Something else was also hard to ignore—Greg's new girlfriend, Jill.

Jill had a freckled face, pale pink lips, and a head full of long, bouncing blond curls. I first noticed them together in the parking lot after school, leaning on the hood of a car and holding hands. Then I saw them in the cafeteria, sharing headphones and Mexican food on Taco Tuesday. Although we shared second-period history class, I didn't count Jill among the small group of less-popular girls I called my "acquaintances."

One day, as we waited to be excused, I watched Jill reading a note from Greg out loud to her friends as they giggled and shrieked.

"Oh my God, Jill!" Paula Simms squealed. "He is SO crazy about you!"

"I know, right?" cooed Jill, clutching the note to her chest and rolling her eyes skyward. "I think I love him!"

As the group of girls tee-heed and swooned, I fantasized that a bolt of lightning would suddenly tear through the roof of the classroom and rip Jill's head clean off her shoulders.

"Are you sick, David?" someone asked me. I turned to see my desk neighbor, Patty Marks, a mousy brunette with pale, meaty cheeks and hazel, almost yellow eyes. Patty was smart, quiet-natured, and generally regarded as a bit of a Jesus freak.

"Oh, yeah, Patty," I answered, realizing that my face had been stuck in a contorted sneer as I watched Jill. "It's just my, uh, stomach."

"Here, drink this," she said, reaching into her brown paper lunch bag. Patty passed me a can of ginger ale and flashed a bashful smile.

"But, Patty, it's your drink and I . . ."

"No, it's okay. I can drink water," she said, nervously fondling her crucifix necklace. "Oh! And this is for you," she added, sliding over a tiny red envelope.

Oh no, I thought. Jill's love note suddenly made sense. It was Valentine's Day.

Seconds later, the bell saved me from having to read Patty's note in front of her. "Thanks," I blurted before running into the hallway to look at the card, which pictured ALF holding an armful of red roses under the phrase "Be mine!"

The rest of the day was excruciating. Girls skipped elatedly down the hallways holding heart-shaped boxes of chocolate. Boys walked bashfully, holding cheap red gas-station roses for their girlfriends. Juniors and seniors sucked face against lockers uninterrupted, knowing that administrators would let their public displays of affection slide. It was all so loud, so cringeworthy, so desperate. I told myself that I was merely offended, but in truth, I wanted to be part of the ritual too.

Looking down at ALF's big, pleading eyes on Patty's card, I thought that maybe it was time to give it a go. After all, I'd been asking God for a girlfriend for two months. Maybe Patty could make me realize that I loved her above Ricky Schroder, Mackenzie Astin, Patrick Swayze, the Tom Selleck look-alike my mom used to date, half of New Kids on the Block, and the entire model cast of the *International Male* catalog.

The next day I slid Patty a card that asked, "Want to go

steady?" She passed it back with the "Yes" box checked, and smiled at me. It was easy as pie. I had a girlfriend.

I was surprised at how much I enjoyed Patty's company that first week. She was a demure girl from a devout Christian family and didn't really have much to say. I could ramble to Patty for hours and she'd barely make a peep. I'd forgotten how pleasant it was to simply talk to someone. It was also satisfying to show the world some living, breathing evidence of my "normality." In the mornings I'd meet Patty near the drop-off circle, where my mom would be able to see us hug as she drove away. In the parking lot I'd make sure Greg noticed me and Patty holding hands near the blue car where he met Jill after school. In the cafeteria I'd get us a table near the lunch line to ensure that most of the student body would see me sharing French fries with Patty Marks, my girlfriend.

One day at lunch, a couple weeks into our relationship, Patty handed me a brush.

"Would you mind?" she asked, turning around to chat with a friend about Bible study.

Running the brush through her hair felt familiar and calming, like a meditation. It took me back to better days with Amber, before the "incident." But Patty was no Amber. Neither was her hair. The brush kept catching and pulling as I tried to work it through her wiry, dull mane, which, upon closer inspection, was flaked with dandruff. As I combed, Patty scooted herself between my legs, which were straddling the lunch-table bench.

"You're sweet," she whispered, looking over her shoulder as her butt made contact with my crotch. "I wanna kiss you soon."

My guts suddenly felt like they were full of turned milk. Bells and whistles began to ring in my head. A blaring internal alarm was bleating, *Danger! Danger! Danger!*

Over the next week, Patty Marks became my least favorite chore. She followed me everywhere. Between classes, during lunch, before school, and after: Patty Marks was there. But something in her eyes had changed. The way she looked at me was different, more intense, *charged*. By the time the weekend came I couldn't wait to be free of her, in spite of our plans to see a movie at the mall.

On Saturday morning I let the answering machine take Patty's call.

"No, Mom!" I yelled as she reached for the phone. "Don't answer it!"

"What is it, honey? Aren't you seeing a movie with Patty today?"

"No," I stammered. "I'm going with some guy friends."

"Oh, that's sweet," my mom beamed, patting my cheek. "A boys' day out."

In the mall I walked toward the theater, two hours earlier than I'd made plans with Patty. I was excited to see *Arachnophobia* on my own, without Patty grabbing me and fawning all over me. But there she was, smiling in high-water pink denim jeans, with her dull-as-dishwater hair up in a crooked ponytail.

"You didn't answer the phone this morning," she chirped. "So when I realized I missed you, I decided to come here early."

"Hey," I said, trying to act happy to see her. "When did you get here?"

"When the mall opened, silly!" she peeped, grabbing my hand.

"Oh," I said quietly, spooked by the realization that Patty had been standing alone in front of the Odeon 14 Cineplex for three whole hours.

As *Arachnophobia* played in the darkened theater she squirmed against me like a fitful baby. "No!" she yelped, grinding against me so hard she was practically in my lap. Her wandering fingertips felt like the spiders in the film, crawling all over me in the dark as she cringed and screamed. As the credits rolled, she swiftly leaned her face toward mine. I turned my head quickly, barely avoiding my first mouth-on-mouth kiss.

"Okay," I said, jumping up from the seat. "I gotta get home."

"Um, okay," she called after me as I wiped spit off my cheek. "See you Monday!"

Throughout the next week, Patty's companionship was an increasingly grueling burden. I disliked everything about her: her weird copper-colored eyes, her dry, brittle hair, and her meaty, clammy paws, which were shoved into mine all the time. It was like holding room-temperature hamburger meat. My mother told me she was sweating because I made her nervous.

But I don't want to make anyone nervous, I thought. *Couldn't we both be adults? Can't I just have a nice, unthreatening girlfriend to watch* Blossom *with every Tuesday?*

I decided to change up my prayer routine. If God had brought me Patty, couldn't he take her away?

Dear Lord, please make Patty Marks dump me. I don't care if she hates me forever. But please help. Amen.

The problem with dumping Patty myself was that I couldn't take the risk that it might make me look gay. I'd have to find a way to make *her* break up with *me*. I started by feigning interest in other girls at school.

"Patty! Look at Jill's blouse. Isn't it pretty? She's wearing her hair in a braid today!"

You know. The way boys noticed girls.

But Patty proved hard to shake. Everywhere I looked, there was her face—a face that was, increasingly often, diving in toward mine with parted lips and a whipping, pink tongue, like the giant plant in *Little Shop of Horrors*. I didn't understand why the prospect of kissing her scared me so deeply. I'd seen lots of people kiss on TV, in films, *and* in real life. People were kissing all the time at school. But no one made it look the way Greg Brooks did. In the parking lot I'd seen him kissing Jill, their lips mashing against each other's as their soft, pink tongues darted in and out. I would watch them and try to imagine kissing Patty with that kind of dexterity. But before I knew it, I was imagining that I was Jill being kissed by Greg.

Shortly before spring break I was sitting in the cafeteria beside Patty with a few other friends when I felt something on my crotch. I looked down to see Patty's pasty meat-paw between my legs.

"Patty," I whispered, trying not to make a scene.

"It's okay, David," she whispered, petting her crucifix with her free hand. "I've been praying about this. And God thinks it's okay."

I'd reached my breaking point. It was time to step things up. That night, I came up with the perfect plan.

A few days later at lunch, I sat next to Patty as she brushed her hair. Once finished, she laid the chunky purple brush down on the table. I picked it up and began gathering a clump of hair from the bristles.

"David, what are you doing with my hair?" she asked with a confused half smile.

"Oh, nothing," I said, feigning surprise at being caught. "I just want a little piece of you with me all the time." I flashed her a creepy smile and stared too hard into her eyes.

"Oh," she stammered. "That's . . . nice."

"I have to go the bathroom," I said, knocking a large book out of my backpack and onto the ground as I walked away.

"You dropped something," I heard Patty say as I left, but I pretended I didn't.

The book Patty picked up was *The Complete Book of Spells, Ceremonies and Magic*, a thick purple tome full of tarot advice, astrological charts, and exorcism how-tos. I'd taken it from my mother's bookshelf, where it lived between Stephen King's *Cujo* and a forensics hardcover called *Explorations in Criminal Psychopathology*. The book was fairly harmless, but I hoped that once Patty found what was hidden in the front cover, she'd be running for her life, clutching her little necklace all the way.

A few minutes later I returned to find the table vacated, save for my witchcraft book, which was full of voodoo-doll sketches and a week's worth of Patty's stray hairs.

That afternoon, Patty's very timid mother called me at home when my mom was at work.

"I'm sorry to say that, um," she gulped, her voice withering at the other end of the line, "and I'm sorry if this is upsetting, but Patty can't . . . Well . . ."

"Go ahead, Mrs. Marks," I said calmly, trying not to laugh. As perverse as it sounds, I got a certain thrill in being dumped by a forty-two-year-old woman at the age of fourteen.

"Well, Patty would not like to see you anymore, David."

"Oh, really," I replied, trying to sound heartbroken.

"Alright, now. I have to go," she said as Patty whispered something in the background. "You take care."

Mrs. Marks hung up, and the line went dead. As the dial tone hummed in my ear, I took a deep breath, feeling accomplished. I was finally free. And in the silence of my bedroom I was alone. As this new reality struck me, so did the dread of how lonely I'd been before Patty came along. And for just a second, as badly as I'd wanted to be Patty-less a few hours earlier, I wondered if her serpentine tongue lashing at my face was really such a bad thing after all. This wasn't a new reality—it was a step back into an old one.

Without a girlfriend, whatever self-delusion of heterosexuality I'd achieved was gone. After a week of solitude all my fears came back, stronger than before: fear of God, fear of my family, fear of my peers, and fear of AIDS. I spent that spring break by myself. As other kids my age went to the beach or movie theater, I sat in my room, masturbating to the underwear section of a Sears catalog. Once, afterward, I thought I'd gotten sperm in a paper cut on my finger. This sent me into a tailspin—I worried that my body wouldn't realize that it was *my* sperm. If it mistook the semen as another male's, my body would know I was gay and instantaneously manifest HIV in my blood, because any gay sex act *must* surely lead to AIDS.

These thought circles were exhausting. My ever-present manifesto was starting to feel less like protection and more like a curse, guiding me through every false smile, nervous glance, and fearful retreat. Even my sleep was fraught with tension, each dream plagued by faceless aggressors, drowning deaths, and cartoon snakes that screamed at me with the voice of God, my father, or Chris Wolfe.

A week before the end of freshman year I woke up in the middle of the night covered in sweat. I'd been dreaming my recurring balloon dream in which I rose into the sky, screaming, knowing that the more I struggled, the higher and faster I'd rise toward the ozone, where I'd burn up. I walked down the hall into the bathroom and opened the medicine cabinet for an aspirin. I swallowed it with water from the tap and started to read the "caution" label on the bottle. Then I read a different bottle's label, then another, and another.

"Honey." I turned to see my bed-headed mother squinting in her terry cloth robe. "David, you've been in here forever. Are you okay?"

"Yeah, Mom," I said, turning off the faucet. "Just a headache."

I lay awake the rest of that night, considering my options, projecting myself into the future, imagining the "what-ifs." Suicide would be forever, but so would being alone. There was no seductive drama to killing myself anymore. It was simply a practical response to my life, the natural antidote to the dull gray thudding in my brain, the only way to undo the realization of what I was becoming.

I stumbled through school that Monday, the last week before summer break. In the locker room I was too tired to notice or care about any of the wet, sinewy boys' bodies around me. In spite of being totally exhausted, I ran laps for forty-five minutes.

I didn't think to fake a stomach cramp or the flu. Gym class was what occupied the 1:30 to 2:30 p.m. section of my daily list of activities. And as long as I honored my manifesto and adhered to the guidelines I'd set for myself, things would be fine. They had to be.

As I stood up from the locker-room bench, my head began to swim. I could feel my heart beating in my temples. Violet dots danced across my field of vision. I braced myself against the wall and carefully walked past the toned torsos of Ethan Gray, Bobby Johnson, and Jason Dermot, trying my best not to puke on their broad, athletic feet. In the bathroom stall at the back of the locker room, I vomited as quietly as I could, not wanting to be the possibly-gay weirdo who was *also* bulimic.

In the gymnasium I slogged up the bleachers toward Greg, who reclined casually while listening to his Discman.

"Hey. David. You okay?"

"I'm fine," I said, not entirely sure if I was hallucinating Greg's voice. "Just feeling a little sick," I added, looking into my bag to avoid eye contact.

"You *look* sick. Why did you even run today?"

"I had to," I said, too exhausted to fully absorb that he was talking to me. "I don't have a doctor's note."

"A note?" he asked with a smirk. "What do you mean?"

"Like a note that excuses you from participating in PE."

"You don't need a note," he smiled, flipping his bangs out of his eyes. "Nerd."

The way Greg called me *nerd* was sweet, as if the word's rightful home had always been on his lips.

"What do you mean?" I asked. "I don't need a note?"

"No. You just . . . sit out."

I repeated it slowly, like someone who didn't speak English.
"Sit . . . out . . . ?"

"Yeah. You show up. You sit here. And you wait for fifty minutes."

"What?" I asked. This simple and obvious possibility blew my mind. Greg howled with laughter and slapped my shoulder.

"You thought . . . all this time that . . . you *had* to do gym class!"

I started to laugh with him, but not the way I usually did with kids who mocked me or adults whose jokes I didn't understand. It wasn't fake laughter intended to let me fit in or save face. It was chest-filling, gut-busting, very loud laughter.

"Hey!" Coach Allen boomed at us from below, "Quiet! You got five more minutes!"

"David," Greg whispered, "another part of 'sitting out' is never looking like you're enjoying yourself. It's key!"

Suddenly it all made sense: Greg's stoic lack of expression, his bored silence, and, most important, his yearlong lack of participation in gym class. No undisclosed disability or top-secret physician's note was required to sit out. All it took to not do it was *not doing it*. I thought back on my entire freshman year: all the push-ups and jumping jacks, and the hundreds of miles run on that blacktop track, all because I assumed I had to. How much time did I waste playing volleyball in those ill-fitting polyester shorts? And how many afternoons could I have spent laughing, albeit quietly, with Greg Brooks in the bleachers?

In the hallway as we left class, a shaft of sunlight hit Greg's handsome face, turning his bronzed hair platinum as he swept it off his forehead. Looking at him made me feel like a shrunken, gray-skinned zombie.

"See you tomorrow!" he yelled, swinging his backpack over his shoulder. "If you don't change out, let's hang out in gym tomorrow."

Waving good-bye, I knew perfectly well I would never change out for gym class again.

CHAPTER 5

Alone in a Darkened Room

Greg and I spent the last week of our freshman year getting to know each other in gym class. We also spent a fair amount of time getting yelled at by Coach Allen for laughing. Coach was so mad by Friday that he made us both change out and run on the last day of school. Greg and I completed our laps side by side, chuckling together as he cursed me for ruining an otherwise perfect record of nonparticipation.

"I hate you so much," he snickered, panting as he picked at the crotch of his gym shorts. "These shorts blow chunks."

"Now you know," I laughed, trying not to look directly at his face in the blinding sunlight for too long.

"Well, I understand why you're so skinny now," Greg moaned, wiping sweat from his brow. I chuckled lightly, trying not to seem excited that Greg had noticed my body changing over the last school year.

After class, we exchanged phone numbers and agreed to hang out that summer. At home that first day off from school, I waited for Greg's call, but nothing. A week later I still hadn't heard from him, and I was starting to feel crazy. I would've clasped my hands and knelt by my bed had I not decided a few weeks back that prayer was a racket. I figured that if God was the kind of architect who would make me fret and suffer that much over his own faulty design, I'd rather not work with him (if he was even there at all).

Although I had Greg's number, I was afraid to be the first one to call. I had to play it cool and wait it out. But after another Greg-less week passed, I was crushed. I was also as pale as a ghost from all the hours spent indoors staring at the telephone.

And then the phone rang.

"Hello," I answered, my voice quivering at the possibility.

"Hey, it's Greg," he said as I hopped up and down as quietly as I could. It turned out that Greg's family's four-day summer trip to visit his great-aunt had become an extended stay when she fell down a flight of stairs. They had only just gotten home. I felt bad that Greg's aunt had gotten busted up, but I could've cared less as the following question flowed from the receiver into my ear.

"You wanna stay over tonight?"

I hesitated—partly out of fear, but I was also executing a favorite courting ritual of my mother's.

"Never seem desperate," she'd remind me while staring at the phone for three whole rings before answering.

"Hello?" Greg asked. "Are you there, David?"

"Sure," I said, staring at the Saturday-night shows I'd circled in the TV guide. "I don't *think* I have any plans."

Two hours later I was in the bathroom, trying to cover a massive nose zit with flesh-tone Clearasil, a product supposedly designed for Caucasian humans, in spite of its peachy-orange hue. After several attempts, my schnoz still looked like a tiny, radioactive tangerine. No matter how thinly I laid the Clearasil on, I still had a huge orange dot in the center of my face. A half hour into washing and reapplying the stuff, my mother popped her head in the doorway.

"David, I . . . Oh, honey. Your face looks like a Twister mat," she sighed. "What's going on with your makeup?"

"Mom, it's not makeup!"

"You know your mother wouldn't mind if you wore makeup," she chirped, styling her hair in the mirror. "Some men live their whole lives as ladies because . . ."

"Mom! I'm not a lady. I'm just trying to cover my zits, okay?"

"Honey, try this Oil of Olay instead," she said, pulling a small tan tube from her purse. "Your face looks like you were drinking a glass of Tang and your mouth missed the glass."

"I don't want your makeup, Mom. It's for women. This Clearasil is bisexual."

"David," she giggled, "it's actually called *unisex*, meaning both men and women can . . ."

"I know, Mom! Just leave and go to Mike's already!"

My mom had started dating Mike a few months earlier. He lived in Seguin, a small town forty-five minutes away, where she was going to visit him for the first time. In the mirror over my shoulder she put on lip gloss, muttering as she hiked up her brassiere. My mom had always been self-conscious about her ample cleavage.

"Honey, do I look like a shameless hussy?"

"Mom," I said to her reflection, "stop worrying."

"Well, I'm nervous about meeting Mike's kids tonight," she said, staring at her reflection and shrugging, as if to say, *I guess this is the best we can do, old gal.* "You would tell your mother if this top made me look like Dolly Parton, wouldn't you?"

"Mom, you look great," I said, rubbing her shoulder. "Besides, where are you supposed to hide those things?"

"You turd!" she yelled, laughing herself to the front door. "Your mother should be ashamed of you."

As she walked out, I yelled, "Good luck on your date, Mom!"

From the stairwell on the other side of the door she absentmindedly replied, "You too, honey."

An hour later I left our apartment complex and began my hike to Greg's. As I walked down Harry Wurzbach Road in the humid sunset, the neighborhood changed. The houses got nicer, the businesses got fancier; gas stations were replaced by high-end craft stores and dress shops. I was entering the ritzier part of San Antonio, near Randolph Air Force Base.

Twenty minutes later I arrived, double-checking the address Greg had written on a pack of gum in gym class. It was a newer house painted a soft eggshell with pale gray trim; the sidewalk was lined with tiny electric candles. The trees on either side of me whispered with the sound of tinkling metal chimes. I stood at the large, frosted glass door and rang the bell. A few moments later Greg's mother appeared, wearing pink-framed glasses and a powder-blue top; a long blond braid rested on her shoulder.

"Hello, dear. I'm Georgia, Greg's mother," she said, wrapping her arms around me.

"Oh . . . hello, Mrs. Brooks," I stammered, ensconced in the smell of roses and cinnamon.

"Welcome," she said with warm familiarity. "Let me show you our home."

"Okay!" I beamed, feeling like an orphan offered shelter on a cold Christmas Eve.

Georgia's floor-length skirt made it seem like she was floating through the house, a stream of pastel gossamer trailing behind her. The floors were covered in Spanish tiles and the kitchen glowed with stainless-steel appliances. The den was furnished with a plush, overstuffed couch and love seat. Georgia slid open the patio door to reveal a crystal-blue, forty-foot swimming pool glistening in the moonlight. Tiki torches softly blazed around the yard and bamboo chimes sang from the surrounding trees. It was so much more than my mom and I had ever had, like my favorite *Architectural Digest* homes come to life.

"We have extra trunks if you want to go for a swim sometime this summer," she said. Torchlight reflected off the pool's surface and danced across her face. Her earrings shimmered as a faint breeze lifted the pastel silk draping of her sleeves. She was Glinda the Good Witch, come to life as someone's mom.

In the kitchen, she poured me sparkling water and gestured to a slightly cracked door off the foyer. "Greg is just down that hall."

I picked up my bag and walked toward the door, saying, "Thanks for having me, ma'am."

"Call me Georgia, honey."

As I raised my hand to the doorknob, it crept open on its own, creaking like a horror-film door behind which gruesome discoveries awaited. I looked back at Georgia at the end of her kitchen, suddenly so far away.

"The house isn't like this once you're down that hallway," she said, bidding me an ominous adieu. "That's the boys' wing."

I could've sworn I heard a thunderclap as I peered down the darkened hallway ahead.

"Hello?" No one answered. I looked over my shoulder, asking, "Georgia, does Greg . . ." But, like magic, she had vanished.

The hallway seemed endless, stretching out ahead of me like the gaping maw of death. As I crept forward, a din of clashing sounds grew louder: car crashes, screaming women, laser guns, electric guitars, like the sound of several thousand televisions on at the same time.

"Greg? Where are you?"

A thudding boom echoed from the recesses of the blackness as a dim shaft of light broke through the passage ahead. A stocky, muscle-bound man with clenched fists appeared. He was covered in a sheen of sweat, wearing nothing but tiny black shorts.

"Who are you?" he barked.

"Uh, I'm . . . uh . . . I'm David." I held up my duffel bag in front of me, like it was proof that I was a welcome guest in this house of horrors.

"Greg! Greg! Greg!" he yelled repeatedly, while staring directly into my eyes. I struggled to maintain eye contact as I remembered my locker-room mantra.

Don't look down. Don't look down. Don't look down.

Greg appeared from a door across the hall, wearing sweatpants and a blue T-shirt.

"Jesus, Greg," the boy barked. "I've been yelling for an hour, dick-slice."

"When *aren't* you yelling, assface?" Greg sneered back.

"Bite me. Is this is your friend, fucktard?"

"No, Johnny. It's a deranged murderer. Of course it's my friend, you idiot."

Suddenly, Johnny thrust Greg down into a headlock. "Say it," he yelled, squashing Greg's neck as he flexed his gigantic bicep beneath his jaw. "Say, 'My name is Greg and I'm a — homo who loves noogies!' "

"This . . . is . . . my . . . brother . . . Johnny," Greg wheezed as his brother rubbed two knuckles back and forth on top of his head "He's . . . a . . . dick."

Maintaining his grip around Greg's neck, Johnny outstretched his free hand and flashed me a crooked smile. "So you're friends with Greg, my little sister?" he asked, shaking my hand.

"Sure," I whimpered.

"Nice meeting ya, Dave," grunted Johnny as he released Greg. "Don't let my brother give you a BJ after you fall asleep."

"Sure thing!" I instinctively replied, like I'd just been given a polite reminder to wiggle the handle when I flushed. As Johnny stomped back to his room, a door behind me swung open.

"Who are you?" asked a redheaded boy in his early twenties.

Greg choked out an introduction. "This . . . is my brother Adam."

"Hi Adam. I'm David. Nice to . . ."

Before I could finish, another door opened behind me. An adolescent boy with shaggy brown hair leaned into the hall, clutching a Swatch phone against his chest.

"Adam, shut the fuck . . . Oh . . ." he paused, noticing me, "who are you?"

Before I could answer, Adam interrupted, "Shut up, Charlie! I'm trying to study!"

"You're too stupid to study, dickweed!"

"I'm not the one making the noise, shit-for-brains!"

Their screaming match continued a foot and a half from my face until Georgia appeared down the hall, carrying a tray. "Calm down, boys," she delicately reprimanded, offering me a carefully arranged platter of Pizza Pockets. "I thought you'd like some snacks." She looked down at Greg hacking on the floor with tears streaming down his face. "Oh, you boys," she smiled, patting my cheek. "It's a kind of hell down here, David. Have fun."

Greg's bedroom was like an oasis in the midst of a nightmare: a clean, well-lit space with two twin beds and a huge window facing the front yard. Across one of the walls was a poster for a band called Erasure.

"David, how have you NOT heard of them?" Greg said, leaping from one bed to the other like a deranged ballerino. He tore through a box of cassettes on the floor. "You haven't heard 'A Little Respect'?" He popped the tape into a boom box and tossed me the cassette case. "They're the best. Check out the cover." Greg bounced onto the bed beside me, propping his chin up on his palms as he began to explain why he loved Erasure. I tried to keep my eyes focused on the lyric sheet as his body leaned against mine. No friend had ever been so close to me on a bed before, or anywhere else, for that matter.

"That's my favorite song!" Greg yelped, pointing his finger at the liner notes in my lap, a mere four inches from my crotch. I instinctively stood up from the bed.

"Your room is awesome!" I said, stretching and yawning to convey the message, *I'm not freaked out by your jabbing at my penis. I'm just feeling really sleepy all of a sudden and need to wake up.*

Greg looked at me quizzically. "Um, do you want to change or something?"

"Uh, sure!" I said, opening my duffel bag and taking out my clothes: two pairs of khaki pants, three polo shirts, two pairs of boxer briefs, and white knee-length socks.

"Are you staying over or moving in?" Greg chuckled, picking at my clothes as if they were evidence from a crime scene. "We're gonna watch a movie, not go to church."

He brushed past me to his closet and opened the doors. "You can borrow something," he said, tossing me a pair of sweatpants and a *Max Headroom* T-shirt.

"Well?" he said, staring at me expectantly. "Are you gonna change?"

"Here?" I asked, not wanting to be naked or partially naked in front of anyone, anywhere, ever. "You want me to change *here*?"

"No, David. I was thinking you'd change in the kitchen."

"The kitchen?" I asked. "You want me to change in the kitchen?"

"I'm joking, weirdo," he said, fiddling with his cassettes. "Change here. Duh."

I began to disrobe at a snail's pace, reminding myself that normal boys changed in front of one another. I tried to jump out of my pants quickly as Greg glanced away from me, but I snagged my right ankle in the cuff. Balancing on one leg like a flamingo, I started to hop to keep from falling over. But it was too late. I face-planted onto the bed, squirming, my legs bound together at the knees by my pants.

"David," Greg chuckled, making the room's cool air feel even colder on my exposed bottom. "You are hilarious."

In the full-length mirror on Greg's closet door I saw myself: splayed out on the bed, legs akimbo, Greg laughing beside me. In spite of my vulnerable position, I started to laugh with him. "Nerd," he chortled. And I swooned.

We spent that night listening to Greg's cassettes, talking about school, and fending off his intrusive brothers as they barged through the door to borrow his clothes, tapes, and CDs.

Four hours later we lay in each of the twin beds, watching TV. A film was beginning that neither of us had seen. A thin man in a nightclub crooned into the camera through a metal fence. On the dance floor, a veiled woman in sunglasses and her gaunt male partner observed the crowd, spotting a red-haired punk girl with her husky, unshaven boyfriend. At sunrise they took a limo to a very dark house, where they started flirting and stripping for each other, inexplicably still wearing sunglasses. Throughout every scene, each character smoked. There were so many smoldering cigarettes in the film that at one point, while a young David Bowie slid his hands up the leather miniskirt of a young Ann Magnuson, I thought I actually *smelled* smoke. As a thick gray cloud drifted in front of the TV, I realized it wasn't a hallucination.

"Greg!" I said, noticing him half-out his window, smoking. "What are you doing?"

"Take a chill pill. I do it all the time. Want one?"

He passed me a Marlboro Ultra Light 100 and a lighter across the threshold between our beds. I put the foreign thing in my mouth as if I'd done it a hundred times before, repeatedly trying to spark Greg's lighter to life until he impatiently ripped it from my hand. Leaning forward with the Marlboro in my mouth, I noticed the perfect musculature of his outstretched arm as he held the flame to my lips.

Don't look down. Don't look down. Don't look down.

As the flame died in Greg's hand, I took my first drag off a cigarette, fully prepared to cough up my guts the way teenagers in movies do. But as the smoke poured down my throat as smoothly as an oyster, I knew it: I was born to do this. It wasn't the first time that something new felt instantly natural to me. Before smoking, there was disco dancing, fashion sketching, and appetizer platter arranging. But this was the first time I felt good at something that was actually *cool*. I caught my reflection in the television screen, superimposed over David Bowie's porcelain face. A cigarette looked as at-home in between my lips as it did between his.

"Want another?" Greg asked. He lit me a fresh one by holding it against the tip of the one he was already smoking; the two cigarettes crackled against each other as a mushroom cloud of smoke drifted upward.

"That's called monkey fucking," he said, handing me the lit Marlboro.

Onscreen, Catherine Deneuve was parting her lips to release a thin trail of smoke, which drifted over her top lip and into her nose.

"I can do that. It's called a French inhale!" Greg leaned into the TV's dim light so I could see him re-create this ageless French vampire's smoking trick. My head began to spin from the nicotine as I watched the smoke move over the soft stubble on Greg's upper lip and into his flared nostril. The hairs on the back of my neck stood up as I shifted in my bed, worried about the flushed, warm feeling in my face and chest.

"David, you try it."

I held the cigarette to my lips and executed the trick perfectly, staring directly into Greg's eyes as he did the same. The two of us finished the entire pack of smokes, monkey fucking cigarette after cigarette like it was a contest. Lit only by faint moonlight and the cold glow of *The Hunger*, we could've smoked forever, like our lives depended on it.

This is Greg doing two of the things that made me love him madly.

1. Being hilarious. Note the catalog pose and fake mannequin hand in his perfectly shredded, acid-washed Guess jeans.

2. Looking perfect: the mock turtleneck, expertly gelled hair, and gold necklace. Half our freshman class wore crucifixes as the Madonna-stained eighties continued to linger into the front end of nineties fashion. But no one at our school wore their faux expressions of religious faith quite as well as Greg did.

CHAPTER 6

Black Celebration

Greg and I spent almost every waking moment together that summer. By then he'd ditched his girlfriend. During the day, we'd hang out in the neighborhood with Greg's little group of great-smelling buddies, who were all easygoing and kind. There was Billy, a slightly overweight boy with freckles who was always making dumb faces and loved playing Pac-Man for hours at a time. There was also Phil, a skinny blond boy who lived on the next block and dated a different girl every week. And then there was Joe, a lanky basketball player with black hair and blue eyes who listened to heavy metal.

I didn't have to work too hard in their presence because they were all such loudmouth buffoons. I could sit in a room listening to them riff on *Beavis and Butt-head* for an hour and not say a thing. They weren't just entertaining; they were also the first group of males I had felt comfortable around in a long time. But none of them made me feel quite like Greg did. As we got closer, it became harder for me to be away from him for more than twenty-four hours at a time.

"You're staying over at Greg's again, honey?" asked my mom, rouging her cheeks in the bathroom mirror.

"Um, yeah, if it's okay?"

"Of course it is!" she said, patting my cheek. "This is your summer!" My mom had been staying at Mike's often, when she wasn't working. The summer was giving her the chance to experience a bit of romance before I went back to school. It was also giving me the chance to form a new friendship. "It sounds like a great environment over there, honey."

Although it wasn't a *bad* environment, Greg and I weren't exactly eating balanced meals, trading baseball cards, and going to bed by ten. Our days with the boys were pretty traditional: video games, movie theaters, and MTV. But our evenings were different, and they belonged solely to us. Every night we'd stay up late smoking cigarettes and drinking gallons of coffee. We'd rewatch *The Hunger* and talk about witchcraft, flipping through my mom's big purple *Book of Spells*, which lived under Greg's bed now. We'd try to figure out how to sneak into over-eighteen clubs and get our hands on this elusive "marijuana."

"Greg's a nice boy from a big, stable family with two parents at home," added my mother as she brushed her hair. "They say that kind of familial bonding can be very good for adolescents from single-parent homes."

I rolled my eyes, imagining which *Is-My-Child-a-Serial-Killer* book my mother had gleaned this information from. "Yeah, you don't want me out there torturing cats."

"Oh hush, you," she yelped, smacking my arm with a hairbrush.

Later that night, after a long day playing video games at Billy's, Greg and I were prepping for our favorite activity: the Ouija board.

Around 8 p.m. we snuck through his house, gathering every candle we could find. We lit each one, until the bedroom was glowing with flickering orange light. Greg delicately placed the Ouija board on the floor between us. Sitting Indian-style across from me, he closed his eyes and inhaled deeply.

"Okay, David. Are you ready?"

"I'm ready," I responded, shutting my eyes and lowering my hands onto the little plastic pointer.

Greg asked the spirits all kinds of questions: about our futures, our friends, how we'd die, who we'd been in past lives. He truly believed in the power of the Ouija board and would heed its advice, taking notes in a small journal he hid in the frame of his bed. I watched him write; he bit his lip adorably as he looked at the ceiling to organize his thoughts. Everything in me wanted to scream out, *You are the coolest, most handsome person I've ever met and if you'd just kiss me one time I swear I'd leave you alone forever.*

"Greg, do you think that . . ."

"Oh my God," he interrupted, wide-eyed. "It's Sunday night!"

We turned on the TV just in time for MTV's *120 Minutes*, a weekly show featuring two hours of our favorite music videos from the newly coined "alternative" genre. That summer we discovered bands like the Cure, Depeche Mode, Bauhaus, and New Order, in music videos featuring dark forests, fog machines, and oodles of black. We listened to an endless rotation of moody British male singers moaning seductively about how sad they were, or sadly about how horny they were, as Greg writhed around his room, dancing. The longer we'd been friends, the more he'd taken to performing outright routines for me.

"David! What do you think?" he asked, slowly swaying forward as he touched his right heel to his left toe on the floor. "Doesn't this look cool?"

"Yeah. It's like you're walking on an invisible line or something."

"Oh my God, David. You're right. I should call this the Tightrope."

"Whatever, private dancer," I said, rolling my eyes.

In truth, I could've watched Greg dance for hours as he spun in circles and pointed skyward. I sang along and thumbtacked different cardboard CD sleeves like makeshift posters to the wall over my bed. And by that point I was really starting to think of it as *my* bed. In *my* room. In *my* house.

Our nights together were a separate thing from our days with the boys, like a secret. Neither of us elaborated on this in words, but a part of me knew that Greg's dance numbers were strictly for us, for me; and I loved it. Slowly, we saw less and less of Billy, Phil, and Joe. Even the days became our own, and by August we weren't hanging out with them at all.

One morning a few weeks before our sophomore year would start, Greg and I walked to the mall. We liked going just as the shops were opening, when elderly folks wearing ankle weights did their early-morning laps around the building's perimeter. Greg and I went straight to the Music Express CD's & Cassettes with our little list of songs we'd heard on *120 Minutes*. After buying as many CDs as we could afford, we set up camp in the food court with our gray Discmans with the orange buttons, excited to listen to our new tunes.

"What's this one?" Greg asked, popping my Pet Shop Boys *Introspective* CD into his Discman. He flipped around the right ear pad of his huge Koss headphones so I could listen too as the opening track, "Left to My Own Devices," began.

We stopped chewing our Chick-fil-A nuggets and froze, immediately transported by the lush, ethereal sound of a full orchestra and dramatic synth hits. A clearly homosexual British man began singing about being "a lonely boy, no strength, no joy / in a world of my own at the back of the garden."

I wanted to scream, *Greg, he's singing about me!*

To be fair, we didn't really have "gardens" in Texas. We had flat, dried-out yards full of burnt yellow grass and stray cat shit. But the music made me feel like I could be anywhere. As the synths and drums built, the vocalist began singing about Che Guevara and Debussy. I didn't know who Che Guevara and Debussy were, but I wanted to. The album continued like a satellite course at Euro-Gay University as Neil Tennant sang about impressionist art, the Russian Revolution, and more British landmarks than you could shake a bag of crisps at.

"They're amazing," gasped Greg, his lips covered in honey-mustard dipping sauce. I considered Greg's love of Pet Shop Boys, Erasure, and Catherine Deneuve. I liked all those things, and I was gay. So, mathematically, shouldn't Greg's appreciation of them make *him* gay too?

I reached over the table with a napkin to wipe his mouth, saying, "Greg, you've got . . ."

"What are you doing?" he snapped, pushing my hand away.

"Oh. Sorry . . . your mouth," I said. "Sorry . . . Sorry . . . I . . ."

"Fuck you, slut!" someone screamed as a flock of birds scattered along the atrium roof.

We looked toward Long John Silver's, where the girl's scream came from. Clustered around a mountain of Taco Bell wrappers and tipped-over thirty-two-ounce cups was a group of kids wearing black clothes and heavy boots. They threw ice and flipped each other off with black-varnished fingers, cackling and yelling at each other with painted lips.

"Who are they?" Greg whispered as a boy in black lipstick noticed us watching. I quickly looked up, pretending to admire the skylights of the mall ceiling, half a chicken nugget hanging from my mouth. These were surely the cult kids we'd heard about on the ten o'clock news, the ones who murdered stray cats on chalk-drawn pentagrams in the park. Or maybe they were vampires who'd realized that covering themselves in a quarter-inch of foundation would protect them from the sun—vampires who, after thousands of years toiling in darkness, had discovered the secret to existing in daylight and said, "Yes! Finally, we've done it! Now we can go to the MALL!"

We watched them for an hour, slyly catching glances as we showed off our brand-new Cure, Bauhaus, and Church CDs.

"Look at that girl in the center," I murmured, noticing a girl in the eye of the goth storm, sitting perfectly still. She was small and Hispanic; her burgundy-tipped ebony hair swept up from the back of her neck and over the top of her head, forming a curtain of strands over her face. Through the chin-length strands we could occasionally see one of her black-framed eyes, peering intensely around her. She was the queen bee of the group, never getting up as drone goths brought her giant Mountain Dews and fresh packs of Camel filterless cigarettes.

"David," Greg whispered in the bustling food court, as if we were in class. "Look at her face . . . When she moves again. Wait a minute. Look right . . . right . . . right . . . NOW!"

As she leaned over to speak to someone, her crusty bangs momentarily moved away from her face. What I saw looked so strange that I didn't quite process what it was at first.

"Greg, does she have a fake nose?"

At one point it might have been flesh-colored, but now it looked ashy and grayish, which made it seem askew on her face.

Two hours later, the goth crew started to gather their things to leave.

"Greg, they're coming this way," I whispered, opening the CD booklet for my Love and Rockets album and holding it near my face to be seen. As they shuffled past, their crooked-nosed leader stopped to tie one of her twelve-hole Doc Marten boots a few feet from our table. Slowly she stood up, staring at me through her veil of fried black bangs.

"Hey," she said. Greg and I looked up at her. "That's an excellent album," she sighed, then stared at us in silence. After what felt like a muted eternity, a boy in a Depeche Mode t-shirt ahead of her yelled "Daphne!," a name that seemed totally at odds with her witchy persona.

"See ya," she said, shooting us a good-bye sneer before shuffling away.

"David!" Greg exclaimed, grabbing my arm. "She liked your CD!"

"I know!" I shrieked back, my excitement amplified by Greg's skin on mine.

We didn't have the guts to say anything to her. But soon we'd have to muster the courage. Because we'd just met a legend, a rare bird, a unicorn.

CHAPTER 7

Warm Leatherette

Son, we need to talk," he said.

There was no reason for my dad to be waiting for me in the parking spot in front of my mom's apartment building after school. He wasn't even supposed to be back in town for another four days. My sophomore year had only started a couple weeks earlier; it hadn't even yielded a report card yet. My mind raced as I wondered what I could be in trouble for. Had my mom found my folder of Antonio Sabàto Jr. clippings from Calvin Klein underwear ads? Had she shown my dad the fantasy writings about Greg, Marky Mark, and the rookie cop from *T. J. Hooker* in my journal? What about the VHS tape full of Mark-Paul Gosselaar's shirtless scenes from *Saved by the Bell*?

My dad stood up from the curb and peered at me over his sunglasses.

"Well?" he asked.

"What?" I said, trying to sound casual.

"Whaddya think?" he asked, grinning from ear to ear and gesturing to the car parked beside him. "I got you some new wheels, DJ!"

"Oh. Um . . ." I looked at the boxy, baby-blue sedan, the car of a low-paid nurse saving for retirement or of one of the old nuns who shopped for yarn at String City in the mall. "What is it?" I asked, trying to muster some excitement for his subpar gift. "An Escort?"

"No, son, but it's very similar. It's a Mercury Lynx."

"What about the Bronco II or the old Karmann Ghia I liked?"

"Well, I did some research, son." My father rounded the car excitedly with a yellow legal pad. "See here?" he said, pulling a pen from his shirt pocket and pointing to his data. "Bronco IIs tip over like clockwork. And they don't even make parts for the other one anymore."

As he rambled statistics, I inspected the car, imagining Greg's ridicule once he saw it. I leaned inside to see the navy-blue interior and slightly cracked plastic dashboard.

"It's lightly used," said my dad jovially, "but it gets great mileage and will last for years and years, maybe even into college."

The nightmare of driving this car for four years worsened once I looked between the seats. "You got me a standard?" I screeched. "A standard? Why would you do that?"

"Now calm down, DJ." My dad rambled through a prepared list of cost-benefit analyses and safety features intended to offset my darkest fear coming true: having to drive a stick shift. For two months we'd sat in grocery-store parking lots and open fields, bucking back and forth in my attempts to drive his stick-shift truck.

"But I can't drive this!" I pleaded, no longer concerned with seeming thankful. "Please!"

"David, calm down." My dad put his hands on his hips and tightened his jaw.

"But I drive Mom's automatic just fine," I whined. "Why did you . . ."

"This is your new car, dammit!" he screamed. "You can let it sit here and rot for all I care. But this is what I was charitable enough to buy for you!"

We barely spoke to each other that night over dinner at Bill Miller Bar-B-Q. I chewed my brisket angrily in silence, too immature to realize how lucky I was to have a car at all, let alone a free one.

I mustered a bitter "Thanks" when he dropped me off in front of my apartment an hour later. As he pulled away, my mother came outside with her boyfriend, Mike.

"You got yourself a car, huh?" he said, noticing the keys in my hand. Mike was a tall, woolly man with a thick beard. He spoke in a laid-back drawl acquired from being born and raised in Seguin, Texas, a small town known for being home to the biggest pecan in the world.

"Oh, honey," my mother sighed, looking at my powder-blue boat. "So *this* is it, huh?"

"Yep," I answered, clutching the keys in my hand so hard I almost drew blood.

"Well, it could be worse, right?" Mike asked with a grin.

"How?" I asked, half-sarcastic, half-hoping for a real answer.

"It could be purple or orange!" my mom exclaimed. "This is actually your mother's favorite color!" She smiled, not knowing she'd just made it so much worse.

"Get in and see how it feels!" said Mike, opening the driver's-side door.

As my mom and I sat down in the front seats, she reminded me, "A lot of sixteen-year-olds don't get a free car, honey. Look on the bright side."

I gripped the steering wheel and settled into the cushy seat. I started to feel better, reminding myself that I finally had my own set of wheels. This positive attitude ended after a moment, as my mother reached to where the tape player should have been.

"Huh?" she queried. "It only has radio?"

I could feel my blood begin to boil on either side of my face. My ears felt hot and my jaw clenched. I was a sixteen-year-old with a car that had no ability to play cassettes or CDs. What was the point of living?

By the end of September, the stereo had proved to be the least of my worries. It was the stick shift that almost did me in.

"We're going to die!" screamed Greg as cars from three directions slammed on their brakes. At the I-410/Perrin Beitel Road intersection I'd gotten stuck while pulling away from a green light. Car horns honked as I turned the key again and again, attempting to start the pastel beast but stalling it every time.

"David! Start the fucking car!" yelled Greg as we bucked forward another few feet. An obese cowboy with a holstered gun stomped toward us, his black truck at a standstill, like twenty others all around us.

"What the fuck is wrong with you, boy?" he yelled, pounding on my windshield.

"He's going to kill us!" yelped Greg, recoiling from the looming giant. "Hurry!"

"I'm trying, Greg! I'm trying!"

After a dozen attempts, I finally released and pressed the clutch and accelerator with perfect timing, sailing forward like a rocket beneath the freeway and through two red lights.

"You're going to crash!" yelled Greg. His flair for the dramatic had been intensifying during the first few weeks of sophomore year, as he'd become more obsessed with our theater arts class. "We're going to die!"

To be fair, I was going to crash. And we did almost die, a few times.

"Pull over, nerd!" Greg demanded. "I'm driving."

For fear of perishing with me behind the wheel, Greg had been driving my car to school a lot. I picked him up each morning with a veneer of sweat on my forehead from the ten times I'd almost flown off an access ramp. But oftentimes, my mom would let me stay over at Greg's, especially on Sundays, which extended the weekend for both of us—she in Seguin with Mike, and I in San Antonio with Greg.

"I just love that you have a new friend," she said. "And from a great family!"

I neglected to tell my mom that Greg's giant bedroom window was easy to sneak out of. I also neglected to tell her that Greg's parents slept in a very secluded room at the back of the house and rarely laid eyes on me. I might also have neglected to tell her about our 2 a.m. walks to Stop & Shop for packs of cigarettes, which would be completely depleted by sunrise.

Every school morning we woke up extra-early, after a three-hour nap, to brew coffee and get our looks together. Greg introduced me to a whole new world of hair products, which added fifteen minutes to my daily process. Side by side in the bathroom, we gelled and moussed our hair into a dozen styles before settling on one. Around 7:30 his brothers would groggily stumble from their bedrooms to find us perfectly dressed, styled, and caffeinated. On the way to Taco Cabana for breakfast burritos we'd smoke a cigarette and watch the sun come up. Then we'd smoke another cigarette and stop at 7-Eleven for more coffee. After another cigarette we'd arrive at school, bucking and rocking into the parking lot in my hideous blue tank.

A few days before Halloween we arrived at school in our usual morning trance, still buzzing from nicotine. I walked into the courtyard wearing acid-washed Guess jeans and a New Order shirt, both borrowed from Greg's closet, which was really *our* closet, in *our* room, in *our* house.

"Hey Greg," said Lisette, a perky, big-haired blonde we called a "Bowhead," a girl whose big, ribboned headband made her head look like an ornate Christmas present. "Hi David," she mumbled plainly in my direction, only because I was standing beside Greg.

"What's up, Lisette?" Greg answered her and slid his Ray-Bans down his nose, looking like Tom Cruise in a movie poster.

"What did you do this weekend?" she asked, batting her eyelashes as she fluffed her new, poodlelike bob.

"Not much. We just hung out at the mall and went swimming at my house," Greg answered Lisette in his bored lower register as she twisted a clump of crimped hair around her finger. Occasionally she glared my way as if to say, "You're *still* here?"

"I got a joke, Greg!" she said, hugging her Dooney & Bourke shoulder bag. "What's red and bubbly and scratches at the window?"

"What?" he asked mock-excitedly, knowing the punch line perfectly well.

"A baby in a microwave!" squealed Lisette, leaning against him as she giggled.

I almost felt bad, watching her bask in Greg's charitable fake laughter. I knew the sound of Greg's real laughter. She probably never would. As we watched her massive crimped bouffant bounce away from us, I whispered out the side of my mouth, "When did her head become a dust mop?"

Greg dropped his books and slowly slid against my shoulder to the ground, roaring with laughter until he was on all fours. I reached down to help him up but was pulled down as well.

"You asshole," I chuckled beside him as papers and pens spilled from my backpack. Students in the courtyard looked at us like we were weirdos, rolling around on the concrete, crying with laughter. Being perceived as a weirdo was an experience I'd thought I wanted behind me. But lying in the courtyard beside Greg, staring up at the sun, delirious from barely two hours of sleep, it felt okay. As long as I had Greg, I didn't care what people thought of me.

A few weeks later we went to the mall on Black Friday, which was a mob scene and made for some great people watching. We hadn't noticed the goth crew in the food court for a while. But after an absence they'd returned with their leader, in all her purple-haired, prosthetic-nosed glory. Greg and I were fifteen minutes into watching the freak camp when we heard a familiar nasal squall.

"Greg!" Lisette giggled from across the food court. Her massive hair bounced in time with a dozen shopping bags as her Bowhead posse approached us.

"Ugh," Greg sighed, ripping the tag off his new Erasure T-shirt.

As the Bowheads neared the freaks, Lisette noticed Daphne putting a cigarette out in a cup of honey-mustard sauce.

"Ewww," Lisette cackled, pointing the freaks out to her friends. "Smoking is so gross!"

Seemingly unfazed, Daphne stood up in front of the group and swept her hair back from her face, revealing a terrifying moonscape of foundation-caked acne. She locked eyes with Lisette as the Bowheads stopped laughing and froze. Daphne let out a shrill scream and ripped away her prosthetic nose, exposing a wet cavity of soft pink tissue that throbbed and flexed with each sirenlike wail.

The Bowheads attempted to escape all at once, tripping one another as woven leather belts and stonewashed shorts spilled from their shopping bags. Scrambling to get up or crawl away, they stepped on each other's fingers and fell over each other's legs. Their screams sounded like the ones you hear in recorded 911 calls. One by one, they ran toward the Macy's entrance as Daphne shuffled forward like a zombie. Lisette finally regained her footing and ran the length of the second-floor balcony, yelling until she was out of sight.

A hundred shoppers looked on in horror, afraid to approach or reprimand the deformed girl in the Nosferatu T-shirt. In their wake, the Bowheads had left a small pile of shopping bags and scattered beads from one of their broken necklaces. Daphne hunched over the mess and made a great snorting sound as she plugged the false nose back onto her face. Two friends joined her and they picked every last bead off the tiled floor, even stopping an oncoming shopper with a stroller.

"Careful, lady!" Daphne warned, picking up the remnants of jewelry.

As Daphne sat back down with the freaks to model some of the abandoned clothes, Greg leaned into my ear and whispered, "Who wouldn't want to be friends with them?"

We had to infiltrate their lair.

On the way home Greg played our favorite Book of Love cassette from the boom box in his lap as we jerked away from stop-lights, causing melees at every intersection. Pulling up to Greg's house as he ejected the tape, we noticed something strange in the driveway. Right behind Johnny, who was doing power push-ups in a pair of tiny onionskin shorts, was a bright-red convertible Cabriolet.

"Surprise!" yelled Georgia as we walked up the driveway. "Christmas is early!"

Greg screamed with delight. "Get in, David!" he yelled, jumping into the driver's seat. I sat down beside him in the beautiful beige interior and relished the rich leather smell of brand-new seats.

"Look! A real stereo!" Greg yelled, pointing to the removable-front tape deck.

"And I installed a CD changer in the back," said Johnny, dripping sweat over me as he reached in to pop the trunk. "You can load it with a dozen discs. It's fuckin' awesome."

"David," Greg exclaimed, "we can listen to music the normal way now!"

"Yeah, normal," I repeated, noticing the automatic transmission stick between us.

"Now you both have cars!" smiled Georgia, momentarily staring across the street at my ugly, azure death trap. In the rearview mirror it looked so decrepit—boxy and boring, with a thin layer of midautumn Texas pollen covering its sides.

Georgia kissed Greg's cheek and went inside as Johnny excitedly told Greg all about the Cabriolet, a car that felt more like the one I should be driving but that I knew was so much more expensive than anything my family could afford.

"Here's the best part," Johnny said, punching a button on the dash.

As the top of the car opened over our heads, we looked up to the cloudless sky. Greg started the car and popped our favorite cassette into the Cabriolet's stereo system. Book of Love's "Boy" blasted from speakers all around us.

"Those are special subwoofers you're listening to, boys," yelled Johnny over the mirror-rattling bass.

"Yeah!" Greg screamed, hugging me as the lead singer cooed the lyric "I want to be where the boys are . . ." We bounced up and down in the seat midhug, knowing that our days of almost dying before first period were over.

"You fags are too much," Johnny said, patting me on the back with a smile. The word sounded different than it had before. And as I hugged Greg, listening to *our* music in *our* car in *our* driveway, I felt a little more like someone's brother.

Here's Greg and me during our sophomore year shortly after we
moved into a more New Wave aesthetic; lots of vests and hair gel
during this phase. I believe we're each wearing matching ankh
charms at the end of those homemade, black yarn necklaces. Our
favorite lunchtime offerings were these scalding-hot hamburgers
that were microwaved in their own plastic packaging. Greg's
excitement over his burger might explain his look of surprise here.
I'm surprised we allowed ourselves to be photographed during
lunch. Eating was never very goth.

CHAPTER 8

This Must Be the Place I Waited Years to Leave

F uckin' wake up!" yelled Johnny, wet and naked, holding a balled-up towel over his crotch. "This fucking phone rang off the hook until I had to get out of the fucking shower," he screamed, shoving a cordless phone into my face before snapping Greg with his towel.

"Jerk!" Greg murmured, wincing in pain as he woke up.

"Excuse me," my mother asked through the receiver.

"Mom? What's wrong?" I asked.

"David. Your father's here to pick you up," she whispered. "Where are you?"

I'd forgotten that we were spending Super Bowl Sunday at my grandparents' house.

"Tell me the address," my dad barked in the background.

I quickly washed my armpits and scrubbed my face to prepare for his arrival, trying to look awake in spite of the three hours of sleep I'd gotten. I went into panic mode, combing the dried gel out of my hair and pacing the bedroom.

"Greg, I need normal clothes. Please! Something for church."

I looked at the options Greg laid out on his bed, the comb shaking in my hand.

"David, it's okay. What's wrong?"

"I just don't want him to be mad," I said, looking out the window as I put on Greg's khakis. "We're going to be twenty minutes late because of me!"

"David, why don't you stay here? Say you're sick or . . ."

A car horn honked. We looked through the window at my dad in the brown truck outside, his jaw locked tight, knuckles flexed around the steering wheel. He slowly turned his head until his laser-beam gaze stopped on us. Greg flinched away from the window.

"God, David. He looks . . . mad."

I hugged Greg tightly and whispered, "He's mad a lot."

My dad and I spent the first part of our fifteen-minute ride in nerve-racking silence. Over the hum of the engine I could hear his teeth grinding against one another. Each red light or delayed exit lane seemed like the final straw, the thing that would push him over the edge.

Every turn, brake, and acceleration was loaded with the possibility of a confrontation. One that would make me sink slowly against the car door, trying to become a puddle that would evaporate in the sheer, blazing heat of my father's anger.

"Why weren't you at your house and ready?" he asked as we arrived.

"I forgot."

"You forgot?"

"Yeah, Dad. Sorry."

"We'll see if I forget *you* the next time we make plans," he said, braking hard in front of my grandparents' house. "Now tuck your shirt in." He got out and walked into the yard. "Hurry up, dammit."

"Sorry," I said, fumbling with the seat belt. "I'm coming. Sorry."

My grandparents had lived in the same pink brick house since before I was born. The garage was a storage area, its walls mounted with taxidermied animal heads that had terrified me for years. A glass jar of dust-covered peppermints sat on the coffee table, untouched since the early eighties. The bathroom was still decorated with the little mermaid figurines I'd given names and told secrets to when I was a little boy. My grandfather sat where he'd been for as long as I could remember: in a beige La-Z-Boy recliner with a television remote in his lap.

"Well hello, stranger," he said, surrounded by a dozen relatives drinking iced tea out of mason jars.

"Sorry we're late," my dad said over the television, shooting me a sideways glance.

"Oh, don't you worry about a thing," my grandmother Oggy said, covering us in salmon-colored-lipstick kisses. "Come out back, y'all. We're about to have venison and chalupas."

The large group moved out to the backyard to have lunch before the game. A massive ten-point buck hung from an oak tree by its hind legs, its chest and stomach splayed open. The men gathered on one side of the deer to listen to my grandfather tell the gory, detailed story of its murder. The women sat in rusty metal chairs around a picnic table on the other side of the deer, discussing their recipes. I straddled the space between the two until my aunt Jean called me over. At first it was a relief. But as my grandmother brought out her famous chalupas, the interrogation began.

"So tell us about all the girls you're driving wild!" said my cousin Janet. "You're so handsome, David. You must have a gal!"

The questions continued as I pigged out on venison, knowing that having a full mouth would give me time to consider my answers carefully. I chewed slowly, hoping a cousin would interrupt or my grandmother would ask for help in the kitchen or the deer would fall from its branch and crush me to death in front of my entire family.

"My neighbor's daughter would love you," winked Janet as cousin Sharla added, "I teach a girl named Robin you should meet."

I wanted to remind them that I was a teenage boy, not a forty-year-old divorcé. As the ladies squawked and gossiped, I looked up into the dripping, scarlet rib cage of the dead creature overhead. With my mouth full of what used to be its body, I thought, *Why can't I be you right now? Swinging in the breeze without a care in the world? Hanging dead from a tree with no one obsessively questioning your burgeoning sexuality?*

An hour later we moved inside to prepare for the game, the women cleaning up in the kitchen while the men gathered in the living room. A half dozen beer cans popped open as the TV screen lit up with crowd shots of painted faces and giant foam fingers. I had no interest in football, choosing instead to hang out with Oggy and her gals. In the kitchen we'd gab about Bat

Boy, UFOs, and whatever else had piqued her interest in the latest issue of *Globe* magazine or the *National Enquirer*. But as I moved into the kitchen, my father stopped me.

"DJ, why don't you stay in here and watch the game?"

I sat down on the couch and watched the pregame coverage as a great-uncle and a second cousin slipped into coma-like slumbers. My cousin Brett started to rail against the Buffalo Bills as my cousin Fred decried the New York Giants.

"They're all damn Yankees," my grandfather interrupted, holding the remote up to the screen to turn up the volume. "What the heck does it matter?"

My dad exhaled loudly. I cringed at the thought that my grandfather's behavior could be another reason for my dad to be upset on the ride home, when it would be just him and me. My grandfather cleared his throat and lowered the remote onto his lap with a quivering hand.

"Bring me some more tea!" he yelled to my grandmother in the kitchen.

Dutifully, she brought him his tea, sneaking me a grin on her way back to the kitchen. As retirees fell asleep all around me, I became transfixed by the pregame interviews on the television. Chiseled, meaty jaws flexed and forearm muscle striations danced as thick-necked Yankee men of various ethnicities discussed the game. As my cousin Bill's sleeping head slumped against my shoulder, the camera lingered on a player's rounded buttocks, the ghostly belt of a jockstrap visible through his sheer spandex tights. I tried to focus on the ladies in the kitchen talking about an endoscopy and then on the deer carcass swinging outside and then on the myriad of black fillings in my sleeping cousin's open mouth, but nothing worked. My grandfather began to snore. The only other conscious person in the room was my father. There I was again, trapped with a rock-hard, brain-burning erection in a small space with my dad.

"I'll be back."

I burst from the room with incredible speed, knowing that the faster I moved, the better chance I had of hiding the lump below my belt. I slammed the bathroom door and dropped my pants, a multiethnic Rolodex of rippling biceps and bulging athletic cups dancing through my head. I unzipped my pants, trying not to think about the pastel bathroom full of *Reader's Digest*s and tubes of Icy Hot, but the inappropriate contrast only made me harder. Thirty seconds later I could feel it rising up in me—that wonderful building of staticlike electricity moving into the tops of my thighs and then higher, centering itself and expanding like a magnificent supernova. I heard a faint ceramic knocking that was getting louder. I realized it was the toilet seat moving back and forth against my shins in rhythm with my strokes. As my knees buckled I bit my lip, muting myself as an amazing rush took control of my body. I opened my eyes just in time to see myself ejaculate all over my favorite mermaid's smiling porcelain face.

"DJ. It's starting," my dad yelled.

I looked around at my grandparents' things: my grandfather's plastic shower seat, my grandmother's giant canister of Final Net hairspray, the tiny tray on the toilet tank packed with geriatric prescriptions. I'd just pleasured myself in their bathroom while imagining complete sexual annihilation at the hands of the Buffalo Bills. I wiped my semen off the tiny face of the magical sea creature I'd whispered to as a three-year-old and felt utterly ashamed.

I zipped up my gay pants and washed my gay hands, avoiding my gay reflection on the way out. In the living room, I was met with an explosion of applause. For a split second I feared that my fantasy football orgy in the bathroom hadn't been as private as I'd thought. But the applause was coming from the television, where a stadium of people was exploding with cheers as a tiny black woman in a white tracksuit began to sing, "Ooo-oooh say, can you seeee . . ."

Whitney Houston belted out the national anthem with more passion, skill, and grace than I'd ever heard. The camera zoomed in on her face, tears welling up in her eyes. The crowd sat hypnotized in quiet, dumbfounded reverie. Whitney's voice was like a siren. As she sang, I could feel something familiar rising up in me: a staticlike electricity moving through my belly, into my lungs, and then higher, centering itself and expanding like a magnificent supernova in my chest. Her gaze rose skyward as she belted out the final note, her expression signifying a kind of hearty thanks as well as a pleading desperation. Watching this beautiful girl with black skin who looked nothing like previous Super Bowl singers, I was reminded that I was free, but that maybe I could be even freer. And maybe I deserved it.

As a wave of applause erupted from the stadium, a silence fell over the living room. A dozen of us stared, wide-eyed and awake, at the television.

"Hmm. That nigger can sing."

My grandfather sat in his chair, arms crossed, staring into the screen with dull, bored eyes.

"Anyone hungry for pie?" asked my grandmother halfheartedly.

Almost everyone walked into the kitchen for dessert, leaving my father, my grandfather, and me alone with the static hiss of the roaring stadium. My dad looked at me with sad, concerned eyes that seemed to say, *Are you okay? Does it hurt? I love you, son.*

As he patted me on the shoulder and left the room, I wondered how it must feel to be that distant from your own father. Then I shuddered at the possibility of one day finding out, albeit for different reasons.

I sat in silence with my grandfather as giant, glistening men ran back and forth across the screen, so many men I wasn't allowed to want. I wondered if that pink brick house was really where I was meant to be. I hoped not, but the back pages of *Interview* magazine suddenly seemed like they were more than a few states away. Those photos were surely taken on a planet in some other galaxy. And on my planet, in this galaxy, inhabited by these people, I knew that I could be only so free.

Staring at the television, my grandfather let out a long exhale and asked, "So, David. How's the girl situation?"

CHAPTER 9

I've Got to Get Through to a Good Friend

Over the next month, I started to feel my newfound optimism slip away. Even in Greg's room on a Friday night, ensconced in the scent of a dozen Glade candles and listening to Depeche Mode, I was preoccupied, unable to shake an invisible weight that was starting to feel unbearably heavy. A small, familiar voice at the back of my mind had returned, and it was getting louder.

You're a liar and you know what's going to happen, it said. *Soon Greg will know. And he won't like you. Go away. Be alone.*

"All I ever wanted! All I ever needed is heeeere . . . In my arms!" Greg sang, bounding from one side of his bedroom to another like a manic gazelle, doing backflips and front flips and generally bouncing off the walls. I watched him spin and leap, wondering how anyone could be that lithe and energized.

I sang along the way I had in church when I was little, my mouth moving but no actual sound coming out. My hands trembled as I lit candles around the room with a butane lighter.

"You ready?" asked Greg, sliding the Ouija board out from under his bed.

"Of course I am," I replied, the words coming from my mouth limply.

Across the Ouija board I stared at Greg's face, softly lit in an orange glow. His eyelashes looked like they were miles long, casting spidery shadows down the length of his cheeks. His brown eyes seemed hazel in the firelight, like they were lit from within. The little facial scar that I rarely noticed looked like a fresh, deep groove on his chin.

"Tune in, Tokyo," he said, rapping his knuckles lightly against my forehead. "David, what is wrong with you?"

"Oh. Sorry. Nothing."

"You're totally out to lunch."

I was trying to be present. All I wanted was to concentrate on the spirits in the room and believe in them. So I tried with all my might to focus on Greg's questions for our visiting ghosts.

"Will David and I have a good summer?"

"Will we go to any good concerts this year?"

"Will we try acid over the break?"

If I could see past my worries and deficits and perversions and just believe in the board, then something mystical would surely happen. Something otherworldly would course through me, if I could only open myself to it. But all I could think about was how alone I felt at that moment. I'd never felt lonely with Greg before. In my head I kept playing the worst after-school special ever made: my father slamming a door in my face; my mother pulling her hand from mine as she broke into tears; my grandmother pretending not to see me in a grocery store; myself, older and thinner, sitting in a waiting room and then a doctor's office and then a hospital bed.

I kept trying to listen to Greg as he spoke to me, just the way I always had. But something had changed. Something was wrong now that hadn't been before. A giant sponge outside my body was intercepting and absorbing all the stimuli I loved: the song playing on the stereo, Greg's ecstatic smile, the flickering amber light against the walls and ceiling of his bedroom. I felt as if my happiness was floating in a cloud overhead and all I could do was watch it hover. I was hermetically sealed away from all my feelings. And I had to get those feelings back.

I looked across the board at Greg, his head tilted back and eyes closed like a carnival fortune-teller. In the dim light of the room I could see the jugular vein in his soft neck throbbing beneath his skin. I imagined that I was a rapidly aging David Bowie from *The Hunger*, locked away by Catherine Deneuve and nearing the end of my centuries-long life. I imagined my teeth in Greg's body, his blood in my mouth, his pulse fading into my being. But the thought wasn't arousing or dangerously sexy. It seemed vicious and depraved. I didn't want Greg to be my victim, or anyone else's. I wanted him to be like me. I wanted a companion.

The thought made me smile for the first time that day.

"Wouldn't it be cool if we were vampires?" I asked.

"Oh my God," he grinned, "I've thought the exact same thing!" Greg took his hands off the planchette and scooted closer to me. "It would be so cool. First of all, we'd totally quit school, right? And we would go to the mall and steal a bunch of awesome black clothes, which we could do, because what are they gonna do? Arrest us? We'll just turn into bats and fly out of Saks before they can catch us. But we'll also be able to be invisible. There are at least three vampire movies where I've seen this happen. So I'm pretty sure it's possible."

Greg rocked back and forth excitedly against my knees, still sitting Indian-style.

"And then we'd write really nice letters to our families," he said, fireworks going off in his eyeballs. "We'd let them know we were okay, but that we'd become creatures of the night and wouldn't be able to maintain contact. My mom would be sad, but I'd send her money and jewels and stuff that I stole from Italy, where we would fly a couple times a year, just for the food. Now, I know we supposedly can *only* drink blood, but I think we'll be able to have lasagna and stuff too. Now, we *will* have to devise some sort of plan for killing people. I mean, I don't wanna be a total dick, so what we'll do is break into police stations by morphing into a fine mist, which happened in *Fright Night* and a few other movies. So, again, I'm pretty sure this is possible. Then you and I would steal criminal records and find people who got off the hook for committing awful crimes, like rapes and murders and stuff like that. And we would only kill THEM! So smart, right? We'd be, like . . . good vampires! But we'd still totally wear black and be sexy and stuff. Like, we would totally hypnotize hot people into making out with us and everything."

Greg slid the Ouija board over and scooted closer, his face a foot from mine.

"The hard part, though, is this: how do we get bitten? The fashion and murder part is easy. Well, anything is easy when you can fly, hypnotize people, and become invisible. But how do we *become* vampires?"

"I don't know, Greg."

"Well, I do . . . Her name is Selene."

"Who?"

Greg pulled out a plastic-bound library book from under his bed and opened it.

"Selene is the moonlight goddess and mother to all vampires. I read about her here, in the *Vampire Bible*."

"There's a bible for vampires?" I asked.

"Well, it's more like a history. We can call her with a vampire spell," he said, pointing at a poem called "Ode to the Vampire Mother."

"Now, you're supposed to read it in the original Latin, but there's a lot of letter *V*'s in this one and I can't pronounce it. So I'm going to conjure her by reading it in English instead."

I imagined our futures, wearing sunglasses in discotheques and nightclubs all over the world, avenging thousands of raped and murdered people by sucking the life from their dangerous yet alluring abusers, flying through the night sky side by side and returning to our glamorous New York penthouse coffins in time for sunrise.

Greg placed the Ouija board between us and put his fingers on it.

"We don't really need the Ouija board for this since it's essentially a spell. But since I'm reading it in English I think it might help or something."

I didn't question his logic, as Greg seemed to have a profound handle on the business of functional, modern-day vampirism.

"Okay, David. Here we go. Close your eyes," he said, tilting

back his head and letting out a moan. I closed my eyes as Greg
began his incantations.

"Oh goddess of the darkness
Mother to the immortal
Let me be reborn as your child
Let your light absorb my own

Allow me passage to the darkness
As from your immortal womb
Into the arms of your children
To whom I will call brother

Oh moonlight
Let me be reborn as your child
Guide the dark ones to me
So I shall be born again."

I opened my eyes and looked down at the board as Greg
finished. Our fingers rested against one another, almost inter-
twined atop the heart-shaped plastic pointer. Seeing his hand in
mine felt more supernatural than if Selene herself had appeared,
hovering at the window in her black veil, politely tapping to be
let in to gorge on our blood.

"Greg, I think I'm gay."

His eyes popped open, but his head remained tilted back, as
if the muscles in his neck had frozen. Nervously, he looked over
his shoulder at his bedroom door and then scanned his darkened room, as if one of his brothers or parents might've silently
slipped in during his vampire prayer.

"David, what did you just say?" he asked.

"I said, I think I'm gay."

He closed his eyes and delicately placed his hands on either side of his face. It was a look of surprise I couldn't decipher: had he just lost his entire family or won the lottery?

"David! Now this might come as a shock to you, but I also have a secret. Um . . ."

Greg hemmed and hawed for a moment, placing his hand to his forehead like Fay Wray in *King Kong*. The drama was palpable.

"It's so hard to say . . ."

Greg's eyes nervously roamed the room until they landed on the board between us. He placed his fingers on the planchette and looked up to some invisible force in the air above us.

"Oh mighty spirit of the Ouija!" His eyes rolled back in his head as he inhaled. "Is someone else in this room *besides* David gay?"

The planchette slowly began to move, my fingers barely touching it. It was like one of Greg's dances; the most magical thing wasn't the supposed ghost in the room but Greg's level of sheer commitment and excitability. As the little plastic pointer moved to the word *Yes*, Greg's mouth opened with glee.

"David! It's ME!"

"You're who?"

"I'm gay too!"

It took a moment for what he said to register. As it settled in, all the pieces snapped into place: the manic dancing, the excessive hairstyling, the endless replaying of "A Little Respect." How could I have been so dumb? Looking at Greg across from me, with his beaming smile, his hundred bracelets, and his perfectly matte face, it struck me that *of course* he was gay! Just like I was.

"One thing, though," he added. "I'm probably bisexual, David."

"Me too!" I blurted without hesitation, knowing it wasn't true but feeling like it provided a kind of safety net. "I still think lots of girls are pretty."

Greg and I spun our wheels for a few minutes, gabbing about how we would totally have sex with women like Madonna, Marilyn Monroe, and Winona Ryder. Once we finished that obligatory little dance, I could say all the things I'd wanted to say for so long.

"There are just so many cute boys at school, huh?" I asked breathlessly.

"David, you know who I really like? River Phoenix."

"Oh God, I love him. But Keanu Reeves is the cutest."

"He's good," Greg shrugged, "but Christian Slater has such a hot voice."

"Yeah, he's got a hot voice, but not as hot as Luke Perry's."

We compared notes and gushed over our crushes for hours. We talked about who we wanted to kiss, what other kids were probably gay, and how nervous we were about what sex would be like. As we heard Greg's parents walk into the foyer at midnight, we went silent, waiting for their footsteps to fade away into the back of the house.

"I worry about my parents finding out," he said, tugging at carpet threads. "And I don't know what my brothers will think."

"I'm scared too, Greg. But I'm glad you know now."

I told Greg about my Sinéad O'Connor suicide fantasy and we laughed. But then I told him about that night in front of the medicine cabinet. He was quiet for so long that I thought I'd scared him.

"Did I say too much?" I asked. "Sorry if that was weird."

"No," he sighed, staring at the floor. "There was a time once when I was maybe eleven, twelve. And sometimes I'd go in the garage to jerk off, because I didn't have my own room yet and I shared a bathroom that didn't lock with my brothers. Sometimes, right after I came, I would feel so gross. And once, right after, I noticed this coil of rope on top of a toolbox. I grabbed the rope and started tugging on it, wondering how sturdy it was. I wanted to know how much weight it could hold."

Greg stopped talking and looked out the window. Maybe he would've finished, but I didn't need him to say any more. So I hugged him. We held each other over the Ouija board for what felt like forever, our bodies limp, as if all the cartilage and muscle inside us had evaporated. I felt light as air, like vapor, like a ghost visiting a place I'd waited years to leave.

As the sun peeked through the window, we decided we weren't going to sleep. Today was a day to stay awake, to celebrate. Greg put on a pot of coffee. I opened the big bedroom windows that looked out onto the lawn. We wrapped ourselves in a blanket and sat in the window frame, our toes resting on the cold soil of the flower bed below. We sipped our coffee and watched the neighbors' windows turn gold, reflecting the sun rising behind Greg's house.

"I was so scared to tell you," said Greg, passing me our shared coffee mug. "You won't tell anyone, right?"

"No, Greg! You're my best friend. Besides, why would I do that when I'm gay too?"

"You mean bisexual?" Greg reminded me with a grin.

"Right," I smiled back. "Bisexual."

I scooted closer to him on the ledge as a cool wind blew past us. Maybe it was a cold front coming through. Or maybe it was a spirit there to transform us. As Greg rested his head on my shoulder, I knew it didn't matter one way or the other.

CHAPTER 10

Scary Monsters

O uch, you bitch!" screamed Greg as blood squirted against my fingers.

"I had to punch it in fast or it would never go through," I said, popping the back of the piercing stud onto the earring. "Now let me put the alcohol on it."

"Fuck," Greg bellowed, the liquid soaking into his punctured earlobe.

"It'll get infected if I don't pour this on!"

"Well hurry up, asshole!"

"Mine hurt too, you pussy!" I barked as I shoved an ice cube against his ear.

You'd think that after two teenage boys admitted a long-kept secret about their sexuality to each other there would be some sort of tentative period, a span of time in which they'd be cautiously honest and play it cool. Nothing could've been farther from the truth. Our coming out to each other was like opening a backed-up fire hydrant, releasing an unwieldy torrent of foul language, sex talk, and fashion experimentation. I stopped stifling my inclinations to wear eye shadow or paint my fingernails, because I no longer had to fear that they would out me to my best friend. Home manicures and Manic Panic hair-dyeing sessions ensued.

We stared at ourselves in the mirror, with brand-new silver studs in our ears. Greg looked at my reflection with a pleased smile.

"We. Look. So. Cool."

"Right?" I answered. "These are awesome."

Over the next few weeks, we encouraged each other to take bolder fashion risks. We didn't have detachable noses, but we could at least cut up our T-shirts and slice holes in the knees of Greg's expensive jeans.

"What are you doing?" Greg's confused mother asked one morning as we dug through the vegetable drawer of her fridge. "If you're hungry I can microwave you breakfast sandwiches."

"We don't eat breakfast anymore," we answered in sync, knowing we'd never look like David Bowie if we continued our morning diet of toaster strudel and Eggos.

"Found 'em!" Greg declared, removing the rubber bands from a bunch of asparagus and snapping them around his wrists. "Voilà, Mom! Bracelets!"

"Voilà?" she quietly repeated, confused as to what the big reveal was.

The next weekend, Greg's little brother walked into his room to find us precariously balancing on a chair beneath his ceiling fan.

"What are you doing in my room?"

"Chill! I'm taking your ceiling-fan chains," Greg said as he jumped down.

"But how am I supposed to turn it on now?" Charlie asked.

"Just stand on a chair," Greg shrugged as we snapped on our brand-new necklaces.

Afterward we went into the boys' bathroom, where Greg bent over and placed the side of his face against the counter. I combed his hair flat against the surface and sprayed it with Vidal Sassoon hairspray before blow-drying it on high heat.

"What the fuck?" Johnny screamed, standing in the doorway with a toothbrush in his hand. As I blasted Greg's hair with the blow-dryer, Johnny shook his head. "You're a pair of fucking weirdos!"

"Fuck you!" Greg yelled over the roar of the blow-dryer, a fine dander of crusted hairspray flaking into his burning eyes. "Ouch! It hurts, David!"

"But it's going to look great!" I asserted, beginning to understand that great fashion should probably be painful to achieve.

With our new piercings, matching half Mohawks, and D.I.Y. fashion accessories, we felt reborn. It was spring break, and these would be the looks to get us the pale-faced, club-going, slightly older, more world-weary boyfriends we'd been dreaming of. Because Greg and I could finally talk about boys, it seemed like they were everywhere, in greater numbers, especially in the North Star Mall food court. Eighteen-year-old jocks, thirty-year-old businessmen, and forty-year-old dads were all there to be ogled and mentally undressed. In the course of a three-hour lunch by the Chick-fil-A, Greg and I would have a dozen carefully narrated sexual relationships with men of all shapes, sizes, and ages. Some guys were just the wham-bam-thank-you-ma'am victims of our virtual, virginal blow jobs. Other men were unknowing participants in imaginary but meaningful long-term relationships. Most of them had sex with one or both of us in a hot tub, the kind of sex they would never forget. Although, in reality, we still weren't quite sure how all *that* worked.

"I bet that guy would be a good lay," Greg said about a college-aged brunet in a polo shirt and glasses. "Look at his crotch, David!"

"Why are you always so into crotches?" I asked.

"Duh. Because that's where their dicks are!"

"But don't you want a small dick at first?" I reasoned. "Like, a starter dick or something?"

"But a big dick just seems better. Like getting a bigger slice of pizza."

"Greg, it's not a meal. Besides, a giant penis doesn't mean he'll be a good boyfriend."

Greg rolled his eyes and shoved a waffle fry in his mouth before spotting another boy. "Look at that one, David! In the blue tie."

"Eww, Greg. He's old." I recoiled from the ancient geezer. "Like, thirty-five at least!"

"Maybe I like them older," Greg said, flashing me a devious smile and beginning to give a chicken nugget a mini–blow job.

"Greg," I whispered, looking around to make sure people weren't watching. "Stop it!"

"It tastes so gooooood," he moaned, flicking his tongue around the edges of the nugget. I could feel my face getting hot; I was partially aroused, but also embarrassed that someone would see

Greg and know what we were. Being identified as freaks was one thing; being identified as queer was another.

"Greg, stop!" I insisted, shoving fries into my mouth as my nerves took hold.

"Bitch, I'm only—" Greg stopped midthought and stared over my shoulder.

"What?" I asked.

"One of them is coming over," he whispered.

I turned to see a pale girl with a nest of fried hair approaching us from the freak encampment. She wore an oversize white T-shirt with a pentagram drawn on the chest and carried a metal lunch box covered in rust. Her short black skirt revealed long, fishnet-bound legs wrapped in two unlaced, dark-green combat boots. She flashed a look at Daphne over her shoulder before stopping at our table.

"Hi, boys," she purred, looking directly at me.

I panicked. *What did she want from us? Why was she here? What would I say with a mouth full of waffle fries and ranch dressing that might impress her?*

"Cool purse," Greg said, gently snapping the produce rubber bands around his wrist.

She flashed us a completely unexpected grin, revealing two rows of perfect teeth behind glossy black lips. "It's awesome you knew what it was. People always call it a fucking lunch box."

Anxiously forcing another fry into my mouth, I bleated, "Yeah, that's what I thought."

"It's my fucking *purse!*" scolded the girl, glaring at me like Medusa. "My great-uncle died with this in his hands, fighting in World War II. Like, they had to pry this from his rigor-mortised grip in a blood-filled ditch. Okay?"

"Names for things are stupid. I hate labels," said Greg, going into damage-control mode. As the girl scooped a handful of waffle fries from my plate, he calmly reasoned, "If it's a purse, it's a purse, right?"

"I think I can feel him in the air when I have this with me," she said, sitting down as Greg flashed me a "be cool" look.

"Like, his ghost is in your lunch box?" I asked, unable to shut my mouth in spite of the waffle fries filling it.

"It's NOT a lunch box! It's a purse," she yelled, slamming it onto the table as Greg jumped in to calm the situation.

"My name's Greg," he blurted. "This is David."

"My name's Raven," she sighed.

I couldn't help but chuckle as Greg kicked me beneath the table and asked, "Um. Your name is—"

Before he could finish, the girl thrust her fist into the air and screamed her own name like a pro wrestler in the center of a WWF ring.

"I . . . Am . . . RAAAAA-VENNNNNN!!!"

Elderly women in wheelchairs choked on their baked potatoes. Parents reached out to shield their children's eyes. I wanted to tell the shoppers, "This is nothing, y'all. If you don't chill out, that other girl will take her nose off!"

Raven proceeded to devour my fries as she told us how much she loved writing poetry, Siouxsie and the Banshees, and female cartoon characters. As she rambled to Greg about how hard school sucked, I scanned her face and body, finally able to see this creature from the wild up close. I could see the thin layer of red polish left beneath the chipping layer of purple polish on her thumbnail. Looking closely at her eyeballs in profile, I could tell that her irises were actually darker than I had thought, but covered in blue contact lenses. From a foot away I could smell the thick scent of funky herbs and musk coming off her body. As my gaze traveled up the back of her head, I realized that her thick, fried shrub of blue-black hair was wrapped around a yellowish stick that looked like a dog's rawhide bone.

"Raven. What's that in your hair?"

With a cold, dead stare she shoved a nugget between her charcoal-crusted lips and answered, "It's a human femur."

She chewed at me for three seconds, her painted irises bulging from their sockets, daring me to challenge her. She gulped down her nuggets as the corner of her mouth started to twitch. Falling forward onto the table, she erupted in a giggling fit.

"Your face! That's fucking hilarious." Just as quickly as she'd started laughing, she stopped. "No, but really. My brother got it, grave digging in Mexico." And with that, she stood up. "All right, maybe we'll see each other at school Monday."

I looked at Greg, confused.

"You go to Gunther?"

"Um, yeah. A lot of us sit under the oak tree in the courtyard at lunch. You probably just didn't notice me. This is my weekend look."

She put her arm on her hip and struck a mannequin pose just as I noticed the safety pin through her earlobe. Suddenly there were ten black-smeared faces flanking her shoulders. A blond girl wearing a dog collar leaned forward and fingered our new Book of Love CD. She tapped the case with her chipped green fingernail and gave an approving nod.

"So good."

"Hey everyone," announced Raven as she smeared on a fresh stripe of black lip liner. "I just met these guys. They're cool."

A limp murmur of lifeless hellos emanated from the group.

"This is Greg and David," Raven continued, throwing her lip pencil into her lunch box and snapping it closed. "And they're meeting us next weekend at Club FX."

CHAPTER 11

Shaking While
We're Breaking

I n San Antonio in 1991 there were three alternative teen clubs: Changez with a *Z*, Phazez with two *Z*'s, and Club FX. FX was out by the airport in an industrial park, a place no sixteen-year-old should be at night, let alone in a dog collar. Trying to seem cool, we'd pretended to know where FX was when we were invited. In an age before every middle-class home had Internet access, this was a problem.

"Greg, we can't just drive around here all night," I said as we circled again through the same desolate maze of big-rig mechanics and barbecue-supply stores. "It's spooky."

"But we can't give up," Greg insisted. "See how great we look."

Greg was in torn jeans, a paisley shirt, and a pale-gray vest adorned with band pins. Hanging off my shoulder was an oversize sweater, the knit so worn you could see my Cure shirt underneath. My hair was gelled back into a ponytail the size of a thumbnail. We were both lightly dusted in a patina of translucent powder stolen from Greg's mother's vanity.

"Fine, David. We'll go back. This sucks."

"I know," I replied, bummed, but happy to know that Greg was all mine for the rest of the night. "Can you stop so I can pee?"

As I peed against the wall of a nursing-shoe factory, I took in the sounds of the night: distant traffic along the highway, a nest of baby birds in a farm-supply sign overhead, a plane landing over the horizon, the pumping bass line of "Bizarre Love Triangle," a train's horn blaring . . . Wait.

"Hurry up," Greg begged, nervously peering down the empty street. "It's freaky out here!"

"Shhh!" I said, stepping carefully back to the car with my finger over my lips. Greg frantically pulled a can of pepper spray from the glove compartment, yelling, "Who's out there? David! GET IN!"

"No! The music," I said, turning off the car stereo as I jumped in the passenger seat. "I think I hear the club." We drove toward the sound as I craned my head out the window like a family dog, but I couldn't hear the distant music over the little Cabriolet's motor. "Kill the engine!" Greg turned off the ignition and we cruised silently through the industrial park, two boys in eyeliner leaning out the windows of a tiny red car.

"David! I hear it," Greg said as we rolled down a gentle decline at three miles an hour.

Greg started up the car and drove in the direction of the sound, through tiny backstreets lined with garbage heaps and blank cement walls. But we'd lost the sonic trail. Greg killed the engine again and we poked our heads out the car windows, leaning into the night toward the sound of what would surely be an amazing discovery. Bored junkyard dogs stared silently at us through barbed-wire fences, as if they'd seen this kind of thing before and wanted to honor our quest.

And then they began to appear: creatures of the night walking along the sides of the road—seventeen-year-old girls with maroon bobs and nose rings, androgynous boys in sunglasses with Mohawks, tiny clusters of ghost-white kids wearing capes in earnest. Our people.

We parked in front of Bubba's Lonestar Propane as a cluster of witches in a cloud of clove smoke wafted past us. Greg turned to me and grabbed my hand.

"David, we did it!"

I smiled weakly at Greg, suddenly doubting that I was cool enough to be there.

"Tune in, Tokyo," he said, lightly knocking on my forehead.

"Oh, sorry," I apologized, grabbing the door handle to leave. "Sorry, Greg. Sorry . . ."

"Hey," he said, grabbing my shoulder, "this is going to be fun. We are going to meet cool people and listen to awesome music. And your hair looks so cool like that, just like Keanu Reeves in *Dangerous Liaisons*! Don't be nervous," he said, and rubbed my shoulder.

I knew that if I didn't kiss him right then and there I was the dumbest boy in the entire world. I leaned across the seat and closed my eyes. I hovered there with the emergency brake impaling my ribs, but nothing happened. I opened my eyes to find Greg staring intensely at his reflection in the visor mirror.

"Am I shining?" Greg turned to notice me leaning over the console a foot from his face. "Oh, sorry. Here you go," he said, and passed me his CoverGirl compact. I dabbed at my face with the pad, feeling like a moron. I couldn't even flirt right.

Greg and I walked down the suddenly desolate street, empty plastic bags and pieces of cardboard blowing by in the wind. At the end of the block we came to the club, a one-story cinder-block building set up high on a subbasement support like a mobile home. We walked past a short cement wall into a big yard, where ghouls and freaks of all shapes and sizes leaned on rain-warped picnic tables, smoking cigarettes. I tripped on a step and almost fell, barely able to see with my sunglasses on.

"David!" Greg smacked my arm and made a peace-sign gesture with his fingers.

"Do you need scissors?" I whispered.

"No, nerd. Get me a cig!"

I fumbled through my pockets for our Marlboros and put two in my mouth as Greg sparked up his Zippo. I tried to light them, but the sunglasses made it difficult to gauge the distance of the fire from my face. I craned my head toward and away from Greg's lighter until I finally landed the tip of each Marlboro in the flame. As they ignited, I could momentarily see around us. A girl with severe black bangs in a miniskirt was sitting four feet away beside a Mohawked person of indeterminate gender wearing a necklace made of padlocks.

Completely nonplussed, Greg reached out for the cigarette without even looking at me, quietly murmuring, "Play it cool, David."

Under a flood lamp at the club's porch entrance, two boys with safety pins through their lips smoked cigarettes. On the other side of the door, two girls looked on as their pink-haired friend reenacted a fight. We walked up the half flight of stairs, where a large man in a black cap sat on a stool. He looked us up and down and grunted, "High tea?"

"Sorry, sir," Greg said, lowering his sunglasses with concern. "What did you say?"

I leaned into Greg's ear and whispered, "Maybe it's code?"

"Oh! Like we have to go by 'Dean' to enter or something?"

"Oh! Dean?" I replied, "I thought he was asking us if we wanted 'high tea'?"

Behind us, an impossibly loud female voice bellowed into my ear. "Bitches, hurry up! Mama has to tinkle, cunts!"

I turned around to see a tiny, busty girl with a stark white face and a giant beauty mark on her cheek. She looked at me quizzically and let out a chortle. "Ha! Nice ponytail, Amadeus. Now can you pull out your fuckin' ID and compose your ass into this club!"

She flipped her bright-blue bobbed hair and flashed a giant Cheshire-cat grin as the people in line behind us laughed. Before I realized what was happening, her hand was plunging into my back jean pocket.

"Look, you silly bitches, the man needs your fuckin' IDs."

"Get off!" I yelled, struggling to remove her hand from my pocket.

"I'm assuming there's a wallet in here, unless you forgot your purse."

Greg tried to resist as she forced her other hand into his pants. "Excuse me, ma'am!"

"I ain't got all night for you two grandmas to adjust your hearing aids and I am not about to piss down the front steps of Club

RX or FX or Detox or whatever the fuck this shithole is called!" she complained, ripping our IDs from our wallets and handing them to the bouncer before storming toward the entrance.

"Miss," the bouncer lazily requested, "ID?"

"Seriously? Oh goddamn, I just came out to smoke five minutes ago. Look at this mug!" she demanded, circling her face with black-painted fingertips. "I know you remember it 'cause it's damn near flawless, but the shit is clearly over fifteen years old. Fuck!"

The doorman handed us our IDs as we watched her disappear onto the crowded dance floor, cutting a furious path through sweaty, skinny teens like they were hanging vines in a jungle. On the ceiling were a few motorized lights, flashing bright-blue beams in time with the music. Beneath them were a hundred sweat-drenched kids who looked like junior morgue employees. They pouted, swayed, and writhed to a Nine Inch Nails song as it boomed from the three-foot-tall speakers on the floor.

"Come on," yelled Greg, pulling me toward the throng of dancing bodies.

"Don't you wanna look around?" I yelled. "Maybe get a soda or something?"

"No! I want to dance!"

"But," I stalled, looking at the otherworldly mob of purple-haired, platform-shoed kids dancing, "I'm thirsty, Greg. I . . . I need to find a bathroom."

"But look at that cute guy over there," he pleaded, gesturing to a shirtless, black-haired boy wearing a long rosary, "and *that* guy in the tie. I wanna go dance with them!"

"Then go dance!" I yelled over the pounding music.

"What?" Greg asked, pulling me closer as a sour-faced girl with four lip rings gave me the once-over. "I can't hear you!"

"GO DANCE!" I screamed.

"Nerd," Greg murmured. He released me and was sucked into the crowd like a minnow absorbed by a great, pulsing, neon jellyfish. I wandered around the edge of the thrashing crowd, past a cheap plywood "bar," where a guy with chunky glasses was pouring Coke and Sprite into plastic cups for a buck. At the back of the club I walked down a long, black lighted hallway. Outside was a patio where thirty teenagers hung out, smoking.

"Bitch! I'm talkin' to you, Mary!"

Out of the darkness stepped the girl from the line. She marched toward me like an angry drum major, trails of black silk flowing behind her. She looked like one of those Halloween ghost decorations you make by throwing a handkerchief over a tennis ball hung from the ceiling. She stopped a foot from my face and pointed at the unlit cigarette between her lips.

"Rock me, Amadeus."

"Sorry, what?"

"Pleeeease." She slowly dragged out the word like I had a learning disability. "Liiiight. Myyyy. Cigareeeette. Pleeeease."

"Oh. Sorry," I said, digging through the pockets of my pants and sweater as she tapped her metallic heel on the ground.

"Holy moley, Mary. How many pockets you got? Are you a boy or a pack mule?"

As I lifted the lighter to her cigarette, it slipped from my hand and fell onto the concrete. I bent over to get it in perfect time with her, bashing the top of my head on hers on the way down.

"Goddamn, bitch! Are you even licensed to operate a human body?"

"Oh. I'm sorry. I . . ."

"Just let me do the heavy lifting."

Slowly, she bent over to pick up the lighter, keeping her eyes on me the whole time while guarding the top of her head with her hand. She sparked the lighter and held it out for me to see before bringing it to the tip of her cigarette. In slow motion she slipped the lighter back into my pocket. It was like watching a magician walk through the beginning of a "now you see it, now you don't" trick. I knew she was mocking me, but I couldn't help but chuckle.

"Glad I could provide *someone* a laugh tonight." She exhaled a mushroom cloud of smoke into my face. "My friend Ray-Ray was supposed to meet me here because he's into some seventeen-year-old piece of ass who can't get into the Bonham 'cause it's eighteen and over!"

"I've never been to the Bonham."

"Of course you haven't, Mozart," she replied, tugging my ponytail. "What old are you? Ten?"

"I'm actually sixteen, okay?" I blurted, defensively. "And my name is David."

"Well well, little miss. There's no need to get sassy."

"Sorry. It's just that my friend kind of left me alone and . . . I've never been here."

"It's okay, girl. Looks like we've both been abandoned. My name's Sylvia, by the way," she said, taking a long drag off her cigarette. "Hey! Wanna get high?"

"High?" I asked.

"Smoke out? Take a toke? Hit the reefer? Dance with Mary Jane? Insert euphemism at will. I'm supposed to save some for Ray-Ray. But he ain't here. So let's smoke up!"

I wanted to tell her I'd never smoked weed before, but she already thought I was ten years old. So I played along. "Okay, let's do it."

"It takes two to tango," she said, staring at me blankly. "You got a pipe or something?"

"Um, no. I . . ."

Sylvia walked to a picnic table where a guy in a kilt was slumped on a bench over a pool of vomit. She slipped a can of Coke from the unconscious boy's hand before yelling into his sleeping face, "Lay off the bagpipe, bitch!" She poured what was left in the can onto the ground and winked at me, saying, "Watch and learn, bitch. Watch and learn."

Sylvia morphed into a flight attendant miming safety procedures, slowly turning the can on its side and denting the top to create a sort of concave bowl. She removed her crucifix earring and poked holes in the can at the center of the dent, the lowest part. Then she sprinkled weed from a Ziploc bag over the pinholes. She sucked on the popped top as she lit the mound of marijuana, making it crackle and glow in the dark.

"Here, girl," she wheezed, exhaling a pungent cloud in my face. "Hit it."

I placed my lips against the hole and took in a long drag. I tried to hold it in, the way I'd seen it done in movies, but I immediately felt an unbearable tickling in my throat. I clutched my chest and hacked a loud cough, a siren call for the stoners on the patio. An ebony-haired girl wearing a long black slip shuffled toward us with pleading eyes.

"Look, Morticia Addams, Mama ain't got no more smoky-smoke!" hissed Sylvia. As she dragged me back inside, I began to feel a strange warmth in my neck and head. Moving through the hallway, I felt woozy and bloblike, like my whole body was a large cotton ball gently rolling down the hall. The eyes of the kids around me glowed a greenish-purple from the black lights hanging overhead. Their teeth looked dead and gray, like little radioactive pebbles glued into their mouths. The bits of dandruff on their black shoulders shone like stars.

"Bitch! Your face!" yelled Sylvia as she pushed me against the hallway wall. "It's a mess!"

"Why do you keep calling me *bitch*?" I screamed over the thumping industrial music. "My name is David. David Crabb!"

"That's a shit last name," she yelled as she rummaged through her purse, which suddenly looked like a twenty-gallon grocery bag.

"Your purse is so big! Are you a bag lady?" I couldn't stop cackling as I rubbed my spine up and down against the wall. "I feel like a cat!"

"Honey, it's weed, not ecstasy. You're acting like you've never been high before."

"I haven't. So thank you, Sylvia," I purred, leaning forward to hug her.

"Now listen, snuggle bug," she said, "you're a sweet boy, but you need to let me fix your face!"

"What do you mean?" I asked as Sylvia flipped open a compact in my face. In horror I screamed, "Ahhh!!! My face!"

While the black lights were bringing out the eyes, teeth, and lint on everyone else, they were bringing out the flesh-tone Clearasil on me. My face looked like a nightmarish galaxy of glowing smears. Each covered blemish was its own green planet floating on my face; a dozen dots shone across my cheeks, nose, and forehead. "Oh my God. I'm polka-dotted!"

"Honey, you're making a scene. Just stay still." Sylvia spit on her hand and begin to rub her saliva into my face with a cocktail napkin. I shrieked and tried to move away, but I was pinned against the wall by her breasts. "Don't move, Mama's gonna fix you."

"Oh my God. Your tits are huge!" I exclaimed as pencils, powders, and creams were applied to my cheeks and forehead. Completely stoned and terrified of this stranger who'd spit all over me, I went limp and let her work. Three minutes later she was done.

"Voilà!" she exclaimed proudly, dropping a handful of makeup tubes into her bag. "Don't ever say I didn't do anything for you."

"David!" Greg yelled from down the hall. "Look who I found."

"Oh. Hi. Hi. Hi . . ." I said repeatedly to Raven and her crew like a broken tape recorder.

"David, are you okay?" Greg asked. "You seem weird. Your face . . ."

Raven leaned in close to me and sniffed, her contact lenses floating on her eyes like blue stars. "He's high."

"David! You smoked pot? Without me?"

"Yeah, he's baked," said Raven. "And it smells like good shit, too. Skunky."

"Skunky?" I asked.

"Yeah, skunky. It means you had some deep, funky shit. Where'd you get it?"

"Sylvia gave it to—" I turned to introduce her, but she was gone. "There was this girl. A girl we met out front who put her hands in our pants."

"Ugh, her!" Greg rolled his eyes. "What a bitch."

"No, no," I said, petting his face, "her name is Sylvia and her purse is full of so much stuff and she did incredible things to a can with her earrings. And . . . this song sounds like razor blades underwater!"

"Um, okay, stoner," Raven smirked as her friends snickered. "Now I want some."

"He's kind of right, though," came a voice from the dark. At the back of the group I saw a boy with shaggy brown hair, wearing a tank top. His eyes were so blue it hurt to look at them.

"This is Jake," said Greg, excitedly bouncing up and down to the beat of the music.

"Hi, Jake. I'm David Crabb," I said, and smacked my forehead with my palm. "Why do I keep saying my full name? Ahhhh!"

As everyone laughed, Jake reached forward and put his hand on my neck, chuckling. "Dude, you're so high!" He slid his arm around my shoulder as we walked down the hall. He smelled like a million amazing things all at once. As the six of us walked up to the bar, Greg shot me a look I'd never seen before.

"Greg, are you mad or something?" I asked.

"No!" He seemed uncomfortable, with everyone suddenly looking at him. "I'm fine. Jeez, you're so stoned!" Through the cloudy haze in my mind, a controlling idea made itself known:

Maybe Greg is upset and jealous because Greg likes me and I'm talking to Jake!

"Greg, wanna have a cigarette out back?" I asked him.

"I can't hear you," Greg screamed over the music.

"Hey David," said Jake, whose bee-stung lower lip was a few inches from my face. "Try this when you're talking to people at a club." Jake slipped his thumb over the little tab in the center of my ear, closing the canal. "See? Now I can yell and you can hear me without it being too loud. Cool, right?"

"Uh-huh," I responded, feeling the warmth of his hand gripping the back of my head. His breath was heavy with tobacco and liquor.

"Want some?" he asked, and pulled a flask out of his jeans.

I leaned in close and ran my fingers through his hair, sliding my thumb over his ear before yelling, "What is it?"

"Whiskey!" He raised it to my lips and then passed it around.

Greg took a swig and then shoved it back between Jake's face and mine. "Here. Let's dance!" yelled Greg before pulling Jake onto the dance floor.

I leaned against the wall with Jake's flask and watched everyone dance for an hour, my head spinning a little faster with each gulp of whiskey. Greg was busting all those amazing moves I'd seen in his bedroom, but now he was doing it for everyone, not just me. He and Jake wrapped their arms around each other's waists as they screamed into each other's ears. It had only been an hour and I was already getting jealous, thinking: *I remember when Jake's thumbs were in my ears.*

Two hours later we all hugged good-bye around Greg's red Cabriolet. Whatever was energizing about the whiskey and pot had faded away, leaving only exhaustion in its wake. I turned to hug Jake, only to find him and Greg sucking each other's faces against a chain-link fence. And a new controlling idea took hold of my brain:

Greg doesn't like you that way. Greg likes Jake that way.

In the car I was quiet, depressed that Greg was interested in someone else but excited about the prospect of meeting other boys who would touch me like Jake did: intimately, comfortably, without shame. I pulled down the visor to fix my hair and was shocked by the person looking back at me.

"Oh my God, Greg. My face!"

"Yeah, it's amazing. What did you do in there when I was dancing?"

In the mirror I saw a face that wasn't mine. It was the face of an effeminate mime or the cruel queen in a Disney film. Both of my eyes were thinly outlined in charcoal black, as were my eyebrows. My skin was covered in a fine, ashy powder and looked like it was carved of bleached ivory. I had a beauty mark under my right eye, and my lips were a deep, dusty pink. Smelling a familiar odor, I touched my face and licked my finger. My face was covered in flour.

"You look fucking amazing," said Greg, smiling and turning up the stereo. "Good job."

"But I didn't do it. Sylvia did," I murmured to myself. "And I never got to say bye."

CHAPTER 12

Kiss Me, Kiss Me, Kiss Me

As Greg and I pulled into the Glenbrook subdivision, we saw them. In the grassy expanse between the main road and the backyard fences, they were easy to spot. Among the wildflowers and drifting clouds of dandelions, four dark figures swayed in the grass. The black-clad pack of teen depressives trudged toward us, a thick cloud of cigarette smoke trailing them.

"Is that them, Greg? Is this it?"

I pulled up a torn sleeve to read the smeared address scrawled on my forearm.

"Wait! That's Raven!" Greg pointed at the kids. From a hundred feet away I could tell it was Raven, her teased thicket of jet black hair magically defying the sweltering humidity.

She waved as the whole clan started running toward the car, a horrifying zombie-film motif most people would be driving *away* from. Jake's hair was in a loose little ponytail, his chin-length bangs dangling over his crystal-blue eyes. Hector was a new friend I'd met a week earlier at *The Rocky Horror Show*. He wore a tattered tuxedo shirt buttoned to the top and sported a freshly bleached platinum pompadour.

"Nice hair, Hector!" yelled Greg.

"I left the shit on too long," he replied, parting his hair to show a cluster of pearly blisters on his scalp. Everyone groaned in disgust, their various bracelets and necklaces jangling as Raven hopped into the backseat and the boys onto the hood.

This was the motley crew whose ranks Greg and I had quickly joined. At FX we'd met more alternative kids who went to our high school, the largest one in San Antonio, where it was hard to locate and corral all these kindred spirits. But weekend clubbing had given us the opportunity to make plans to meet at school. There was a spot beneath an oak tree in the courtyard populated by a ragtag mob of fishnetted freaks and black-clad cadavers chanting Joy Division lyrics and reeking of patchouli. After school we'd meet in the parking lot around my little Mercury Lynx or Greg's Cabriolet, making plans to go to someone's parentless house to smoke weed or drive downtown to buy CDs from Hogwild Records. We'd effectively fused our Monday-to-Friday lives with our weekend lives at FX.

"Hey boys," screamed Raven, hugging us around our seats.

Jake gripped the roof of the car and slid his torso up the glass, grinning as his crotch dragged the windshield wiper.

"Hey Davey," he purred, reaching through the open window to tousle my hair.

"Uh, hi Jake." I could feel the blood rush to my head as he began to hump the hood of the car. Greg shot me a death glare, unhappy with this forward flirtation between Jake and me. Hypnotized by his blue eyes, I didn't realize that my foot was slipping off the brake. Suddenly the car jerked forward, almost sending the boys sliding off the hood.

"Oh, I'm sorry!" I yelled my apologies out the window, knowing that getting out of the car would reveal my slight erection.

"Onward, chauffeur!" Jake yelled, reclining against the windshield like it was a lawn chair.

"But you're on top of my car. What if a cop . . ."

"Be cool," Greg demanded, slapping my arm.

"Yeah, David," whispered Raven, pinching my nipples from behind. "It's my birthday!"

My car lurched forward with Jake and Hector on the hood, rolling along at five mph. People on their way to church services craned their heads as we passed, their mouths agape. Young families and elderly couples flashed their lights and honked, as if I might not be aware that a small horde of teenagers was covering my car.

As the sun beat down, Jake stripped off his shirt. He shook out his ponytail and stretched out on the windshield, his skin tan and wet against the glass. As he squirmed to get comfortable, his baggy jeans slid down his hips, showing the top of his butt crack.

"Take it off, baby!" yelled Raven, chugging Mountain Dew.

Jake slid his pants down and pressed his bare ass against the glass, turning to smile at me before licking the windshield.

"David, stop the car!"

I'm not sure how long Greg and Raven were yelling before it actually registered. Greg's knuckles rapped lightly on my forehead.

"We're here, crazy! Wake the fuck up."

"It's okay, David," Hector said, lingering behind to light his cigarette as everyone piled out. "His ass *is* kind of hypnotizing."

To say that Raven's front yard was messy is an understatement. It was deeply unloved. Trudging through the plastic children's toys and knee-high grass, I wondered how the surrounding neighbors hadn't shut the place down. Inside, Raven's mother greeted us.

"I'm Barb! How are y'all?" she bellowed, a stream of Parliament 100 smoke streaming from her lightly mustached lips. Barb was no taller than five-foot-six and no lighter than 250 pounds. She appeared to be wearing a muumuu, but it could just as easily have been the floral fitted sheet from her bed, rolled up off the mattress that morning and stapled at either shoulder. She had long, dry hair that hung to her waist like graying streaks of hay.

"Have some snacks and shit, y'all!" She walked us through two dust-covered rooms full of yellowing newspaper stacks and ticking grandfather clocks. In the kitchen she presented a display of paper-plated food before lighting a new cigarette off the open flame of her stovetop. Raven rolled her eyes and hugged herself in embarrassment as Barb laid out the "snack station."

"This is a pimento loaf I got at Piggly Wiggly. It's delicious. These are my mama's famous 'ants on a stick,' which are celery sticks full of cream cheese and raisins. I got some butter crackers here and bacon Easy Cheese for y'all, but I think Jenny took it into the living room. JENNY!" she hollered past us with unimaginable force. A tiny face covered in orange spray cheese turned away from the massive television and smiled.

"That's my sister," Raven moaned. "Don't talk to her, or she'll never shut up."

"Don't you talk that shit about your sister! She fucking loves you!" Barb screamed.

The tiny, golden-locked girl giggled, liquid cheese streaming down her chin, as Axl Rose fried in an electric chair on the big screen in front of her.

"She's very cute, Mrs. Gunner. And your home is lovely," I said, nervously trying to cut the noisy tension as Axl screamed, "Numma numma numma need-need. I wanna watch you bleed!"

"That's *Mizz* Gunner, honey. I'm divorced," Barb huffed, softening as she looked at me. "Well, *you're* new. Where have you been hiding this one, Milly?"

"Don't fucking call me that, Mother!" Raven groaned as Barb pinched my face.

"David, you are just a little cup of sunshine." Barb released my cheek and led us into the living room, her massive smock swaying from side to side.

I leaned against Jake and whispered, "She's like a walking duvet." He chortled quietly and wrapped his arm around me. I could feel the warmth of his chest against my shoulder. As I glanced at Greg, he quickly looked away.

"Y'all can hang out in here or the backyard if you wanna smoke," Barb said, furrowing her brow at Raven. "And by *smoke*, I mean cigarettes. Not weed!"

Barb lit cigarette after cigarette as she continued the tour of her home, each room containing a hidden stash of Zippos, matches, and butane lighters. Barb lingered in each room for several minutes as it filled with hovering shelves of smoke. Mid-sentence she'd stop and clutch her chest, shocked at the rays of sunlight suspended in tobacco clouds around us.

"Oh, good God," she shrieked, reaching for one of an endless array of air fresheners that were stashed all over the house. She doused each room in Vanilla Fields or Cinnamon Stick or Ocean Breeze, waving the air around her with genuine surprise as we followed her out.

"Does she not realize that she's the one filling this place with smoke?" I whispered to Jake, who buried his face against my shoulder to stifle his laughter. As Barb showed us a wall of family photos in the smoky den, little Sara began to hack like an elderly truck-stop waitress. Barb sprayed a noxious cloud of Tropical Summer through the gray haze.

"Mom, we want to hang out," Raven interrupted. "My friends don't need to know the whole fucking lineage of our family!"

"Oh damn! I'm sorry, baby," Barb said, retrieving Jenny from the coffee table. "Let your big sister and her friends have some fun." Leaving the room, Barb grinned at Raven over her shoulder and winked. "Okay kids, I'm off to watch my *LA Law*. Mi casa es su casa." Then she disappeared down a clock-filled hallway through a corridor of smoke, like a gorilla in the mist.

Over the next hour a half-dozen kids showed up, each covered in an array of rubber bands and metal bracelets, torn jeans and safety-pinned T-shirts. We smoked cloves in the backyard and Hector taught us a few Santerian love spells with Mexican candles. I thought of casting one on Greg or Jake, which made me realize that they'd disappeared. I looked around the living room as Raven brandished an empty wine bottle and declared, "It's time for Spin the Bottle!"

My stomach sank. I'd never kissed anyone, not even as a joke. I needed support. I needed my best friend.

I walked into the front yard hoping to find Greg and Jake smoking, but I saw nothing. Then I noticed my car rocking. The windows were misted and hard to see through. Every few moments the car would shake, and then there would be a muffled laugh, followed by a quiet groan. I wanted to open the door and yell, *How can you* both *be doing this to me? You're the loves of my life!* But I wasn't going to be the uptight one, the jealous one, the prude. I marched back into the house to find a dozen kids gathered in a circle on the den floor. I took my seat in the group and began assessing the situation in a positive light. I thought, *I don't have to feel insecure about this. I'm sixteen years old. I'm practically an adult.*

"Where are you going?" I asked Hector as he walked outside.

"This shit is for little kids," he deadpanned. "I'll be outside. Have fun getting mono."

I wanted to escape with him, but I had a job to do. If Greg could make out with someone, I could too. I took a deep breath and looked around at the circle, reminding myself, *You can do this, David. You can kiss any of these people.*

And then the doorbell rang.

A shaft of blinding sun cut through the smoky room as the door creaked open. A massive silhouette appeared, with long, wavy hair and a bright-pink headband. She wore bifocals that made the top half of her eyes gigantic and the bottom half microscopic. A too-tight belt cinched the middle of her blubbery abdomen. She looked like a fat, upright-standing ant. Worst of all, at the center of her face, where a normal person's nose would be, was a complex network of bandages, like five or six thick slabs of bacon strapped horizontally above her mouth.

"Ooh, Spin the Bottle!" she squealed, revealing a mouthful of silver braces.

"Oh," said Raven. "This is Pam." As the girl shut the door behind her, Raven leaned in to whisper, "She's the daughter of my mom's friend. Ugh!"

"I'm Pam," the girl repeated, breaking into the circle between Raven and another girl across from me. She lowered her ample bottom to the ground and sat Indian-style, adjusting her yellow plastic barrettes and grinning at anyone who dared make eye contact. And then she locked eyes with me, staring with her giant half-moon orbs as every ticking clock in the house came to a stop. A flirty smile stretched across her face, revealing an intricate network of neon-colored rubber bands attached to her dental work.

"Hi," she whispered coyly, offering me a tiny, four-fingered baby-wave.

"Looks like David has a fan," said Raven. Everyone in the group laughed, and Pam blushed. "Awww, cutie's first kiss."

"I've kissed someone before! Don't be stupid!" I said, realizing too late that Raven wasn't talking about me. "Oh, yeah. Pam. Ha . . ." I mumbled.

The tension was palpable as we began, each person's spin nearly a death-defying risk. At any moment, someone would be kissing the gaping, metallic maw of Pam, whose loud mouthbreathing and laser-beam gaze remained focused in my direction.

Finally, it was her turn. She picked up the bottle, turned the spout toward me in midair, and then laid it back down on the carpet.

"You!" she beamed, baring her teeth and giggling. I looked around for someone to call foul on Pam's technique, to save me from mashing faces with this escapee from the *Texas Chainsaw*

Massacre family. But everyone looked away, relieved that I'd be taking one for the team.

"I just had sideus surgery," Pam said, mispronouncing *sinus* through the deformed inner workings of her mangled head cavity. She closed her eyes and leaned forward. Before I could take a breath her lips were on me, chewing and gnashing against my mouth like a dog on a rawhide bone. I could barely hear the group giggling through the mélange of sensory overload.

First there was the metallic taste of her dental work, like licking the inside of an empty can of tuna fish. Then there was the odor. Her flesh and hair smelled like synthetic fruit, or the stale plastic innards of a Strawberry Shortcake doll. I could feel the delicate scraping of metal edges against my gums, each dart of her tentacle-like tongue holding the promise of some gruesome oral injury. After what seemed like a minute I tried to back away, only to feel the immense pressure of her bearlike paws on my shoulders, thrusting me back into her mouth.

At this point, the group's gentle snickering gave way to nervous laughter, the kind emitted before something brutal and life-changing happens to a victim who at first simply can't believe he is looking at a *real human head*.

"Come on, Pam," Raven said, awkwardly chuckling.

As the strength of her embrace intensified, so did the powerful suction of her piehole. As this face-eating persisted, I realized the extent to which kissing is made possible by possessing a functioning nose. Without it, the act becomes a dangerous game of breath-play, complete with gagging, mucus-y sound effects. At one point, Pam formed a seal around my mouth so tightly that I could feel her drawing breath from inside my body.

"Pam, I think he's had enough!" I heard Raven plead.

And then Pam coughed into my mouth. Sure, it was positively disgusting, but it freed me. My head jerked back like the guy listening to his stereo in the Memorex commercial. I wiped a pint of saliva from my face as Pam heaved and retched.

Catching my breath, I noticed Barb down the hall through a small crack in her bedroom door. She was laid out on her bed, lit only by the glow of *LA Law* through a haze of cigarette smoke. A grin spread across Barb's face as she gave me a thumbs-up and a deeply unsettling wink. What had already been a disturbing first kiss was now, improbably, much worse.

For the next half hour we all tried to enjoy ourselves, but the party was unsalvageable. My new friends would chat with me and be extra-touchy, offering little hugs or shoulder pats as if to say, *I know that was hard, but we're all proud of you.* I would take solace in this just as I noticed Pam watching me from twenty feet away, her face peeking around the corner of a storage shed in the backyard or partially obscured by a gauzy drape blowing in the living room. At every turn I could sense her there, sheepishly smiling whenever I caught her gaze.

I found Hector smoking on the front porch as a big brown station wagon tapped its horn.

"Who's that?" I asked.

"Sasquatch's mom," he answered, straightening the cameo brooch at the center of his shirt collar. "She's been here the whole time."

The front door opened behind us as Barb helped Pam onto the porch.

"You get home okay, sweetie. And tell your momma hi for me, okay?" said Barb, patting Pam's butt as she stepped into the yard.

"Bye, Daniel," Pam giggled, with her creepy little finger-wave.

Hector chuckled. "Wow, your first love doesn't even know your fucking name."

Pam's mother got out of the front seat and walked around the car to open the back door. She strapped her daughter in and got back in the driver's seat, like a chauffeur. Pam leaned her face against the window and continued to wave good-bye, the glass in front of her mouth fogging up with hot, strawberry breath. As it occurred to me that Pam might be even more "special" than I'd first assumed, Greg and Jake emerged from the backseat of my car. Gazing out on the tableau as Pam and her mother pulled away, I couldn't help but compare Greg's party experiences and mine. Greg had made out with Jake. Jake had made out with Greg. I'd made out with a large, semideformed simpleton with a mouth full of razor blades.

I could taste blood on my lip as Greg tucked in his shirt and asked, "What did we miss?"

I glared at him silently as he went inside with Jake. Hector passed me a lit clove. "Don't worry, dude. You'll hook up with Jake eventually. Everybody does."

I took a long drag off the clove, reminding myself that I could finally cross "first kiss" off my list. Watching Greg lean against Jake through the kitchen window, I hoped my second one would be better.

CHAPTER 13

Under the Milky Way Tonight

I don't understand how it can get you high if it's just a piece of paper," said Greg, fingering the tiny blue square in his palm.

We'd been sitting in Greg's room for half an hour, contemplating our hits of acid. We'd gotten them from a dealer at school a few days earlier, and we'd been waiting until the weekend to take them. My mother had gone camping with Mike and was letting me spend the next four days with Greg, whose parents would be away the entire time.

"What if we overdose, Greg?"

"You have to stop being such a pussy. You can't OD unless you take a whole lot. Like that guy who stuck the whole sheet down his shirt and then ran from the cops for half an hour!"

"That guy went to Judson High School! I heard he's going to be in a padded cell for the rest of his life!"

We'd all heard of the guy who absorbed a sheet of acid through his sweat, and the girl who took too much and cut off her face, and the guy who thought there was a bee in his head and ripped his ears off with a corkscrew. These were the ghost stories of the alt crowd. Bowheads and preps told campfire tales about the deformed Donkey Lady who lived under a bridge by the river, while all the kids in black whispered about the girl who took five hits of white blotter and, thinking her beloved Persian cat was too cold, blew it up in the microwave.

"David! This is the perfect time. My parents are gone."

"I guess we can call Jake or Raven for help if something goes wrong."

"No, David! I want to do this with *just* you the first time. What if I freak out, or look weird, or it's like a truth serum? I'll tell Jake I think I love him and it'll be awful!"

"Fine," I replied, miffed that Greg's crush was becoming love.

Sitting on our tiny bed islands, we looked into each other's eyes.

"Whatever happens, David, I love you!"

"I love you too, Greg! You're my best friend."

We placed the bits of paper on our tongues and sat motionless, staring at each other from across the room.

"What happens now?" I mumbled through closed lips.

"Uh-oh-uh."

"Huh?"

"I. Don't. Know," answered Greg, careful to keep the hit on his tongue.

Twenty minutes later we were angrily stomping around the kitchen.

"I can't believe we gave that dude ten dollars for that!" Greg complained, taking a hot cookie sheet of pizza bites out of the oven. "He gypped us!"

"What a jerk! And we could've gone to FX tonight," I said, popping a pizza bite into my mouth. As Greg poured a second round of Captain Morgan and Coke, I noticed that the pizza bites tasted odd. Something wasn't right with the texture. I had to have another one to figure it out. I chewed carefully, with intent, trying to suss out each element of flavor and understand what was going on in my mouth. But the pizza bite eluded me. I popped another one in my mouth and closed my eyes. My mouth was suddenly full of the most disgusting material ever created by man. I opened my eyes to see Greg staring out the kitchen window, tracing his wet finger along the glass and humming.

"Greg! Who is outside?" I asked.

Greg turned to me with giant black eyes and whispered, "Everyone!"

I looked down at the empty cookie sheet. I had eaten twenty pizza bites.

"Greg! I ate too much. Drive me to the hospital."

"We can't drive, David."

"You're right. Oh no! I'm afraid I'm going to drive!"

I imagined myself the victim of an ill-intentioned hypnotist, sobbing as I pressed my possessed foot on the gas pedal and flew off the I-10 overpass to my death. I pulled out my car keys and threw them at Greg. "Here! You've got to keep me out of that car!"

Greg looked into his hand like he was holding the key to launch a wad of nukes. "It's too much responsibility," he said, throwing them back. "What if I end up driving? What if I can't stop myself?"

"Greg, you've got to be strong!" I threw the keys back at him. We stood in the kitchen like this for several minutes/ hours/weeks, throwing the car keys back and forth in a psychotic game of hot potato. And then it happened. Everything clicked into place. Every single thing made sense. In some wordless, inexplicable way, the truth of the whole world came crashing in.

"Greg! I understand everything!" I looked into Greg's dilated pupils.

"Wait!" He raised his finger to shush me, like he was figuring out the tip on a bill. "David!" he gasped. "I understand everything too!"

I grabbed his shoulder. "Greg, it's happening. We're tripping!"

"Oh. My. God. David! We're tripping!" We threw our arms around each other, laughing as we hopped up and down in the center of the kitchen.

"What the fuck is going on?"

Greg and I looked toward the foyer, mid-embrace, to see Johnny.

"We made food!" Greg blurted out as I realized that we were both wearing oven mitts.

"Jesus Christ, you're a couple of weirdoes," Johnny grunted. Greg and I remained frozen in each other's arms, staring at Johnny, as if stillness might camouflage our altered state.

"Um, okay, freaks. I'm going to work out." As Johnny trudged down the hallway, we remained entangled. Hearing his door shut, we tiptoed to Greg's room.

"Shhh," whispered Greg, shutting his door. "I want to show you something."

Greg pulled out a shoebox from under his bed and removed the lid, revealing the most beautiful pair of bright-blue, ten-hole Doc Marten boots.

"My mom got them yesterday," Greg said, handing me the boots. "They were a hundred and forty dollars." We rubbed the smooth heels on our faces and inhaled the thick odor of leather and rubber. Greg leaned toward me and said, "I think these shoes are magical." The whites of his eyes glowed from within.

"It's true," I whispered back. "Hey. Let's listen to some music."

"David, why are we whispering?"

"I don't know!" I whispered back loudly. Moments later, The Smiths' "Shoplifters of the World Unite" began blasting through the stereo and we were immediately on our feet, reenacting our favorite FX dances: the "I'm Balancing on a Tightrope" walk, the "Help, I'm Caught in a Sexy Spiderweb" sway, the "Here, Let Me Erotically Deal this Deck of Cards" hand flourish.

Reaching to the ceiling with my eyes closed, I heard Greg say my name. Snapping into the moment, I realized that the entire Smiths CD was almost over.

What had happened to time? Who stole my hour?

"I have an idea!" said Greg, pirouetting toward me in his bright-blue boots.

"I know!" I screamed. "I have a *million* ideas right now!"

"We need to get into a gay club where there are *real* gay people," Greg announced, jumping onto his bed. "Just imagine it, a place where anyone you meet might have sex with you!"

"Or be the love of your life!" I swooned, spinning myself in Greg's comforter like a whirling dervish.

Greg came to a stop and dramatically grabbed my shoulders. "I mean, don't you want to meet someone?" he asked. I wanted to tell Greg that he was my "someone." He peered into my eyes, his face a foot from mine, his sun-kissed bangs hanging over his warm brown eyes. He was perfect.

"Your face is weird, David."

"Oh no!" I yelped, raising my hands to my face. "Don't look at me!"

"Your pores are just gigantic!" he said as I recoiled from him. "It's okay, David. I have another idea!" He took my hand and led me down the hall into the boys' bathroom, a filthy nightmare of mildewing towels and uncapped deodorant sticks where random pubic hairs clung to every surface like tinsel on a Christmas tree.

"You have to try this! It feels amazing!" Greg said as he wiped a cool, wet pad over my face. A tingling, crisp sensation braced my skin as if it was slowly freezing.

"It's a Stridex pad, and it's incredible for tightening your pores."

"Oh, wow! I can feel the air on my cheeks."

Greg blew on my face as a rush of electricity zapped across my forehead. I could feel my eyes roll up into my head as Greg held my neck and continued to blow on my face.

"What the fuck are you freaks doing now?"

Johnny stood in the hallway, wearing the mere suggestion of underwear.

"I'm sick!" I replied instinctively.

"Stop being homos and get out of the fucking bathroom." Johnny stomped away as I remained frozen, with my head in Greg's hands.

"Greg," I whispered, "we have to get out of here! It's not safe."

Although neither of his parents was home and it was bare-ly midnight, we snuck out from Greg's window and into his front yard. The sound of cicadas was almost deafening. Up and down the fluorescent-lit block, the grass of every lawn glowed an almost toxic green. Not a soul could be seen or heard; there weren't even any cars.

"Greg! Where are we going? Isn't it dangerous out here?"

"I don't know," he whispered back. "On the count of three, we'll run across the street."

"To that church? Really? A *church*?"

"We have to get away from this house!" Greg looked into my eyes with the urgency of an action hero about to dismantle a bomb. "On the count of three! One. Two. Three!"

Hand in hand, we ran across the street and into the church parking lot. Around the back we stopped, breathless, with our bodies pressed flat against a brick wall.

"Look! A swing!" Greg pointed to the playground at the top of the hill. "I haven't been on a swing since I was a little kid."

"Doesn't that seem like a million years ago?" I asked as we ran up the hill toward a red plastic swing.

"Yeah. I miss being a kid," he replied as he jumped on the swing. "Push me!"

"Really? I don't miss it."

"Why?" he asked as the chains supporting him squeaked above. "Didn't you have fun?"

"Yeah, but I have friends now," I said, pushing him harder and higher, up to the stars.

Greg looked over his shoulder and smiled at me, his face glowing blue in the light of the half moon. "You know, you're like another brother to me?"

I smiled back, knowing that he meant it. "Me too."

That night we walked around Greg's neighborhood for hours, stopping to look at flame-red tulips writhing in the ground, growing up toward the sky before our very eyes. Obsessing over any plant in sight, we'd stop and sit in someone's yard for just a moment to watch them grow in high-speed LSD motion.

"They want to grow so bad!" I whispered, amazed at nature but still keenly aware that I was sitting in a flower bed beneath a stranger's bedroom window at 1 a.m.

Later, we came across a mass of a hundred beetles stuck on their backs beneath a streetlight. Greg reached out and flipped one over. As it skittered away, he pulled me close and opened his eyes wide in amazement, exclaiming, "That beetle thinks I'm God!"

We skipped and danced down the length of an endless, empty drainage ditch running through Greg's subdivision, twirling our cigarettes in the air over our heads to make figure-eight traces that lingered like fireflies.

This world felt endless. It was like I'd become part of a new thing, and that thing connected to another new thing, and so on and so on, until I was a part of everything. And so was Greg. Looking into the homes around us, I felt like I was a member of all those families, like a little, invisible piece of me had slipped inside each window we passed and would live there forever in a kitchen drawer or magazine rack or beneath the glass of a framed family photo.

Greg ran ahead of me, the bright-orange flame of his cigarette chasing him like a shooting comet. I wondered how I had ever been so lucky as to meet him and how implausible the math was that had led us to each other. I thought of what he had said on the swing a few hours earlier. I realized that it was too important to *not* mean everything, and it all became clear: he didn't need to love me the way I wanted him to, because the way he loved me meant I wasn't alone. And that was all that mattered.

Watching his blue feet and tiny tobacco comet fade into the blackness ahead, I thought, *Who needs a boyfriend when you have a brother?*

I can honestly say I have no memory of this photo being taken. I can't tell you anything about the night in question or why I'm wearing that hooded mustard pullover, an item of clothing that I am *sure* was not mine. The top of the glass leads me to believe we are all at the twenty-four-hour diner Jim's, which probably means this was taken after the midnight *Rocky Horror Picture Show*. There's a level of inebriation here that's so intense I actually don't recognize myself. I mean, I know it's me. But the features, expression, eye shape, and everything else make me feel like I'm looking at an askew doppelganger of myself. Looking at it for too long gives me the chills.

CHAPTER 14

Ask Me

Why didn't Greg want to be my boyfriend?

That was all I could think about while I watched Carla writhe over Greg's crotch as the curtains behind her went up in flames. Slumped against the corner of Carla's living room, I found myself tripping much harder than I'd anticipated on a tab of acid called Blue Ice, which was tame-sounding compared to others we'd had, like Black Widow or Fire Ant. Blue Ice sounded like something soothing you'd take after injuring a tendon.

But Blue Ice was the opposite of cool. The sun-drenched curtains continued to burn behind Greg and Carla as they unbuttoned each other's jeans. Everything was on high heat. It wasn't all burning up so much as collapsing like a soufflé: the kitchen counter, the chandelier, the Kitty Kat wall clock ticking so loudly I thought it would shatter the windows. Each of these things seemed to be warping in an unfelt nuclear heat, rippling and bleeding down the walls and cabinets. As Greg's forearm moved back and forth beneath Carla's crotch, the illuminated drapes brightened. Watching my best friend finger-bang this girl, I realized that the sun itself was going to burst through the walls. It was the end of the world.

But my Pineapple Crush tasted so good. Watching it melt in my hand, I couldn't stop thinking, *My God, this is the most delicious and refreshing beverage I've ever had.*

Carla's loud moan snapped me back into the moment. I thought about reminding them that I was there, slumped against the wall in the house of this punk girl I'd only met that day at lunch. Her house was the polar opposite of Raven's. It had a grand staircase in the foyer and a giant skylight in the vaulted living-room ceiling. I sat on the floor hugging my knees to my chin, perfectly content to watch Greg and Carla make out as the sun ate us whole. Carla threw her head back and let out a muffled groan, her shoulders shuddering. As I watched a girl orgasm in front of me for the first time, I thought, *How does Greg do that?*

I tried to imagine myself, with my scrawny rib cage and big pores, letting someone straddle me as I made them come, and I couldn't. But Greg could. As the sky exploded behind him I was filled with admiration, lust, and rage. How could I feel all those things so intensely at the same time for the same person? Maybe it was the Blue Ice talking.

"What are you looking at?" asked Carla, pushing the lavender-tipped bangs on her otherwise hairless head behind her ear. As she dismounted Greg and sat beside me, her multizippered pants and dozen earrings jingled like a sack full of spare change.

"The sky's on fire, right?" I asked casually, the way someone might inquire about a bus route, as we stared out the window.

"Oh, wow," she said as Greg sat down on my other side.

"It's beautiful!" Greg rested his head on my shoulder, his scent enveloping me. I looked down at the top of his head and could swear that strands of his hair were weaving themselves into a rug.

"Guys. What if hair enveloped the world?" I asked.

Greg let out a chortle. "What the fuck are you talking about?"

"Well, imagine it. What if hair never stopped growing and crept across the globe slowly and no one could stop it? Even if you cut your hair, it would just revolt by growing faster. All kinds of hair too! Straight hair, braided hair, Afros! And soon the weight of all that hair would crush people's homes and suffocate them and creep to new continents across the ocean floor! And these long clumps of hair would lash up out of the beach like . . . like . . . big hair waves!"

"Hair weaves?" asked Carla, with genuine terror in her eyes.

"No, hair *waves*, retard!" corrected Greg as they laughed.

Carla pinched my cheek. "David, you are *so* cute."

"Guys! It could happen. I mean, the sun *is* eating us, after all!"

This just made them laugh harder. Greg leaned over me to cackle in Carla's ear, the length of his torso warm and heavy in my lap.

A month ago, the night we'd dropped acid for the first time, I'd felt like I'd built a bridge that had gotten me closer to him. We'd tripped until five in the morning every weekend since, sneaking through his bedroom window to fall asleep as the sun rose. Then, after six hours of fitful slumber, I'd wake up angry and confused as Greg talked about whatever random guy he'd kissed at FX the night before. That was enough to bear without Greg making good on this whole "bisexual" thing, let alone right in front of me.

Carla? But not me? I couldn't wrap my head around it.

More often than not, all Greg talked about was Jake, who was suddenly with us all the time. Jake was under the tree with us for every lunch, lying in some girl's lap and complimenting her bracelets while Greg massaged his scalp. Or stretching as he stood up, and *unintentionally* showing the top of his ass crack as his jeans slipped down his hips. He was there every day, talking about some great punk show he'd snuck into or some awesome piercing he was going to get. A half dozen girls and boys would be totally enraptured, Greg at the front with stars in his eyes.

That said, I was right beside Greg, swooning as well. We gazed into Jake's ocean-blue eyes as his words became the wah-wah voice of Charlie Brown's teacher. The thick funk of pot stench from his clothes drifted over us as he dramatically recited Misfits lyrics like they were Walt Whitman poems. Greg would laugh as his arm grazed mine and I'd drift away, imagining him kissing Jake, or Raven kissing Jake, or Jake kissing Greg while undressing Carla and jerking off Hector as Raven gave a blowjob to some muscular senior quarterback we all hated.

"What the fuck are y'all doing?" The three of us turned from the flaming window to see Jake hanging in the doorframe. His threadbare *Meat Is Murder* T-shirt rode up, exposing his lean, tan stomach. "Hey, let's go for a walk!"

As I started to get up to leave, Carla grabbed my arm, saying, "Hey, wait up."

Greg bounded out of the room with Jake like a happy puppy, leaving me alone with Carla on the cold marble floor.

"I saw you watching," she smiled at me.

"Um, uh . . . well . . ." I stuttered as the blood rushed to my face.

"Oh my God," Carla sighed, holding my face in her hands and smiling. "You're blushing. That's so cute." Before I could say anything, she put her lips against mine. I froze, feeling her hand creep down my chest and stomach toward my crotch.

"You're gay, right?" she asked.

"I'm bisexual," I countered.

"Seriously?" She laughed. "You're a double-stuff virgin, aren't you?"

"Double-stuff virgin?"

"Yeah. It's when you're a virgin who's bisexual. It's so sad."

"I'm not sad! Morrissey doesn't have sex and he's happy."

"Yeah, but he doesn't want to have sex," Carla reasoned. "He's asexual."

"Look, I'm just tripping really hard and . . ."

"Here," she interrupted before shoving my hand down her pants.

"Whoa!" I yelled, trying to pull my arm back.

"Shhh," she whispered, her long legs wrapping around me like a spider. "I saw you watching us." She wriggled closer as the burning sky brightened behind her. "Feel that?"

"Yeah," I said, not sure what part of her vagina she was referring to.

"Not that," she snickered, reaching down to adjust my fingers. "That."

"Oh, that!" I said, resting my thumb against a fleshy nub.

"That's the part that feels really good when you touch it," she whispered.

"Huh. It's like a little button," I snickered, rubbing it faster.

"Oh yeah," she moaned, bucking and panting as she laid back on the floor. I sped up and slowed down repeatedly, tittering quietly at the amazing amount of control my thumb had over Carla's movements and vocalizations. My diddling was getting a much bigger reaction than Greg's, which I was quite proud of. I wasn't repulsed at all, the way I thought I might be with a girl. But I wasn't turned on either, her body seeming less like a sexual object and more like a deceptively simple lab set.

"Come here," she moaned, hiking up her shirt and pushing my mouth against her exposed nipple. I began to suck instinctively, thinking, *Gee whiz. I haven't done this in years.*

I continued to nurse and diddle, playing her body like an arcade game that would eventually spit out twenty more tickets if I operated the controls correctly.

"I want your——." She stopped as her hand touched the loose fabric of my pants crotch. "Oh."

"What?" I grinned. "Am I doing it wrong?"

Carla gently took my hand from her pants and chuckled, tousling my hair and kissing me softly on the forehead. "You're cute, Crabb."

"Hey, are you guys—Whoa!" yelled Jake in the doorway. "Didn't know y'all were doin' the horizontal mambo in here!"

"It's fine," said Carla, standing to adjust her pants. "We were just coming out."

As Jake left, I stood up, feeling like I'd done something incorrectly. "Sorry if I messed up."

"You were great," smiled Carla as she took my hand. "But I think now I know why you were watching."

At the end of the hall we found Hector and Raven sitting at

opposite sides of the dining-room table. Greg and Jake watched as Hector held up the flame from a blue plastic lighter.

"Shhh!" he said, although none of us had said anything. "Thirty seconds."

Taking his thumb off the lighter, he leaned over Raven as she pulled up the crushed velvet sleeve of her shirt.

"Hurry," she demanded, gritting her teeth as Hector plunged the hot metal top of the plastic lighter onto her forearm. "Fuck, that hurts!"

"Just a few seconds," he said, blowing on the lighter as it sizzled against her flesh.

"Don't fucking blow on it, dickweed! It has to burn to make the mark!"

Thirty seconds later he removed the lighter and grinned down at his handiwork.

"Oh, Hector! It's beautiful!" Raven turned to us, holding her arm out so we could all see the blistering scar of a perfect happy face branded onto her skin. They hugged each other and waved us toward them. We formed a group huddle and began to sing along to our favorite song.

"Shyness is nice, and shyness can stop you from doing all the things in life you'd like to!"

"Ask" by The Smiths was like our theme song, full of lyrics about the dangers of introversion and shame. It's an unusually sunny song until the halfway mark, when, in typical Morrissey fashion, the listener is reminded that a bomb is more likely than love to "bring us together."

"I want a happy face!" yelped Carla, beginning a slow procession as all of us held out our arms to Hector for branding. When it was finally my turn, Raven threw her arms around me.

"No, you can't hurt Davey."

"I know," chimed in Carla, "he's our cutie-pie."

"No. I want to," I said, sitting across from Hector and offering my forearm. I'd been the cutie-pie, the funny one, the sweet boy, my whole life. As Hector lowered the lighter onto my skin, I kept the pain at bay by thinking about who I could become and how I might change. I wanted to feel things I hadn't felt, touch things I hadn't touched. I wanted to break someone's heart and keep secrets of my own. Carla and Greg smiled at me from the couch as another cool blast of Blue Ice crept up my spine and into my cerebellum. There was so much left to hear and smell and taste, and I wanted all of it.

Thirty seconds later, it was over. I smiled down at the fresh scar on my arm smiling back at me. Through the patio door I could see the sun disappearing over a horizon line of burnt lawns and dull beige homes. It might not eat us after all.

Before you get all judgy concerning the over-the-top nature of this particular photograph, know that it was Halloween, the one night of the year when I could let my general fashion sense become a mockery of itself. I made those vinyl pants myself, which explains why the ass split on the dance floor an hour later. All things considered, it was a blessing, as my undercarriage was a moist pit of discomfort. Sylvia mocked my complaining, saying "Honey, vinyl doesn't breathe. Bitch, you got swamp-ass!" Luckily the cape covered my exposed butt the rest of the night. Also, I think we can all agree that the spookiest thing about this photo is the china hutch behind me.

CHAPTER 15

Smash Every Tooth in Your Head

As the credits to *Fried Green Tomatoes* rolled, Mike silently wept beside me. Over the last few months I'd discovered that my mom's boyfriend was a big softie.

"Aw, hell. My allergies are killin' me," Mike murmured as my mom handed him a tissue from her purse. His son and daughter, Mickey and Sarah, sat beside me as their father had one of his "allergy attacks," which commonly took place during reruns of *Little House on the Prairie* and ASPCA commercials.

"Oh honey," my mother said, rubbing Mike's back.

"I'm fine. I'm fine. The air's just so gosh-darn dry in here."

Sarah covered her face and giggled at her dad as her older brother shot her a look. Mickey was twelve and Sarah was nine.

As a queer, goth sixteen-year-old, I couldn't have had less interest in two preadolescents who were growing up on a farm in a town known for its giant legumes.

"Can I go now, Mom?" I asked, impatiently twirling the pentagram pendant hiding under my shirt. "Greg and I are watching a movie tonight, and he's waiting for me."

"But I thought you were going to have dinner with us?"

"Oh, Teri. Let the boy go have fun with his friends," Mike said, patting my leg. He handed me a twenty-dollar bill. "You mentioned you needed gas earlier. So take this."

I thanked Mike and pocketed the cash as he wiped his cheeks. In truth, Greg and I wouldn't be watching a movie at all. We'd be going to FX. I was the designated driver, which meant I couldn't get too fucked up. So tonight, I was going to be the adult. Tonight, I was going to practice moderation.

A few hours later I was tripping my balls off in the FX parking lot. I had tried to be good, but the setting made it impossible. How was I supposed to be good with Jake and his flask sidling up to me on the dance floor?

"No, Jake. I don't want a drink. But . . . Okay. I'll have a sip. *One* sip."

Later, on the patio, Raven handed me a joint as our favorite song played.

"I can't. I'm driving. Well . . . Okay, but I'm only having *one* toke."

Around midnight Greg cornered me in the bathroom and took out a tiny hit of acid.

"Greg, I can't! I'm driving. Well, okay . . . I'll just have a corner of the tab."

Over the course of three hours, this kind of "moderation" equaled one very fucked-up sixteen-year-old.

By midnight I was a mess. The four quarter-hits of Blue Angel acid I'd eaten had taken hold. I couldn't organize my thoughts. I was trying to get some fresh air and clear my head in the parking lot, but everything I saw warranted committed investigation. Concrete, tree bark, corrugated metal, and car windshields all demanded my deep and profound reflection. "Acid spiders" were creeping in and out of my peripheral vision, like a million little daddy longlegs crawling at the edges of my eyes. The muscles in my jaw kept involuntarily twitching, as if tiny hives of larval worms were uncoiling beneath my molars. I kept hearing a bizarre, metallic vibration coming from somewhere in the night.

Oh wait. That's my teeth.

Over the muffled din of Nine Inch Nails I heard the sound of an approaching banshee getting closer and closer, until my ears felt like they were bleeding. Then it appeared above me in the sky: a plane coming in for a landing at the edge of the tarmac a few hundred yards away. The plane seemed so close that I tried to reach up and touch it. As it disappeared behind the club's roof I noticed the Pepper Creek Family Dental sign: a fluorescent light box depicting a glowing, smiling tooth with feet and Hamburger Helper–gloved hands. He held a big red toothbrush and offered a hearty thumbs-up, his bright-blue eyes peering into me like they'd seen things . . . awful things.

This sign sent me into an existential crisis.

Does that tooth know what it is? I thought. *Does that tooth have teeth of its own?*

I touched my jaw as it flexed and quivered behind my skin. As I stood there all alone in the parking lot, listening to the distant thump of "Down in It," it hit me.

My teeth have teeth!!!

As the nightmare of these infinite dental Russian dolls took hold of me, the door to the club opened. Two girls in baby-doll dresses stumbled down the stairs and came to a sudden stop upon noticing me. I realized that most of my right hand was inside my mouth. I quickly removed it, nonchalantly wiping saliva on my pants.

"I'm out of cigarettes," I blurted, thinking in some spontaneous fit of drug-addled logic that this would explain why I was devouring my hand. The girls ignored me and proceeded to make out on the hood of a VW Bug. Carefully I crept back toward the entrance of the club, strangely worried they might catch me and demand I stay.

No. You! Weirdo. Stand here and continue to fist your face as we kiss!

Back inside, the lights looked like they were melting from the ceiling in great, glowing drips. I had a bad case of the Icky Strickies: stomach cramps from the strychnine in the acid. My heart was pumping out of my chest to the beat of the kick drum. I thought to myself, *How is the DJ still playing Nine Inch Nails? Has he played even one non–Nine Inch Nails song since I've been here?* As Trent Reznor screamed, I found that I couldn't think of a single song in the world that wasn't a Nine Inch Nails song. "Down in It," "Sin," "Enjoy the Silence," "Like a Prayer," "Mr. Bojangles," "The Greatest Love of All" . . . ALL by Nine Inch Nails!

I neared the dance floor and passed a hippie-goth chick covered in a thousand pimples and an oversize 10,000 Maniacs shirt.

She screamed in my face, revealing a horselike set of chompers covered in braces. Her teeth seemed to swell from her mouth like tiny white balloons trapped in metal cages.

"Be careful! THE SKINHEADS ARE HERE!"

A chill ran down my spine. Skinheads had invaded FX three times in the last month. They were the mortal enemies of freaks. To an extent, they were just like us. We were all stuck in Texas aspiring to be like the New York punks and angsty European bands we loved. But skinheads' idols and interests made them dangerous. Their identities were based on a sociopolitical divide that simply didn't exist in the suburbs of San Antonio in 1990. These guys weren't neo-Nazis or a burgeoning labor party in Manchester. They were just jerks who met at Dairy Queen for Butterfinger Blizzards to talk about who they'd finger-banged. They didn't spend the weekend picketing labor laws; they spent it bashing "fags." And that was the problem. Skinheads: they ruined everyone's good time.

As my eyes refocused in the darkness, I saw six of them gathered in the middle of the dance floor. They were marching in slow motion around some poor sucker they were about to beat the hell out of. All the FX regulars were pressed against the walls, sipping their sodas and peering timidly through their teased bangs, waiting for this episode to come to an end.

And then I heard it: Greg's sharp, high-pitched yelp.

The poor sucker trapped in the center of that skinhead huddle was my best friend. I noticed Carla in the corner, covering her eyes as they began to beat him. I wanted her to look at me, as if we'd lock eyes and instantaneously conceive a plan of attack and jump in with crazy ninja skills to save Greg. I tried to picture our small clan of pale, calligraphy-loving bisexuals fending off seven massive skinheads. It wouldn't work.

The club began to empty as the beating continued to blaring industrial music. I stood there under violet strobe lights and watched the whole thing play out like a flickering slide show, photo after photo of wet skin and bared teeth, mouths in the shape of the word *faggot* and strings of spit suspended in the air like ice sculptures. The kick drum of the music was impossibly loud, but somehow I could still hear Greg screaming. And then I noticed that the DJ had stopped spinning. There was no music. That incessant, pulverizing beat was coming from behind my sternum.

After a while I opened my eyes, not realizing they'd been closed. I'd retreated twenty feet back into the narrow hallway leading out of the club. I inhaled a waft of warm, strawberry-scented smoke from the fog machine as the skinheads approached me. Their oily, shining heads reflected the club lights above like domed mirrors. I pressed myself against the wall and watched them pass by, laughing and tossing a pair of bright-blue Doc Marten boots back and forth.

In the car, Greg was hysterical and barefoot. The passing streetlights looked like glowing streamers, and my spine was melting into the driver's seat. I tried to filter out Greg's psychotic screaming as the little white dotted lines in the road became albino gerbils and scattered all over the highway.

"David! What the fuck happened in there?"

"I'm sorry, Greg. I'm sorry . . ." I repeated, grinding my molars against one another as the streetlights ahead became an on-ramp to a spaceship.

"I was just minding my own business and they crowded around me! They took my fucking SHOES!!!"

"I know, Greg. It's really—"

"My favorite Doc Martens! They TOOK them! And my face!" Greg pulled down the visor and shrieked at his lumpy eye in the mirror. "My face is deformed forever!"

"Just calm down, all right?" I said, my trip intensifying as Greg ramped up the theatrics. "We're going to follow Carla to her friend's house and put ice on it!"

"Ice?! I have been through a *trauma*, David! I'm going to look like Sloth from *Goonies*!" Greg leaned over to show me his eye under the interior light. "Look at my eye!"

"I'm trying to drive! I can't look at your eye! I'm tripping really hard, okay?"

"Is there blood? It feels wet now. Do I have a weird blood-eye?"

Greg yelled and punched the dashboard for another ten minutes before we arrived at George's house at 3 a.m. George used to go to Gunther High School with us until he turned eighteen and inherited a bunch of money from his dead mother's life insurance. He immediately dropped out, bought four cars, and moved into his own place, which became a halfway house and party destination for all the runaways, drug dealers, and delinquents from our school.

As we walked in, two guys in Sid Vicious shirts were doing lines of blow off a glass coffee table. My eyes were tricked by the table's reflection, and for a moment I thought the table was a box with two guys inside who were popping out to kiss the pair of men sitting on the couch.

I plopped Greg down on the black leather couch and rushed into the kitchen.

"Where are you going? David! My face!"

"Move!" I screamed to a tranced-out girl who was staring at

water rushing over her hand beneath the faucet. She looked at me with large, empty eyes.

"It won't come off," she murmured.

I gathered ice in a plastic bag and looked down at her pink, pruning hand, which was completely free of any marks.

"Here," I said, shoving a roll of paper towels at her. "You already got it off!"

I could hear Greg wailing in the living room as I left her in the kitchen, smiling at the realization that she'd finally removed something that had never been there. I ran down the hall and tore through the bathroom cabinets, looking for a towel.

"David! My face!!!" Greg screamed hysterically as I entered the living room. I turned the corner, prepared to smack his perfect face, but I was totally unprepared for what I found. Bright-red blood projectile-squirted through Greg's fingers as he held his face. Wet crimson cascaded down his arm and neck as various inebriated weirdos gathered around.

Stone-cold sobriety took hold of my entire being. Greg wasn't overreacting. His face truly was ruined, and now my best friend would be blind. As I stepped forward to help him, a small black mass of velvet and crucifixes appeared between us. The smell of cheap perfume and Lubriderm enveloped me. A familiar girl with a nest of peach-colored hair glared at me from behind her black tarantula eyelashes and blew a huge plume of Marlboro Light smoke into my face.

"He's not bleeding, Miss Thang!" she blurted in a nasal South Texas whine. "I just put a raw steak on his nellie face to stop the swelling." She reached up and flipped over the slab of pink beef covering Greg's eye. "Girl, you gotta keep the cool side on that shit!" she wheezed as bloody tears dripped down his cheek.

It was my unlikely angel: Sylvia.

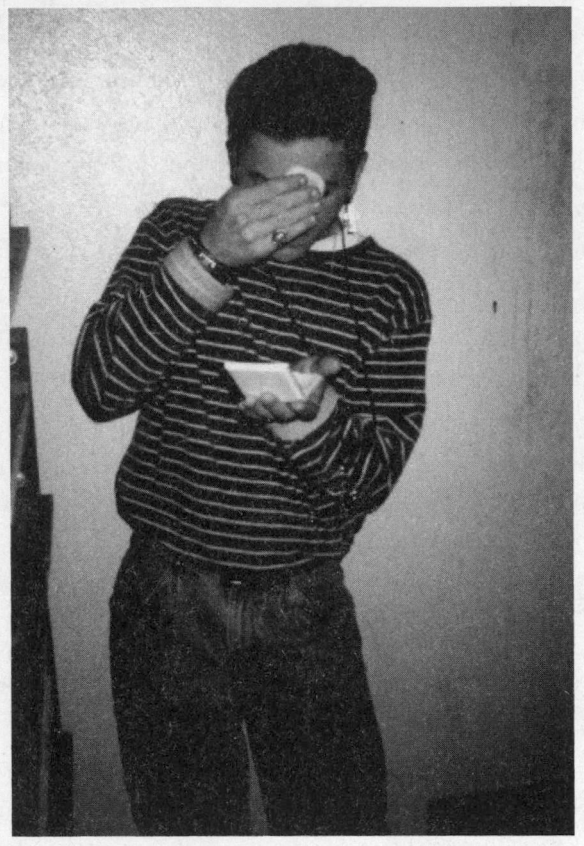

"Am I shining? What about over here? Am I shiny in this light?
What about my forehead? Is it shining? My nose? Is it shiny?"

Here is Greg beating the fuck out of his face behind a bleacher in
3rd-period gym class. Although our looks were still pretty tame
during this time this was taken, we both already understood the
value of having sheenless, matte faces. Greg carried this damn
compact with him everywhere, eradicating any perceived shine the
moment he felt the slightest humidity, which was all the time in
San Antonio.

CHAPTER 16

She's in Parties

Author Jacqui Rivait is credited with the quote "If you don't have anything nice to say, don't say anything at all." Dorothy Parker would later famously say, "If you don't have anything nice to say, come sit by me." Sylvia, had she written, would have said, "If you don't have anything nice to say, I'll say something worse. And if it's about me, I will read your hair for filth!"

Reading was one of the many gay terms I learned from Sylvia. She'd shown us a documentary called *Paris Is Burning*, about drag queens in the New York City ball scene. Greg and I became obsessed with the movie and added a liberal dose of terms like *shade*, *work*, and *Miss Thang* to our daily vocabulary.

Hearing Sylvia's "language" evolve on the spot was quite an experience. When we'd introduced her to Raven at a party, they'd had a disagreement over the true meaning of a Yaz lyric.

Things got heated, as they usually did between Sylvia and any-one else with a vagina, and Sylvia called her a cunt. As Raven stormed from the room, Sylvia continued to scream.

"You're a cunt. Goodbye, cunty! Whatever, Kunta Kinte! Keeping walkin' back to your slave shack! [*Tongue clicking and lip-popping*]"

Sylvia had drawn a phonetic comparison between *cunt* and Kunta Kinte, a character from the PBS slave saga *Roots*, which led to a series of racist jokes and, finally, vague insults in some made-up African dialect. Not only was it incredibly offensive, but it also made no sense. There weren't many people whiter than Raven or Sylvia, in ethnicity *or* actual skin color. Addi-tionally, Sylvia didn't have a racially-biased bone in her body. It wasn't so much that she singled out any one type of person for her disparaging remarks as it was that everyone in her path was fair game. And once you crossed Sylvia, every aspect of your person was up for *reading*, regardless of whether or not it was politically correct.

One night on the FX patio, after digging through her purse for five minutes, Sylvia found that she was, as usual, out of cig-arettes and cash. She nudged Raven, batted her eyes, and in a baby voice asked, "Girl, can Mama bum a smoke?"

"Seriously?" Raven replied. "I've already given you so many."

"But massa!" Sylvia feigned fear and dropped to her knees on the cement. "Peeees! Me just want one smoke, massa!"

"You are awful," Raven laughed, rolling her eyes as she hand-ed Sylvia a cigarette. They smiled together for a moment before Sylvia murmured under her breath, "There's a sucker born every minute," then proceeded to click and pop her way into the club.

Raven's smile turned into a sneer. "I can't stand that bitch," she hissed. "Why do you guys hang out with her?"

Greg and I shrugged in silence, but we both knew the answer. Sylvia could be insensitive, but her insensitivity was strangely inspired and wonderfully absurd. And for some reason, she liked Greg and me. Simply by not harassing us, she made us feel like special members of a very exclusive club.

Sylvia was also a professional fag hag, a title she'd chosen for herself that was as offensive as the ones she applied to other people. At eighteen, Sylvia was not only an adult who could get into clubs, but she was also pretty much the queen of every gay bar in town. And soon she was going to get us into one of them.

Walking up to the entrance of the Bonham Exchange, downtown San Antonio's premier gay club, I felt butterflies in my stomach. Sylvia walked ahead of us, her voluminous breasts bouncing under countless layers of gauzy ebony fabric.

"Thank God we're out of that fuckin' teen bar. I was about to catch a bad case of puberty up in that joint." She looked over her shoulder and saw us, several feet behind her. "Why the fuck are y'all in the back of the goddamn bus, Rosa Parks? Let's put some fucking hustle in it!"

"Sylvia, we're nervous," Greg said. "What if they don't believe the IDs you got?"

"IDs? What the fuck is this ID business?"

"Well, isn't that how you're getting us in?" I said.

"David, listen to me." She turned to us and placed her hands on our shoulders. "You are babies who are about to be men. I am going to make this possible, okay?"

We nodded and smiled as Sylvia sweetly patted our faces.

Suddenly and with painful intensity she pinched our cheeks and dragged us around the side of the club. "One! Do NOT question Mama! Two! Just FOLLOW Mama! Three! Do whatever Mama tells you to do!"

"Ouch! That fucking hurt," Greg whined as she released us in the alley behind the Bonham.

"Why are we here?" I demanded, rubbing my burning cheek.

Sylvia raised her small clutch and lightly smacked my head with each word of her command. "Do! Not! Question! Mama!"

The light over us flickered as she caught her breath and fixed her hair, which had been dyed an almost iridescent violet. Greg, trying to calm her, said, "Sylvia, your hair is such a nice purple color."

"Bitch! It's called EGGPLANT!" she screamed. Taking a deep yoga breath, she straightened her teardrop-shaped brooch. "Now, just stay here by this fence and you will be in this club in five minutes. *Capisce?*"

We nodded in silence, muttering a quiet "Thank you" as she clicked away.

An hour later, we were still waiting by the tall wooden fence. The alley was somehow darker, and distant sirens had been sounding closer and closer.

"It's getting late, huh?" Greg was pacing up and down the alley.

"What if this is a prank?" I asked.

"I know she's a little bit crazy, but why would she do that? I mean . . ." He stopped as we heard a slight scratching.

"A rat!" Greg winced and fell against the chain-link fence on the other side of the alley.

"Pssst. Bitches!" a voice whispered. "Are you there?"

"Sylvia?" Greg asked.

"No. It's Anne Frank, fagotron!"

As I snickered, Greg backhanded me in the chest and replied, "What do you want us to do?"

Suddenly the two-by-fours of the fence busted out with brute force. A small four-inch heel kicked the planks from side to side as they swung back and forth, still nailed to the top of the fence. Sylvia's tiny face peeked out from between them and flashed us a bloodred Joker grin.

"Heeeeere's Johnny!"

We crawled through the narrow space in the fence and snuck through the patio. Inside the club, Sylvia kept reminding us to keep our cool. "Close your mouths, whores. You trying to catch flies?"

But it was amazing. The Bonham Exchange wasn't any old dance club. It was a palatial converted synagogue, complete with a three-story vaulted ceiling over the dance floor and four full bars. Muscular men in tiny thongs gyrated on boxes to thump-heavy music. The Bonham's speakers and laser lights made FX seem like a school dance.

"Look, David. Everyone's drinking out of *real* glasses!" Greg exclaimed.

"Isn't it fancy, ladies?" grinned Sylvia. "Welcome to the Bottom Sexchange! Now let's go."

"Wait! Why are we leaving?" Greg begged as Sylvia pulled us away from a hairless Mexican guy who was thrusting his banana thong in our faces.

"It's last call, Gregorian Chant! Come on, Crabapple!"

I looked at my watch and saw that it was already 2 a.m. I hadn't realized how long we'd been waiting in that alley.

"Don't worry, girls! Night's not over yet. We're going to an after-party!"

Thirty minutes later we pulled into the Elmira Inn, a shady downtown hotel. Even if you never went downtown, you knew about the Elmira from its appearances on the ten o'clock news. It was where prostitutes got busted and drug deals went wrong. Greg and I were genuinely thrilled to be there.

"Oh, wow! This is the place where those drag queens started that fire!" Greg chirped as he parked the car. "I've always wanted to see it!"

"Well, you're about to, Mary," said Sylvia in a half-welcome/half-warning. She dug through her clutch and pulled out a small glass vial. "Here. Sniff a little of this before we go in."

"What is it?" I asked as she took off the lid and inhaled the stuff.

"Oh, don't be such a stick-in-the-mud, Minerva!" she replied, her eyes rolling back in her head as she slumped into her seat.

"Yeah, Minerva," chided Greg as he took a snort, clearly confused about who "Minerva" was. "Oh, wow," he said, leaning back. "My head is so warm . . ."

I took the vial from Greg and snorted, my head filling with a thick, hot jelly that slipped down my neck all the way to my tailbone. "Oh, fuck. It feels amazing." I could only imagine what high-end, designer drug I'd just taken. "Sylvia, what is this?"

Her eyes rolled down from her skull like venetian blinds. "It's VCR head cleaner."

"What? You mean I just inhaled—"

"Let's go, cunts!" And, like that, she was on her feet and up the stairs. On the second floor, we walked into a smoke-filled lair of thudding club music and pungent male musk. My brain was buzzing with a pulsing crackle, like the staccato hum of an old television right after you turn it off. Dizzy, I grabbed Sylvia's arm. "I feel . . . spinny."

"I know, bitch. It's called the wah-wahs. Isn't it fabulous?"

I tried to focus my eyes through the smoke in the dimly lit room. The door to the next suite was open, as was the one after that, and the one after that. Dozens of people, mostly men, filled the space as far down as the eye could see, like an endless mirror reflecting itself, forever and into eternity. I realized that Greg was gone and suddenly became aware of the immediate space around me. I looked down to see two men rolling around on the carpet in their underwear.

Are they fighting? Or . . . Oh wait . . . They're not fighting.

To my right, a girl with fluttering eyelids was grinding her shoulder blades into an air-conditioning unit.

It's not that hot in here. Does she feel sick? Oh wait . . . She feels just fine.

I felt a smack on my arm and turned to find Greg beside me with a plastic cup.

"Hey, I made you a rum and Coke, but there's no Coke. So it's just rum and ice."

I downed the glass and noticed that Greg was now only wearing a tight white tank top.

"What happened to your Psychedelic Furs shirt?"

"I felt overdressed," he said as a skinny boy in red underwear stumbled past us.

"Where's Sylvia?"

"How should I know?" Greg could barely focus on me. "Oh my God, that guy is totally checking us out."

I tried to aim my vision on one point in the spinning room, but everyone seemed to have a twin. "Which one? The little blond guy on the bed?"

"No. That forty-year-old in the red tank top drinking Zima. You should go talk to him."

"No, Greg. I feel weird. I don't want to."

"Of course you don't want to. I have to do everything." Greg handed me his drink and coiffed his hair. "How do I look? How's the light? My skin?" Greg angled his face in several directions. "Am I shiny? What about here? Am I shiny like this? Okay. Give me back my drink."

Greg confidently strode up to the man and introduced himself. "Hey, I'm Greg."

"Hey, I'm Paul," he replied, slipping his thumbs into the front of his low-slung jeans. "How old are you, Greg?"

"How old do you think I am?" Greg flipped his bangs and gave Paul a smoldering stare. Paul leaned forward and whispered something in Greg's ear. Greg laughed coyly and slipped his thin red straw between his lips seductively. "You're funny."

How the hell does he do that? I thought, followed immediately by, *I need to find a bathroom now.*

I stumbled through the connected suites, trying to find an unlocked bathroom, as strange men looked at me with an intensity I hadn't experienced before. *Are they angry?* I thought. *Why do they all want to fight me?* As a mustached man in a bandanna palmed my bottom, I realized that these men didn't want to fight at all.

I wanted to be like Greg, to turn to this man confidently and simply say, "Hello." But I couldn't even hold his stare. It shouldn't have been so hard for me to look into the eyes of another man, if only to say, "Hi. I'm David."

"David!" I spun around to see Sylvia sitting at a small table with a few men. "Crabapple! Come to Mama!"

A half hour later I was even more obliterated, curled up beneath the table against Sylvia's leg. I started to nod off as she entertained a gaggle of adoring gay fans, one of whom offered her a small bag of cocaine.

"Come on, stick-in-the-mud," she whispered to me. "A hit of this will keep you up."

"No, Sylvia. My head feels like a brick. I don't feel well."

"Suit yourself, pussy. More for Mama." I heard her snort a giant line as an old, haggard woman entered the room. She shuffled toward us in flip-flops, wearing a dirty denim skirt that revealed bruised knees. Her short auburn hair was arranged atop her head in an unnecessary banana clip. Her entrance stirred the masses, and as she sat, a hush fell over the room.

"If y'all don't know me, my name is Leona," she announced with a gravelly rasp. "And when Leona gets to the party, that's when the party starts!" Leona erupted into a fit of coughing and removed a small glass pipe from her bag. "Who wants to hit it first?"

"Excuse me, ma'am. He does!" Sylvia grabbed the pipe and passed it down to me. "Here, Minerva."

"No, Sylvia. My head . . ."

"Oh, come on! It's just weed."

"But I feel so sick and . . ."

"Come on, Crabby. Don't make Mama get high alone."

Sylvia looked at me with the big, wet eyes of a pleading child. Leona stared at me sleepily, a thousand wrinkles at either edge of her permanently down-turned mouth. As the song on the stereo faded to silence, the eyes of every man in the room were on me.

All their stares felt like a dare, compounded by Sylvia's insistence. I unfurled from my tiny fetal ball in an attempt to rise to the occasion. I would not be shamed by all these strangers with eyes I could barely look into, all these men to whom I could not simply say, "Hello. I'm David."

The first odd thing I noticed was the crackling sound the pipe made as I lit it, like someone ate a bunch of Pop Rocks and opened their mouth to my ear. Then my head felt like it was in a microwave, severed on a dish while slowly spinning in waves of radiation.

I collapsed under the table onto all fours as my throat closed. My eyes watered as I tried harder to move air past the prickly blowfish that was expanding in my neck. The lights in my head were starting to go out. I reached up from under the table as tears streaked down my face.

"Sylvia . . . Help."

She looked at me with blank, tired, pink-hued eyes, eyes that said, "I'm sorry. Have we met?" Slowly, a smile spread across her face as one of her eyes went a little googly, like the wandering, displaced eyeball of a broken doll. She let out a slow wheeze of a laugh, like air escaping from a slit tire.

"Bitch, you just smoked CRACK!"

The room erupted in laughter around me. As quickly as I'd thought I was going to black out, I felt an urgent rush of electricity course through me. My entire nervous system was on fire and my eyes felt like they were being pulled open by tiny, invisible wires. In the midst of the laughter, I slowly raised my head up. Beneath the table across from me were Leona's legs. As my vision cleared and my brain began to process at lightning speed, I found myself looking up Leona's dirty acid-washed denim skirt.

There they were: her withered, pendulous penis and testicles bouncing in time with her deep, cacophonous laughter.

The door across the room opened and Greg entered with the older guy in the red shirt. As he tucked in his tank-top, Greg scanned the scene before him.

"What happened?"

I was pretty sure at that moment that Greg had enjoyed a better night at the party than I had.

Between Greg's skin tips and Sylvia's eyebrow tweezing, I had a lot of look going on. Here I am posing with Greg, whose insane shoulder pads made him look like a power lesbian from the cast of *L.A. Law*. I wish Greg would've confronted me about my paisley button-down over the turtleneck t-shirt, but my pout almost makes up for it.

Almost.

CHAPTER 17

Boys Don't Cry

Honey, we're getting married! Mike is going to be your step-father!"

Mike smiled at me across the restaurant table with tears in his eyes, presumably a symptom of that day's high pollen count.

"David, I want you to know that I love your mother very much. I think I can make you both very happy. I promise." Mike's desperate insistence made me feel like I was buying a car. My mom shifted uncomfortably and shot him a look as he continued. "I just want you to know that Seguin is a great little town."

And then I got it. The desperation, the sales pitch, my mother's forced grin as she twisted her dinner napkin into a little paper rope.

"We're moving to Seguin?" I asked.

"Honey, listen to your mother," she begged. "Mike has a great job and a house in Seguin. His kids are near their grandparents and they're really settled there."

"Well, I'm really settled *here*!" I snapped.

"David, we won't be moving until your school break! That's something, right?" My mother reached out and took my hand. "It's going to be great, and— What's that?"

"What's what?"

"This thing on your arm here," she said, touching my happy-face scar.

"It's nothing!" I said, pulling my arm away. "I'm happy for you both. I just . . ." My mother stared at me hopefully, like she was waiting for my blessing. "Of course I'm happy," I lied. "I'm sure Seguin will be great!"

"I am *not* moving to Seguin," I declared, banging my fist on the steering wheel as Sylvia handed a joint to Greg in the backseat.

"Don't let them tell you what to do!" wheezed Greg.

"Emancipation, bitch!" screamed Sylvia. "Be your own man, girl!"

The three of us were driving half an hour outside of San Antonio to a town called New Braunfels, inexplicably pronounced "New Braun*s*fel" by those who lived there.

"Why do those hicks relocate their *S*'s?" asked Sylvia, her glazed eyes half-closed.

"You're the one who wanted to come out here," sighed Greg, perturbed that we were headed to the country instead of sneaking into the Bonham Exchange.

"Come on, bitches," Sylvia moaned, teasing her freshly-dyed blood-red hair in the visor mirror. "Once you see fine-ass Tommy you'll understand. He's got a Mohawk and did time for graf-fiti," she squealed dreamily.

I'd agreed to go as long as she paid for the gas and cigarettes. But halfway there, with an empty tank and no smokes, Sylvia realized something.

"Oh, sorry, Minerva. I forgot my wallet at home."

"You'd forget your pussy at home if it wasn't attached to your crotch," Greg said, starting his and Sylvia's weekly cussing match.

"Look, Gregorian Chant, do you really want to start with me?"

"You forget your wallet a lot for someone who doesn't seem *that* stupid."

"Whatever, cunt. Love your hair. Hope it wins."

"Okay, Sylvia. At least my hair is tinted less than thirty colors."

"Bitch, what you got ain't a tint. What you got is a frost!"

"Ah!" Greg's nostrils flared in offense. Sylvia had crossed a line. It was time to intervene.

"Guys, just stop fighting, okay? I've got enough for gas and smokes, all right?"

"David! Don't be a pushover," Greg said, punching my shoulder from the backseat.

"Thanks, Crabb," said Sylvia, snuggling her painted face against my arm. "Don't be mad, Miss Thing."

A few minutes later I reached into the Walgreens drugstore bag in my lap and removed a small white plastic Vicks inhal-er. With scissors from her purse, Sylvia cut through the rough, tubelike casing and removed the fibrous, cylindrical, menthol-soaked core, which looked like a cigarette filter with the paper stripped off. She cut it into three pieces and handed one to each of us.

"So what did Joey tell us to do with these?"

"I think he said you just wash it down with a drink," she calmly answered.

I stared at her blankly.

"What?" she asked. "He said it's like cheap ecstasy. You just take it like a pill. It's called . . ." She looked down at the package in her hand. "Vicking?"

"Uh, that doesn't seem right, Sylvia."

"Oh my God, David. Are you afraid to fucking eat a Vicks inhaler?" dared Greg, thus beginning his and Sylvia's weekly "make-fun-of-David" session, their version of make-up sex.

"Davey is afraid of getting too fucked up," scolded Sylvia, twisting her fists in front of her eyes like a baby.

"Ha-ha. You are such a bitch, Sylvia," said Greg.

"My name is David and I—" Sylvia jumped, as if surprised by something. "Oh, that's just my own shadow!"

Greg kicked the back of my seat in hysterics. "Girl, you are throwing some shade!"

"Come on, Mary! Take the goddamn thing."

"Seriously, David."

"Just swallow it, Stick-in-the-mud."

"Come on, dude."

"Do it, Minerva!"

Their imploring became too intense.

"SHUT UP!" I interrupted, popping the fuzzy little cylinder into my mouth and swallowing.

"Ha-ha! You're fucking insane," cackled Greg, throwing his Vicks chunk at Sylvia and falling over in the backseat. "You actually ate it!"

Sylvia threw her Vicks out the window and squealed with

laughter. "You are crazy, Crabb!" she cackled, trying to catch her breath. "I can't . . . believe . . . you ate it . . ."

As my stomach emitted an ominous growl, I braced myself for what was coming.

A few minutes later we pulled up to a shabby mobile home with several smaller trailers attached to its sides and roof, like a white-trash M. C. Escher painting. After I applied some powder, fixed my ponytail, and straightened my Siouxsie and the Banshees T-shirt, we headed to the front door. I could hear thrashing music inside as we walked onto the porch, which was littered with cigarette butts, beer bottles, and a waterlogged recliner. In the dimly lit living room were about thirty people, although the bed in the center made me think it might not be the living room after all. Some skinny, hairless boys looked at me from a dark corner as I neared the wood-paneled kitchen bar. Glass broke behind me after an enormous guy in a puffy jacket threw a beer bottle against the wall. As two boys in tank tops started to punch each other, I realized that these people, although freaks, were not my kind of freaks.

These freaks were skinheads.

Sylvia and Greg were nowhere to be seen. I could feel the piercing stares of every bald, steel-toed, suspender-wearing dude in the room. I was suddenly the correct answer in a very dangerous game of "one of these things is not like the other." I felt like a Vegas showgirl in full regalia stranded deep inside Rikers Island. Sweat beaded on my forehead as I rushed back onto the porch. By the blue light of a crackling bug zapper I tried to de-fag myself as quickly as possible, shaking my hair out from its ponytail and rubbing makeup off my face. I unrolled my jeans to cover my Doc Marten boots while scanning the cigarette embers glowing in the backyard, hoping to see Greg or Sylvia attached to one of them. My hands trembled as I tried to light my Benson & Hedges Ultra Light 120, thinking, "Dammit! Why don't I smoke butch-er cigarettes?"

From the darkness came a spark and flicker. A flaming Zippo gracefully rose to my cigarette. I felt like Marlene Dietrich in a noir film.

"I gotcha," said the hulking Cro-Magnon with cropped brown hair towering over me. "I'm Max." He popped the Zippo closed in a single swift motion. Max wore a white T-shirt with an Irish slogan on it. Tiny suspenders dangled from his pants, which were rolled up high around sixteen-hole Docs.

"Uh, hi. I'm David," I stuttered.

"I've never seen you around here. Where do you live?"

"Uh, San Antonio. I'm from there. You know, I was born there," I continued, unable to stop speaking due to my nerves. "But we're supposedly moving to Seguin."

"Oh yeah. That's the town with the big nut."

"Yup. It's the biggest pecan or some stupid shit like that," I croaked, trying to sound ultrastraight while avoiding too much direct eye contact.

"Your hair reminds me of someone," Max said, squeezing the cigarette between his lips with his thumb and index finger.

"Mine?" I raised my hands to my head, realizing that my scalp felt unusually sensitive. "Probably Dave Gahan from Depeche Mode. I get that a lot."

"Hmmm. I was thinking it looked more like that chick from Deee-Lite."

I paused, wondering if I should feel threatened. But as my skin began to tingle, I wasn't offended at all. Perhaps it was the

Vicks inhaler I'd eaten, but I found Max's comparison hilarious. Once I began laughing, I couldn't stop. And as Max laughed with me, he seemed transformed. He might have been laughing *at* me, but it didn't matter, because suddenly he had dimples and chubby cheeks like a giant, overgrown baby.

"You're funny," Max guffawed, handing me a warm beer.

Over the next hour everyone came outside to say hi to him. Each partygoer gave me the once-over and looked to Max, who gave a straight-faced nod, as if to say, "This guy's okay." One by one, each skinheaded boy and Mohawked girl shook my trembling, clammy hand. I felt like I was holding court with Max, who was apparently the mayor of freaks in New Braunfels.

As I started to Vick harder, I could feel my hair growing, and the wind on my neck. I couldn't stop stretching.

"Dude. Are you a yogi or something?" grinned Max as I reached down to touch my feet. "Who are you here with?"

"Oh, they ditched me," I said, sliding into downward-facing dog on some skinhead's patio.

"Fuck 'em, dude," proclaimed Max, clinking his beer bottle against mine.

"So, Max. You seem cool," I said, raising my leg onto the deck railing like an extra from *Fame*. "But how can you be a skinhead?" The rush of Vicks in my bloodstream was making me a little cocky. "Aren't they all fascists and racists?"

"Dude. Hold up," barked Max, slamming down his beer. "I'm not a bigot. I'm a SHARP."

I froze midstretch, confused by the term. "Huh?"

"A SHARP: a skinhead against racial prejudice. We take the aesthetic of the enemy and subvert it," he explained. "See, skins wear white laces for white power, but we wear multicolored laces for unity. Skins are straightedge, but we'll smoke pot, drink beer, huff shit, whatever. Plus, skinheads are always looking for a fight. SHARPs only fight if provoked."

"So you're like the hippies of punks or something?"

"Ha-ha! Oh fuck, that's funny. Sean!" he yelled over my shoulder. "My friend Dave just said SHARPs are like 'the hippies of punks'!"

Max popped open another beer and told me about the little town that might be my future home. "You know their football team is called the Seguin Matadors, right?"

"Like a bullfighter?" I asked.

"Yeah," he chuckled, taking a long drag off his cigarette. "But at away games, no one knows the little shithole. It gets mispronounced. So as they rush onto the field they get introduced like this." Max made his wrists limp, and in a fey, high-pitched register, cheeped, "Welcome the Sequined Matadors!"

That night, the two of us joked and drank for hours, talking about good music and news propaganda and racial intolerance and our single moms. Hanging out with Max felt like reuniting with someone I'd always known, someone familiar. I had a genuine feeling that Max was going to be a good friend.

And then I had a different feeling: the kind you get when you've eaten a toxic chemical meant for topical use. The wind felt ice-cold. My muscles started convulsing. My scalp was covered in fire ants. I gripped my belly as the contents of my stomach came to a boil.

"Are you okay, dude?" Max asked.

I opened my mouth to answer, but instead of words, a projectile spray of vomit erupted from between my lips. I puked repeatedly off the side of the porch, hoping between each bout that it was almost over. Finally, as I wiped the last bit of vomit off my mouth, a glass of water appeared in front of me.

"You okay, friend?"

"Sorry," I answered, totally ashamed. "I ate a Vicks inhaler on the way over."

"You ate . . . What?" he asked before roaring with laughter.

Max laughed at me all the way to his house, where he lent me a clean, puke-less shirt with a leprechaun on it and allowed me to crash on his bedroom floor. I woke up the next morning around seven, still unsure what had happened to Greg and Sylvia. I dressed quietly and looked around at Max's room, barely lit in the rising sun. The floor was littered with dirty clothes and a dozen pairs of boots. The walls were covered in posters for the Misfits, Bob Marley, and Operation Ivy. On a dresser by the door was a collection of framed photos: Max and his mom, Max with two girls, Max in a huddle of boys with cropped hair.

I grabbed my keys and prepared to walk back to my car in Max's oversize leprechaun shirt. As I crept into the hallway, a shaft of light filled the bedroom. Max was still asleep on his bed, curled up into a tiny ball. It seemed impossible that anyone as large as he'd seemed the night before could suddenly look so small.

I left a note on his door before I left. "Thanks for everything. PS—If anyone ever offers you a Vick's inhaler, DO NOT eat it."

CHAPTER 18

Barbar(ian)ism Begins at Home

"David, I'm so sorry I took off from that party," explained Greg as we chain-smoked in his bedroom. "But those skinheads triggered a bunch of deep-seated trauma for me. I had to get out of there."

"But where have you been since then?" I asked. "No one's seen you for two weeks. Your mom wouldn't tell me on the phone. Raven heard you OD'd and Carla told me that you got sent to rehab!"

"Rehab? I wish! But I *do* have big news," he announced, leaping onto the bed and plopping down beside me. "So that night in New Braunfels, Sylvia called her hot friend Paul to come pick us up from a gas station. After Paul dropped off Sylvia at Bonham we made out in his backseat! He's so hot and he's super-old. Like, almost thirty!"

"And then?" I asked, feeling jealous but still wanting to know more.

"So the next morning my mom was being a total bitch and we started fighting. And in the heat of the moment, I screamed—" he paused for dramatic effect—"Mom . . . I'm GAY!"

"What? You came out to her?"

"Yes! But I got so nervous about the whole 'gay' thing that I blurted out a bunch of other stuff to make it seem less scary. I said, 'Mom! I'm also an alcoholic! And I'm addicted to acid! And I take allergy pills every day to get even more fucked up!' David, I don't even know if allergy pills do anything. I even told her I was becoming an anorexic, which is so dumb because I eat like, four bags of Funyons a day!"

"And what happened?"

Greg was trembling with excitement as he lit his cigarette. "So get this! My mom wants me away from bad influences for a little while. So I started doing a month of home school last week, which is like zero commitment," he said, a long snake of smoke trailing from his mouth into his nostrils. "I also have to go to one Narcotics Anonymous meeting a day, where I have been meeting the hottest older guys you've ever seen. I made out with this thirty-four-year-old Mexican air force guy who's trying to kick as addiction to prescription painkillers and . . . I think we're in love!"

My blood started to boil with that familiar mix of envy and arousal.

"David! We need to talk," he said, stamping out his cigarette. "Things haven't gone that far with Jose, but they might. And when they do . . . I need to be prepared." Greg reached under the bed, taking out a handful of condoms and a jar of pickles. "Listen, David. I know it's weird, but we have to understand how this is going to work. If we're going to be gay, we have to know how gay stuff works. If things go further with Jose I need to know what to do. And now that you're maybe moving to Seguin . . ."

"I'm not moving!"

"Well, you say that now, but your mom *is* moving. What are you going to do?" he gasped. "I'm sure there aren't any gay people in Seguin. So how will you learn?"

"Maybe with a real person and not a hamburger topping!"

"Listen to me! We are going to do this!" Greg countered sternly. "You're going to take your pickle and rubber and stay here while I turn off the lights. I'm getting into *my* bed and getting under the covers. And we're going to walk each other through this. Whatever happens, no matter what I say, DO NOT come over to my bed, okay?"

"But isn't this dangerous?" I asked, taking a slimy pickle from the jar.

"What's dangerous?" Greg snapped. "Never getting laid? Ending up some old virgin living in a trailer park with a bunch of pornos? It's time to be a man, David!" he barked, like a personal trainer at an elliptical machine. "Now put the condom on the pickle before I turn off the light!"

I looked down at my soggy dill, annoyed that I was going to experience intercourse via vegetable while ten feet away from the guy whose pickle I *actually* wanted.

"Three seconds!" Greg warned.

I fumbled with my condom, dropping the pickle on the bed.

"Three . . ."

"Greg, I'm trying. It's just so . . ."

"Two . . ."

" . . . Slimy."

"One."

The light went out just as I slipped the condom over my pickle. Across the room I heard the click of a button. "I thought I'd play some music to get you in the mood," Greg said as the sound of Madonna's "Justify My Love" filled the room.

"Nothing can get me in the mood for this!" I replied, the pungent odor of vinegar and Trojan lubricant smacking my olfactories in a decidedly unsexy way.

"Ooh!" Greg exhaled. "I got the tip!"

"What?" I asked, shocked. "You already got a condom on it and put it inside you?"

"I'm a pro with condoms, David," he barked, "because I PRACTICE!"

"My rubber smells like old seafood."

"Woo!" Greg exploded with a giggle. "It's so cold!!!"

"You could've warmed them up first!"

"Stop complaining! Do you really want a warm limp pickle in your butt?"

"I don't want a cold *hard* pickle in my butt, Greg! I can't do this."

"Just surrender to the fantasy, David. I'm pretending mine is Marky Mark."

"I'm pretending mine is NOT a pickle!" I said, fumbling with the slippery thing beneath the sheets. "Don't you have a gherkin or cornichon something I could start with?"

"Shut up, David!" Greg snapped. "The only other pickles we have are those bread-and-butter ones!"

"Well, I'm not about to shove a handful of sliced pickles in my ass!"

"Then shut up and use your dill!" he snipped.

"But Greg, if the condom breaks it'll sting so bad!"

I tried to muster the courage to fuck myself with the pickle, trying to imagine it was Greg. But even with him groaning in the darkness, I couldn't get myself turned on. I tossed the pickle beside me, deciding it was all too weird.

"Oooh, yes," I feigned, trying to sound authentically turned on.

"See, David?"

"Ahhh," I moaned again, playing along so that we could experience this "first" together. I moaned and panted in the darkness for fifteen minutes, faking my first, and hopefully last, orgasm with a perishable food.

The next morning was awkward as Greg and I got ready for school. It was almost like we'd had sex with each other. Hair gel and safety pins were passed in low, hushed voices. Direct eye contact was avoided. In Greg's car we barely spoke, allowing "Just Can't Get Enough" to drown out the discomfort between us. Greg lit a joint and passed it to me. At the red light at the entrance to our school's parking lot, I accidentally dropped it on the floorboard, sending Greg into a maniacal frenzy.

"What the fuck?" he screamed, leaning over my lap to retrieve it. "My car!"

I took a certain pleasure in watching him sweat it. He was always so together, so cool. After pounding the floorboard with his hand for a few seconds he went to sit back down, accidentally jabbing his hip with the emergency brake.

"Ouch! I almost sat on that."

"Well," I grinned, "at least it's not a pickle."

Greg's head turned slowly to face me like an oscillating fan on low speed. We glared into each other's eyes for what felt like an eternity until the corners of our cotton-dry mouths began to twitch. We laughed until we collapsed against each other, coughing and choking on a thick mist of marijuana smoke. We didn't realize that the light had changed until all the cars behind us started honking. Preppy kids in Jeeps yelled and honked on either side as they passed us. A cowboy in a pickup with a big Texas flag in the window gave us the bird.

"Move, you fucking faggots!"

We skipped first period in the school parking lot, hotboxing the car and screaming "Just Can't Get Enough" until we could barely breathe. We spent lunch beneath our tree with our friends, exchanging knowing looks and breaking into constant laughter over the previous night's escapades.

"What the fuck are you cracking up about?" Jake asked us as Raven rubbed his feet.

"Yeah, you've been giddy little bitches all morning," added Carla.

"Oh, nothing," Greg answered her, grinning at me with bloodshot eyes.

That night my dad called me from the road. I pleaded my case, knowing I had only one option if I wanted to stay in San Antonio.

"Look Dad, I know you work on the road and keeping a place here would be unnecessary but I'm doing great in San Antonio and moving me away from school this close to graduation could really hurt my GPA and negatively affect my chances of getting into a well-respected college of my choosing. So—"

"David," my dad interrupted. "Wait a minute. Slow down. Are you saying you want me to get a place there with you?"

"Yes?" I answered.

"Well, it would be nice to have a home base instead of just keeping all my stuff in storage. But I'd only be home for a few days every couple weeks. We'd have to get you a bank account that I could deposit money in for your groceries and things. I hope that would be okay for you. I'd hate for you to be lonely."

Fireworks were exploding in my brain. I tried to camouflage my excitement about this prospect, and in a mature, carefully measured voice, I replied.

"Dad, I think I would be okay with that."

CHAPTER 19

Left to My Own Devices

Greg, Sylvia, and her friend Ray-Ray had decided to take hits of acid and ecstasy at the same time, or "candy-flip." At midnight we broke into the grounds of the McNay Art Museum, a beautiful compound full of landscaped gardens, vine-covered gazebos, and small ponds full of giant goldfish. We did this on a dare from Sylvia, whose drug-addled challenges were getting increasingly dangerous.

A week earlier she'd dared me to drop acid in a hospital ER, where we sat for an hour watching bloodied, crippled people come and go. We must have looked out of place: Sylvia with her flame-orange bob in a deep-necked gown, her lace-covered boobs pressed up to her chin; me with a gelled-up Mohawk, amethyst bolo tie, and penciled-in eyebrows. At 3 a.m. I reached my breaking point when an unconscious man in a neck brace with a bloody eye socket was wheeled in. I ran through the hospital parking lot to my car, where Sylvia held me in the backseat as I sobbed against her heaving bosom.

"Oh God. Sylvia! I'm going to die. You're going to die!"

"Shhh, Minerva," she calmed in her morose way. "We're already dead."

My weeping jag lasted for an hour. But Sylvia was there, like she always was, to help me through the psychotic break she herself had triggered. She was like a morose Pied Piper, leading anyone who got to know her on a series of harrowing field trips to experience troubling things. Sylvia was loud and campy, but she also kept dried roses pressed in the pages of her Anne Rice novels. In the last year she'd captured and found homes for no fewer than five black cats. On two separate occasions I'd walked in on her crying by candlelight while reading Percy Bysshe Shelley.

Tonight, in the museum garden, she was sketching plants in her journal as Greg bounded back and forth across a babbling brook in nothing but his underwear.

"I'm a sprite. A fairy. I'm Puck!" he tittered, his arms and legs smeared with mud.

Ray-Ray, a thin boy with a curly blond ponytail, was bent over a concrete bench in one of the gazebos, busily weaving the long leaves of a tropical plant into shirts for us.

"We can live off this land," he declared. "We'll work this soil and harvest our own food!"

For a moment I believed him. *We can live in nature*, I thought, the steady traffic of Austin Highway zooming in and out of a strip-mall parking lot sixty feet away. Sylvia and I curled up beneath the stars with a flashlight to read the party pages in *Interview* magazine.

"Look how gorgeous she is," Sylvia said, pointing at the model Linda Evangelista hugging a famous fashion designer who was wearing a chandelier as a hat.

"This one's great," I said, transfixed by a picture of Kurt Cobain laughing with the famous drag queen RuPaul as she held his crying baby.

"Oh, Crabb. I wanna go there!" she sighed, snuggling up against me. "I wanna be with those people!"

"Me too, Sylvia. But what would we do?"

"We have marketable skills, bitch! Maybe you can get into performing or something. And I can get some poetry published!"

"We'll be like a gay-straight, art world power couple!" I declared. "We'll live in a brownstone and our friends will be gallerists, junkies, drag queens, and performance artists!"

"It'll be fabulous!" Sylvia sighed as she took my hand. "A real life."

We lay under the stars in each other's arms all night, imagining that future together in a better place.

The next morning I met my dad at my mom's apartment to move. She was headed to Seguin and I was moving in with my dad down the road from Gunther High. I'd had just enough time to put a crisp white button-down over a torn, pit-stained T-shirt that was covered in Sharpie drawings of anarchy A's and crosses.

"Sorry I'm late," I told my dad, still pulling chunks of dirt and moss from the soles of my shoes. "Greg's brother thought it would be funny to turn off the alarm clock."

"It's okay, son," said my dad, patting me on the back.

"Boys will be boys," my mother added, emerging from the kitchen with a suspicious look. My mom was upset that I wasn't moving with her and knew perfectly well that I'd kept my new social circle a secret from my dad. "I'm sure your father is going to love your friends."

Over the last month of sporadic apartment-hunting I'd managed to downplay the "new me," wearing baseball caps over my short-on-bottom/long-on-top haircut and opting for bright, clean sneakers in lieu of my usual scuffed-up boots. In small doses, I was a pro. But now I'd be living with my dad for several days in a row a few times a month, which was going to be challenging.

"Well, visit your mother when you find the time," said my mom, without looking at me. Directing a synthetic smile at my father, she added, "I'm sure you're both going to enjoy living together." My mother and I both knew that living with my dad could be difficult due to his temper. But as he closed the door to his pickup truck, I knew it was a done deal. I felt a pang of guilt as we all drove away. My mom was making a family with someone she'd always hoped to find, and I knew she pictured me as a part of that future. But I reminded myself that regardless of the occasional tension with my dad, I was going to be free. And it was going to be awesome.

My dad couldn't leave soon enough. It had been four days of nonstop complaining and griping. The landlord was an asshole, the traffic was bullshit, and all the local restaurants were crap.

"Goddamn piece of junk!" he screamed, bouncing up and down on an overstuffed suitcase. I wanted to explain that his anger would never change the simple physics of his situation, but when my father was having a spell, I'd learned to do what I did best: disappear. I sat quietly on my bed in a red baseball cap reading an algebra textbook and listening to Aerosmith, the most benign and heterosexual CD I owned. After a few more minutes of violent grunting, my father stepped in to say good-bye to his all-American, rock-and-roll-loving bookworm of a son.

"All right, DJ. I'm giving up on that goddamn thing," he said in the doorway, holding a garbage bag of toiletries and clothes by his side. "The checkbook is on the table for food and stuff. I'll see you in a few days."

We hugged good-bye and I watched him walk down the stairs. With the phone in my hand just outside the frame of the window, I waved to him as he pulled from the parking lot, knowing that a dozen teenagers awaited a call from my newly parentless home.

By nine o'clock the apartment was packed with people. A mist of cigarette smoke hung in every room, and Solo cups full of vodka and Big Red soda covered every surface. Jake had brought a container of impossibly strong weed cookies that had slowly turned everyone into woozy zombie versions of them-selves. Carla and Raven hummed along to the lilting shoegaze of Cocteau Twins on the couch as Greg and Jake reclined against each other on my bed.

"David, come here," called Jake, holding up a joint.

I sat on the edge of the bed and took a hit as something shat-tered in the kitchen.

"Ignore it," he said, pulling me down on top of him and Greg. He held the joint to my lips and I took a long toke. "Doesn't that feel better?" he asked, slipping his hand beneath my shirt to rub my shoulder. Greg cleared his throat and rolled to his side, shift-ing Jake's hand out of my shirt.

"Oh. Sorry," Greg said, maneuvering farther beneath Jake in

a way that pushed me farther off him. "This bed is so small for three people."

The doorbell rang. Greg smiled and snatched the joint from my hand as he rubbed Jake's chest. "You should probably get that, hmm?"

I opened the front door to see Sylvia in giant black sunglasses with a bun of bright lavender hair atop her head. She had a huge suitcase, her massive purse and a pet carrier. "Finally, Minerva. I've been ringing for five minutes! Oh dear," she said, noticing my guests. "What's the average age of this gathering? It's like fuckin' *Romper Room* in here!" Sylvia barged past me, knocking over Raven with one of her suitcases. "Shift it, creatures of the night! Is my room down here?"

"What?" I muttered as she waddled down the hall into my dad's room. "You can't go in there!"

By the time I walked in, she was already unpacking her suitcase, stacking black satin on black chiffon on black velveteen atop the dresser. A tiny Siamese cat jumped on my dad's bed.

"A cat? You brought your cat?"

"His name is Voltaire! Not after the industrial band, after the poet." She removed a newspaper from her bag and starting tearing it into strips as she walked into the master bathroom. "Voltaire! Poop in here, okay?" The little cross-eyed cat walked into the bathroom as she dumped a small bag of kitty litter into the newspaper-filled bathtub. "You. Poop. In. Here," she said, kissing his face. "I swear, this little bastard understands every fucking word that comes out of my mouth! Girlina!" she announced. "Mama's home!"

"I thought you might stay over, but I didn't realize it would be so permanent," I said.

Sylvia cocked her head to the side like a dog who had just

heard a confusing sound. "Well, of course, munchkin. Where else would Mama stay? We're roomies, Crabapple!"

Before I could muster a reply, she was dragging me down the hallway to the kitchen. "We can make me a key tomorrow. I'll stay here until your dad comes home, at which point I'll stay with Ray-Ray for a few days until we have a fight and he kicks me out again, which generally takes about four days . . ." She rambled on and on, bopping from the fridge to the utensil drawer to the microwave, making herself a drink as she heated up one of my dad's Mexican TV dinners.

"I can't really pay you anything right now," she continued, "but Mama is on a job hunt and once I get on my feet, I'll chip in for bills. Not too much. It's not like *you* have to pay anything."

"Yeah, but my dad—"

"—Is a wonderful man," she cackled, filling a 7-Eleven tumbler half-full with his Jack Daniels. "Thank you, Mr. Crabb!" she said, filling the whiskey bottle up with an inch of tap water and placing it back in the cabinet. "I'll be ready to leave for the club at eleven. I'll be in my room until then," she said, going down the hall.

"But I'm having a party. I don't wanna go to . . ."

"David, where are you?" Jake yelled from my room.

I walked in as Greg laced up his shoes and Carla put on her jacket.

"Where are you going?" I asked.

"Duh," said Carla, kissing my cheek. "It's a school night. I gotta be home by ten."

A line of kids started to stream out the front door.

"I'm not going anywhere," said Jake, lying back on my bed as Raven kissed his cheek. "I'm too baked to drive."

"Have fun, boys," she said, winking as she left.

"But you're coming with me, right?" Greg asked me as he slung his bag over his shoulder. "Aren't you staying over at my house?"

I looked past him at Jake, whose shirt was riding up, exposing the faint line of fine hair leading from his navel to his belt buckle. "I'll hang with you, David," he said. "My dad's out of town."

"Greg," I stammered. "I'm going to stay here. I have my own place now."

His face collapsed like an overdone soufflé. "Fine, David. I guess you don't need to stay with me anymore, then."

I had never chosen anyone over Greg before. But tonight, my libido was winning. Greg stomped down the hall and out the front door, slamming it behind him. I stood in the center of my room as Jake stared directly into my eyes.

"It's cool if I stay here with you tonight, right?"

"Of course!" I blurted before he was actually done asking.

"Come here," he said, each bicep flexing as he rested his arms behind his head. I'd taken one step toward him when someone screamed from the living room.

"Sylvia!" a man's voice called. "Where is Mama?"

Sylvia erupted from her room, emitting a high-pitched squeal.

"Jake, I'll be right back." I ran down the hallway to find Sylvia jumping up and down with Ray-Ray and another man with a matching blond bob.

"Minerva, it's Sterling and Ray-Ray. They're going to the club with us tonight!"

"But Sylvia, I drank too much to drive."

"But Sterling's drivin' us! Mama's gonna get ready. Y'all make yourself at home."

"But I live here!" I yelled as she skipped down the hall.

Sterling turned on the TV at top volume and flipped the channels, one per second. "Ugh. Your cable selection is the *worst!*" he complained in a queeny, nasal voice.

As Sylvia did her hair, I sat awkwardly between the boys on the couch, "making myself at home" in my own apartment. Down the hall, I could see a light under my bedroom door. I imagined Jake behind it naked, sprawled out on my bed unconscious, waiting for me like a pornographic sleeping beauty.

"It's time to put on my face!" screamed Sylvia from my father's room.

"If she's just starting, we won't be out of here until midnight," I moaned, eliciting unexpected laughter from the chilly Ray-Ray and Sterling. I spotted Jake's backpack by the TV, and it hit me: since I wasn't man enough to bail on the club for fear of Sylvia's wrath, couldn't I just make it impossible for us to leave?

"Hey guys," I asked sweetly, "you like cookies?"

Thirty minutes later Sylvia came out of "her room" holding Voltaire. She was dressed to the nines. "Whaddya think, boys?"

"Hush, bitch!" said Sterling, shoving his eighth cookie into his mouth. "We are halfway through this MTV *True Life* with Serena Altschul!"

"It's about an Amish community who've all become addicted to crystal meth," added Ray-Ray, greenish crumbs cascading from his lips.

"But girls, it's almost midnight and I'm all dressed up!"

"Shhhh!" demanded Sterling. "We're too fucked up to drive and we *have* to finish this show!"

The two of them devoured more cookies as Sylvia stomped to the kitchen and poured herself a cocktail. Eventually, she sat with us and surrendered to the fact that this would not be a big night out. At 2 a.m. we were transfixed by our fourth straight episode of *True Life*, glued to Serena Altschul's chilling, in-depth exposé on a tiny Texas town torn apart by a string of cult-related animal sacrifices. Even I'd fallen victim, so stoned after my sixth cookie that I'd totally forgotten about the smooth, tan boy with crystal-blue eyes lying in my bed.

Around three in the morning I woke up alone on the couch.

"Hello?" I called as someone in the apartment giggled. There was an odd taste in my mouth and something sandy and brittle in my teeth. I walked into my dad's bedroom, looking for Sylvia. In the bathroom mirror I looked at my brown tongue and noticed something on my lip. I removed a small piece of newspaper from my mouth and caught a whiff of my own rank breath. Looking into my dad's bathtub, it hit me.

"Ha-ha, bitch!" howled Sylvia in the mirror over my shoulder. "You ate cat shit!"

I bent over the toilet and retched, slamming the door in Sylvia's face with my foot. After five minutes of vomiting I stormed into the living room, where she was shutting the front door behind Sterling and Ray-Ray.

"Now, David. Before you get too mad—"

"You fucking bitch!" I screamed, pushing her against the wall. "Get out!"

"I'm sorry, Crab-Cakes. I just got too fucked up. I was a little mad," she pleaded, her bloodshot eyes filled with tears. "I don't mean to hurt people," she sobbed. "I just lose control sometimes. I love you. Please, I don't have anywhere to go." Barefoot with crooked lipstick, she became the victim again, a transformation she excelled at, partly through manipulation and partly in truth. "Please, Minerva. Just let me stay here tonight."

As I looked into her sad, bloodshot eyes, I saw a girl who, for all her faults, had become the closest thing I'd ever had to a sister. But I couldn't bear to give her permission. Instead I walked away, leaving her to cry alone. In my room, Jake was passed out, curled up into a cocoon under my bedspread. I lay down next to him, feeling a total lack of horniness, the taste of cat shit still ripe in my mouth. After an hour I was still too enraged to sleep. And I knew what I had to do.

Next door in my father's room, Sylvia was passed out on her side, still fully dressed. I snuck past her and into the bathroom, where I leaned over Voltaire's makeshift litter box and retrieved a small turd with toilet-papered fingers. Quietly, I crept toward the bed, the rising sun just beginning to peek through the blinds. At the edge of the bed I stopped, seeing Sylvia's journal open on the floor. I leaned over it and noticed my name. It was a letter to me.

In the letter, Sylvia apologized profusely for what she'd done, writing that she'd never meant to hurt me and regretted how she'd behaved. She ended the note by reminding me that I was her best friend and hoped that I could trust her again one day.

In the mirror over my dad's dresser I caught my own reflection: standing there with a piece of cat shit in my hand, prepared to feed it to one of my best friends. Not only was it a cruel prank, it wasn't even clever, doing the exact same thing to Sylvia that she had done to me. It was pathetic. She hadn't even locked the bedroom door. She could've. But she trusted me. Just as I thought this, Sylvia rolled over to face me in her sleep, revealing a star-shaped tapestry of a dozen Band-Aids covering her mouth. Still holding the wad of Voltaire's poop at my side, I looked down at her messy face. Sylvia: my loving, *trusting* friend.

I woke up around 1 p.m. the next day with Jake beside me. In the night, he'd kicked off all the sheets and removed his underwear. I was curled up against his side fully clothed, my face resting against his chest. He smelled musky and the skin on his belly was soft as I rubbed my hand across it. I looked up to see him staring at me with those pale-blue eyes, close enough that I could see every beautiful line and detail in his plump pink lips, which I'd never wanted to kiss so badly.

"Hey David."

"Yeah," I replied, pulling him close to me as my erection grew against his hip.

"You wanna suck it?"

"What?" I asked, thinking I'd misinterpreted the layered nuance of his romantic gesture.

"My dick," he clarified. "Wanna suck it?"

I looked down at his penis, which was brightly lit by a shaft of midday sun creeping under the blinds. It was flaccid and wrinkled. I'd never seen a penis so brightly lit before. The head was more purple than I'd expected. The balls looked far too hairy to belong to Jake. The urethra seemed way too big, like the mouth of a dehydrated sandworm from *Dune*. Jake cleared his throat and hocked a loogie into a glass on my bedside table. The musky odor of his body was suddenly pungent and overpowering, like a bunch of old onions.

"Well?" he said, gesturing to his penis like I was a child who hadn't finished his dinner. I looked at it again, a little bit repulsed.

"Um," I stuttered, unable to answer him.

"Oh. Uh, okay," he said, sitting up stiffly in the bed. "Well, I gotta go, dude."

Jake jumped up and dressed quickly, either too mad or too embarrassed to take his time. After he left I felt ashamed that I couldn't perform, without being entirely sure that any part of me had actually wanted to. I'd had him in the palm of my hand, but I let him get away. What was my deal with sex? Why was I so afraid of intimacy that I couldn't even do it with a pickle?

Sylvia stumbled out of her room around 2 p.m., lit a cigarette, and curled up with me on the couch. She was rude, foulmouthed, and untrustworthy. But she was the devil I knew. I spent the day with her watching TV and drinking screwdrivers while Voltaire ate leftover pizza on the dining-room table. Cigarette butts were everywhere and a potted plant in the corner had fallen onto my dad's turntable, but I couldn't be bothered to clean any of it up. This was my castle. And I was its prince.

CHAPTER 20

Taking a Ride with My Best Friend

The ceiling was made of pudding. Wave after wave of thick tapioca hovered above me. Or was I hovering above it, suspended over an endless ocean of heavy cream? Somewhere, a chain saw revved as a woman screamed. The ceiling shifted to my left as the carpeted floor slid out from under my face to meet the soles of my feet.

Oh, wait. I'm standing up now.

The room was dim. A foot with black-painted toenails stuck out from a down comforter on the floor. A digital clock read 7:05. It meant nothing to me. *Am I early for school or late for dinner? What day is it? What town am I in?*

Sitting on the edge of someone's bed, I noticed a raccoon watching me from a window. And then something fell into place.

Suddenly the pudding ocean was just the ceiling. The chain saw was just a stereo. The screaming was a girl laughing outside. The feet belonged to Greg. And the raccoon was my own face in a mirror, reflected back at me. My eyeliner had been perfect last night, but now it had gathered in two smeared pools beneath each eye. I looked like one of those Mexican skeleton dolls.

I stood up as a Mohawked girl in panties ran past the doorway. A moment later, a boy in a red elephant-trunk thong ran after her, a houseplant cascading out of his backpack.

The stereo was too loud.

I am the son and heir of a shyness that is criminally vulgar.

I crept onto the floor and underneath the huge comforter, whispering, "Wake up, Greg."

"David, where are we?"

"I don't know."

Suddenly Greg and I were both very awake, which always happened quickly the morning after we dropped two hits of acid.

"Greg! My mom!" I yelped, remembering that I was supposed to have spent the night with her in Seguin. "She must be so pissed!"

"No, David. It's fine. You had me impersonate my mom and call her. Remember?"

"I had you call my mom while we were tripping and fake your mom's voice?"

"Yeah. It worked fine. I told her you were staying over because we got food poisoning. We talked about the Botanical Garden for, like, a hundred years."

"Really?"

"Yeah. Then we talked about how great our sons are and how, of all the Designing Women, she feels most like the Annie Potts character. Your mom is so vulnerable. I love Libras. They're so—"

"Wait. You talked about *Designing Women* with my mom on acid?"

"Yeah. She's a firecracker! Woman-to-woman, I can really sense that kind of manic Annie Potts energy about her," said Greg, slipping into his fake mom voice. "See? I'm good, right?"

Just then, a shaft of light crossed the floor. We looked toward the bedroom door, where a girl with bright-red lips stood in a sequined yellow jacket and golden top hat. She held a Mountain Dew and started to slow-motion tap dance like she was trudging through imaginary maple syrup.

Greg rolled over and looked at me excitedly. "David! I remember! We went dancing with Carla and then dropped acid at *The Rocky Horror Picture Show*."

And then the rest of it fell into place: sneaking Carla out her bedroom window, meeting Greg at the Dumpster behind the Bill Miller Bar-B-Que, huffing whippits by the mailboxes at Sylvia's apartment, snorting ephedrine in a bathroom with a stranger, getting into a fight with Jake about Depeche Mode's pre-*Violator* work, gorging ourselves on Taco Cabana guacamole and queso, driving to *The Rocky Horror Picture Show* at the Northwest 14 Theatre, holding Sylvia's hair out of her face as she puked up Taco Cabana guacamole and queso in the movie theater parking lot, and finally ending up at George's apartment for rum and Diet Cokes.

"But we're not at George's," Greg said, scratching his head and looking around. He blurted to our visitor, "Hi, Columbia!"

She stopped moving, like a deer caught in headlights.

"Don't startle her. She's fucked up," I whispered.

"David, are we still tripping?" Greg whispered back. "I mean . . . my favorite character from *The Rocky Horror Picture Show* has just come to life right in front of me!"

Her body hung limply like a broken-down robot, her arm barely swinging from the flimsy joint of her elbow.

Greg screamed, "Hello!"

With a jolt, she suddenly came to life, put her hand on her hip, bent slightly to her left, and with cold, black eyes stated matter-of-factly, "I am a teapot."

Greg and I laughed nervously as she swayed. I could feel my guts aching from the acid we'd taken. Every burst of laughter cramped me to the core. We retreated beneath the comforter and curled in toward each other until our knees were touching.

"Whose car did we drive here? Yours or mine?" Greg asked.

"I don't know. I guess we should get out of here and figure it out."

Ten minutes later we tiptoed through a minefield of sleeping freaks on the living-room floor. Holding hands to balance each other, we navigated our way through a forest of fishnet-wrapped limbs capped in Doc Marten boots. Black-painted fingernails peeked out like creeping moss around graffitied jackets and shrubs of teased purple hair.

Five feet from the door, I felt a hand grip my ankle. Instinctively I screamed, "I don't know anyone!" as if being a stranger here somehow protected me from this person.

A girl with fuchsia hair wearing a silver choker stared up at me with giant, dilated pupils. Wiping a long strand of spittle from the corner of her mouth, she began to weep.

"Where are Brian's keys?"

"Um . . . who's Brian?" I asked her.

Greg pulled me toward the door. "David! Don't engage her!"

"WHERE ARE BRIAN'S KEEEEYS?!?!?!"

As she wailed, the human floor shifted to life. Crushed velvet tree roots became snakes made of human arms and legs.

"Run!" Greg shrieked.

We flew out the door as the fuchsia-haired girl screamed, "KEEEEYYSSS!!!"

Around the side of the building, we found ourselves in the complex's parking lot. I tried to catch my breath and shielded my eyes from the scorching Texas sun.

"Greg, I need air-conditioning. Now."

As we scanned the parking lot, I could feel the armpits of my shirt began to fill with perspiration. Greg drove a tiny car that was always a pain in the ass to find, especially in the sea of massive vehicles that filled most San Antonio parking lots. We stumbled from row to row of parked cars. Greg pointed his key-ring remote in different directions, hoping to hear a chirp from his little red Cabriolet, a strangely happy car considering that it was driven by a guy in a bat necklace. My mouth was bone-dry and beads of sweat collected on my forehead. I threw my head back in exhaustion, my mouth hanging open like a broken Pez dispenser.

"Where is your caaaaaaar?"

I was going to puke. Or maybe I needed to eat. In the distance I saw a fifteen-foot-wide sombrero hovering in the sky. It wasn't a hallucination. It was a Taco Cabana. And it was all I needed. I could almost taste their breakfast tacos. I imagined every combination possible: egg, bacon, cheese; carne asada; chicken fajita with guacamole; bean, cheese, potato . . .

"GREG! Where's the motherfucking car?!?!"

"Bitch! Stop screaming at me already! You already hooked up with the love of my life!" he yelled. "Can you at least not scream at me?"

He hadn't brought up that night at my house since his first day back at school a couple weeks earlier. I wanted to tell Greg that I'd failed miserably at hooking up with Jake. But soothing his feelings would mean embarrassing myself. It seemed better to let him think something had happened. So I mumbled, "Sorry," and left it at that.

We strolled through the parking lot, getting looks from suits holding coffee thermoses on their way to work: Greg in his combat boots and dangling earrings, me with my dirty, shoulder-length hair and raccoon eyes, wearing a thousand rubber-band bracelets. Greg kept aiming his key-chain remote into the expanse of pickup trucks and sport-utility vehicles surrounding us, like someone hopelessly trying to find water in the desert using a forked stick. Finally we heard it: the high-pitched, sissy chirp of Greg's car alarm beeping from his Lilliputian red convertible.

Once inside, we collapsed into the seats, as if we'd arrived home with no intention of actually driving anywhere. Greg lit a Marlboro Ultra-Light 100 and French inhaled a long strand of cigarette smoke. He studied himself in the mirror as if I wasn't there, admiring the perfection with which he passed the toxic smog from his lips to his nostrils.

"David, should we go to school today?"

I flipped the wall calendar in my head. "Is today a weekday?"

Greg noticed an Alamo Bank sign towering above us. "Well, it's 7:25 a.m. and ninety-one degrees, and today is May 29."

We stared at each other, hoping to somehow transform that

information into a clue regarding whether it was a Tuesday or a Sunday.

"What do we do, Greg? Today is Wednesday . . . I think."

"Well, we can't go to school like *this*."

We pulled down our visor mirrors and inspected our bloodshot eyes, crusty hair, and cosmetic-blotched skin.

"David, I think we should rest today."

"But we haven't gone in a few days. Because I remember Raven—"

"Hey," Greg interrupted. "Sorry I yelled at you about Jake."

"I'm the sorry one," I apologized. "I should've stayed with you that night. I'm really sorry that—"

"Shut up!" Greg yelled, smacking my forehead. "Stop saying sorry all the time about everything, okay?"

"Oh, sorry," I instinctively said again.

Greg glared at me, trying not to smile. "Look, nerd. Are we going to school or not?"

I shrugged and waited for Greg to make up my mind for me, the way he always did.

"Fuck it," he said, lighting a roach from the ashtray.

A few minutes later as we pulled away from the Taco Cabana drive-through with our breakfasts, we pieced together the rest of the previous night: who kissed whom, who took what, who was hot, who seemed cooler than we'd thought, who'd been lame. Greg blasted the Cure's *Disintegration* from his car stereo and we drove past our school. Rolling by slowly, we watched our friends, enemies, and peers march through the huge brick arch leading to the courtyard. They looked so tired, their shoulders slouching as they shuffled to first period. Their backpacks looked so heavy, like they were full of stones. It seemed too early in the morning for anyone, including us, to have obligations.

"Suckers," Greg hissed. He pushed a button and the convertible top retracted over our heads, releasing the huge cloud of marijuana smoke we'd been hotboxing on our drive. In the rearview mirror we could see a clan of preps cough and gag on our mood-altering exhaust.

Greg convulsed in a maniacal fit of laughter, shredded lettuce and salsa spilling out the side of his mouth.

"Enjoy the contact high, bitches!"

I felt bad for all those kids: all the preps, jocks, kickers, Bowheads, punks, nerds, potheads, and goths stuck in that academic jail on such a beautiful day. But I felt guilty too, ashamed of all the lies I'd told and would continue to tell to remain the way I was that day: absolutely and perfectly free.

This is the kind of half-assed drag that lots of alt-youth boys attempted at least once at the hands of their Bowie-obsessed, Martin Gore–loving, New Wave girlfriends. Here, the girls turned Greg and me into their own living, breathing, life-size dolls. Although we had partial say in our "looks," I have to blame the girls for the final outfit choices. While Greg got to look like a saucy, shapely pole dancer, I was reimagined as a Puckish stewardess with kerchief and headband. We stayed inside sporting these looks, drinking Strawberry Hill, and listening to Yaz's "Upstairs at Eric's" the rest of the night. Later in the evening there was makeup application and some light hair-crimping. I can only thank God that those pictures haven't surfaced, as I looked like a candy-faced, ghoulish Raggedy Ann in all of them.

CHAPTER 21

Age of Consent

Just gimme your keys, crack whore!" yelled Sylvia.

"But why?" I slurred back, swaying with my big red Solo cup of rum in some stranger's living room.

"Just give me your keys!" she screamed again.

"But I don't want to leave!" I yelled back, placing my drink on a shelf that wasn't there. As it smashed to the floor, Sylvia reached into my pocket and ran away with my car keys.

"Hey, Sylvia . . ." The next word came out in the form of vomit—all over the carpet, a chair back, and my shoes. A roll of paper towels hit me in the face.

"David, fucking pull it together!" Greg was standing with Jake in the kitchen. "Stop fucking drinking!"

"Fuck you," I said, laughing to myself as I squatted down. I'm not sure if it was the weed, the rum, the bump, or the ephedrine pills I'd bought from the truck stop, but my equilibrium was shot, and I ended up sitting in a pile of my own puke. After cleaning the floor and myself, I stumbled to the front yard, where Sylvia had popped the hood of my car.

"What are you doing, Sylvie?"

"I'm getting' high!" she yelled, leaning over the engine as Ray-Ray started the car. "Your AC isn't working 'cause you got a coolant leak!"

Sylvia leaned over into the engine and put her mouth on a small metal tube.

I stumbled forward, confused. "Wait. You're sucking on my car engine to get high?" Falling back onto the cement, Sylvia held her belly and rolled around, laughing in a deep, demonic voice.

"What's happening to her?" I asked Ray-Ray as he pulled back his golden locks and leaned beneath the hood.

"We're getting high off this Freon leak! It'll give you major wah-wahs, but be careful, 'cause that shit constricts your throat and can suffocate your ass."

"That's crazy," I said, leaning under the hood for a hit. Soon a small group of partygoers was lined up at my car. A dozen of us rolled around on the lawn, the satanic timbres of our laughter creating more laughter until we sounded like a pack of goats.

The next day I sat in second-period algebra focusing on one thing: not vomiting. Watching Ms. Kelsey's arm fat flap around like a rooster's neck as she wrote on the board was making me ill. I was just about to ask to go to the bathroom when the PA system came to life.

"David Crabb, please report to your guidance counselor's office." I sat still for a moment, doubting what I'd heard, until it repeated: "David Crabb. To the guidance counselor's office."

I walked down the linoleum-tiled hallway, stoned out of my mind. Greg and I had gotten super-baked two hours earlier to fend off our hangovers. At the front office, a secretary gestured to the door of my guidance counselor, Brownie Richardson.

Brownie was a man. Yes. A full-grown, fifty-year-old man with thick spectacles and a salt-and-pepper bowl cut had chosen to work in academia with the name "Brownie." He stood up from his desk and straightened his baggy suit.

"Well, hello, David," he said cheerfully in a froglike baritone.

"Hi, Mr. . . ." I paused, realizing that every note I'd ever forged to skip school was laid out on the desk before me—more than a dozen letters with my dad's faked signature.

"I think it's time we had a talk, David. Don't you?"

I was about to answer when I sensed movement in the corner of the room. I turned around to see my father. His beet-red face made his bald head look like a tiny, scarlet stress ball. He gripped the arms of his chair, his jaw tightly clenched, staring down at the floor like he was trying to burn a hole through it.

"Have a seat next to your father," Brownie said with a broad smile.

I sat cautiously in the vinyl chair a mere foot from my dad. I was trying so hard to act sober that I felt like the attempt was actually counteracting my goal. Every move I made or thing I said seemed strained or over-pronounced.

"How are YOU do-ING, *Mr.* RichardSON?" I asked, emphasizing all the wrong syllables. My elbow was having a hard time securing itself against the armrest, slipping back and forth against either side.

"Well, David. As you can see, we seem to be having a problem with honesty, which is disappointing," said Brownie, patting the notes on his desk. "I can tell from looking at you that you're a nice guy. You never fight or wind up in detention. But you apparently never wind up in class, either." Brownie chuckled lightheartedly at his little joke and looked at my father, who continued to glare hatefully at the carpet. "I'm going to ask you a few questions now, David."

"Sure. Okay." My voice broke a little in response to the silent waves of fury radiating from my father.

"So, David. Would your father understand if you told him you were on drugs?"

"What?" I replied with immediate incredulity. "How could you think that? How could you accuse me of such a thing?" Meryl Streep would've eaten her heart out as I pounded on the desk, demanding, "Give me a cup. I'll pee in it right now and you'll know the truth!" Ironically, being stoned out of my mind was really helping my performance. Before I knew it, I was standing over Brownie's desk, dramatically pointing to the door, as if someone with a portable urine-testing lab waited on the other side. "Give me a cup and I'll PEE IN IT!" I yelled.

"Calm down. No one's on trial," Brownie said, even though someone was. "Would your father understand if you'd gotten a girl pregnant?" he asked, reverting to what I could only imagine was one of his stock "troubled youth" questions.

"Yeah. He'd understand," I answered, my lower lip beginning to tremble. I glanced beside me for a response, but my dad still wouldn't look at me. Brownie cleared his throat and in a low, hushed tone asked, "David. Would your father understand if you told him you were gay?"

As the ground slipped away beneath me, I felt like Wile E. Coyote. Like I'd jumped off the edge of a cliff and was hovering over a pit of rocks, my little cartoon legs spinning.

It's not supposed to happen like this, I thought. *It should get to be my choice.*

"No. He wouldn't understand," I said.

Why did I just say that? Shut up, David. Shut up.

Brownie squinted, like my answer had confused him. "He . . . wouldn't?"

This second question was a golden opportunity to explain that I'd just misheard him. I could say I was simply too high on LSD and Freon to have accurately represented how very heterosexual I was. I could fix it. But again I said, "No. He wouldn't understand."

I couldn't tell if I was really high or suddenly stone-cold sober, but there were tears in my eyes. As much as I'd felt accepted during the last year, this admission to my father made what I'd thought I'd come to terms with real. Everything was about to change. I started wishing myself out of the room, wishing myself somewhere else—not with Greg or Sylvia or Raven but somewhere alone, hermetically sealed in a vacuum, untouchable. My father looked into my eyes, not with anger or sadness but blankly, like he'd just been punched in the solar plexus and was stuck in that moment right *before* the pain hits.

In the car on the way home, a new mantra kept repeating in a horrible loop.

My dad knows I'm gay. My dad knows I'm gay. My dad knows I'm gay.

It's humiliating enough being outed to your father by your guidance counselor. But it's especially emasculating when his name is Brownie. I'd hardly noticed him at school before, but now he found me in the halls two or three times a day to pat me on the back and ask me how my father and I were doing. He was trying to be kind. But all I saw was the man who'd ruined my father's happiness forever.

My dad took time off work so that we were together every morning and night. I'd even heard him creep into my room at 3 a.m., presumably to make sure I hadn't shimmied out the window of our third-floor apartment. I was gay. I wasn't Spider-Man.

After a week of awkward, nerve-racking meals together, I hoped things were improving with my dad. I'd been attending all my classes and had hardly seen my friends. One night, we sat over our plates eating steaks and watching *Wheel of Fortune*. My mouth full of squash, I said, "Do you think Vanna White ever has alphabet nightmares? Like being devoured by vowels and stuff like that?"

My dad laughed hard for a few seconds, looking at me with an expression I'd missed. But all at once, the warmth vanished, as if he'd realized that laughter was something he couldn't offer me anymore. His warm chuckling was suddenly replaced by an intensified scraping of fork against knife. He stared at me with the saddest eyes and asked, "You know what they do, right?"

"What?" I had an idea what he meant, but I was hoping I was wrong.

"Homosexuals. You *know* what they do, don't you?" he asked again before returning to eating his steak.

After dinner I locked myself in my room, attempting to call

my lost and missing friends. Outside, I could hear cabinets slamming and angrily washed glasses ringing against one another. I tore open *Behaviour*, the new Pet Shop Boys CD that Hector had given me, and popped it into the stereo. The first song "Being Boring" began quietly with the sound of a digital flute and gentle wah-wah guitar licks. I turned the track up louder, hoping to tune out my father and transport myself anywhere but that tiny, lonely bedroom. The lyrics tell the story of a man's life from boyhood to middle age, the first few verses detailing "invitations to teenage parties" and the tentative thrill of leaving home. The first half of the song mirrored exactly how I felt in that moment; ecstatically impatient for the future, but frightened about the loss my freedom might bring about. I played the song again and again, each spin holding me like an invisible blanket in my bed.

Half an hour later, there was a knock on my door. My dad walked in carefully, the way you would around an untamed animal. He pulled up a chair across from me and sat down, pulling something from his back pocket. "I want to show you something," he said, revealing the August 1987 issue of *Penthouse* magazine. For a moment I was happy. *Rolando!* I thought, happy to see my long-lost G-stringed Latin or Italian or Greek lover.

"David. I want to ask you, and there's no wrong answer here. Well, there is a wrong . . . Um . . ." My father hesitated, searching for the right words. "Anyway . . . I want to ask you . . . Who are you more attracted to? Her . . ." he said, pointing with a grin to Candy and her satellite-dish areolas, " . . . or *him*?"

This was different. Answering this question wasn't like committing to a simple label. This was saying to my father that I wanted to do what "they do" with "that guy"—the ripped, tan one with the broad shoulders and the sweaty bulge in his thong.

I took my time answering the question, hemming and hawing in hopes that a ringing phone or knock at the door would keep me from having to tell my father the truth. But eventually, the silence became more unnerving than the possibility of admitting the truth.

"Him," I said quickly, like I was ripping off a Band-Aid.

In the stillness that followed, I thought that this was about to be the moment my dad stopped loving me or called me a name he wouldn't be able to take back. I braced myself, afraid that this would be the instant I stopped having a father. Leonard stood up slowly from the chair and rolled up his magazine. I waited for his response, knowing that his sprinkler system of rage was about to be firmly aimed at me and no one else.

"Well, son," he blurted with forced excitement, "tomorrow we're having fajitas for dinner!" Then, before I had time to reply or process his response, he spun on his heels and left.

I spent the next several weeks coming out to my father over and over again. It was like a gay *Groundhog Day*. He'd point out a pretty woman at the mall. I'd agree, and then he'd ask me how I could know if I was *really* gay.

"Dad! I'm gay, not dead!"

I would mention that I found Freddie Mercury weird-looking and my dad would smile, as if finding a gay person unattractive somehow made me straight. Regardless of how many times I said it, it always seemed like the first to my dad, who would look at me with sad, confused eyes and then go silent.

After a few weeks, my dad decided to go back on the road full-time. I'd be moving in with my mom and Mike in Seguin. I didn't put up a fight. How could I? He'd rearranged his life and spent thousands of dollars to support his secretly gay, school-skipping, drug-addled son. A part of me was almost relieved to get away from the tension, even if it *was* to Seguin.

On our last night in the apartment I was packing up a box of journals and sketchpads when I found an old greeting card. My father had sent it to me when I was little and away at summer camp. On the front was a drawing of a big, orange lion with a little, smiling cub at his side. Inside, my father had asked how my summer was going and if I was making new friends. At the end, he wrote something that he said to me a lot when I was little: that the reason he loved me wasn't just that he was my father. He loved me because I was a "neat person," and he thought that even if he wasn't my father, I was someone he would want to know.

I took the card across the hall, where my father was packing up his things. I crept into his room carefully, the way he'd crept into mine three weeks earlier. He wasn't so much an untamed animal as a zombie, shuffling from closet to dresser to bed, unaware of his conniving son's presence in the room.

"Dad?"

"Yeah, DJ?"

"I'm sorry. I love you."

"I love you too," he said into his suitcase.

"Why do you love me, though?"

He paused, wearily looking up from a pile of two suitcases' worth of clothing he was trying to cram into one. "What do you mean?"

"Just tell me why you love me," I asked again.

He sighed and tossed down a ball of socks. "I love you because you're my son," he answered, looking at me blankly for a moment before returning to his packing.

Later this night, lying in my bed with my headphones on, I stared at that old, wrinkled greeting card. I read and reread it for half an hour, unsure whether it belonged in the box of things I'd be taking to my new life or in the garbage.

CHAPTER 22

A New Life

A lot changed after Brownie-gate. I hadn't been the only one called into the school office that day. It had been a shake-down. One by one we'd fallen like dominoes when con-fronted with our forged letters, admitting to a myriad of bad be-havior. A few of our friends got sent to alternative school. Some were forced to go to rehab. Others just disappeared.

It was a sad time made sadder by my leaving, and we all couldn't have been happier to feel so sad about it. If you ever want to see goth kids step up to the plate and own their brand, just give them a reason to say good-bye. My last week of school was a black celebration of morbidity, as evidenced by my grow-ing collection of dark poetry, sad mixtapes, and moody char-coal sketches. Greg performed a suicide-themed dance for me at school, choreographed to Depeche Mode's "Blasphemous Rumors." In it, he bounded across the small black-box theater

232 • BAD KID

in a black cloak with a red silk scarf, which he used to simulate sprays of blood and swinging nooses. It was disturbing and baroque, and one of the gayest things I'd ever seen. It was also the most amazing gift anyone had ever given me.

After class we all reminisced in the grocery-store parking lot next to school, chain-smoking and drinking whiskey from Jake's flask. I had to be in Seguin by 6 p.m. for dinner. So at five o'clock I started saying good-bye, which takes forever when goth teenagers are involved.

"David," said Greg, "let's hotbox in the car real quick."

Greg and I jumped in his little Cabriolet and rolled up the windows, letting it fill up with pot smoke. "Oh L'Amour" played on the stereo, reminding me of all those road trips we'd taken together when so much was still unspoken. The car looked different now than it had a year ago. The dashboard, like the bumpers, was matted with Cure and Bauhaus stickers. Every few feet of the interior was marked with a cigarette burn or a splash of dried nail polish.

"I'm gonna miss you so much," said Greg. I would only be an hour away, but we both knew things were about to change.

"I don't think my mother's going to let me do anything for a while. She says I can't leave Seguin at all until the end of summer."

"I know. I think my mom's clamping down too," said Greg, taking a deep puff on the joint. "Fucking Brownie."

"Yeah," I sighed. "Fucking Brownie."

"Hey," said Greg, taking a toke. "Come here."

Greg leaned toward me, his hand reaching up around the back of my head. He closed his eyes as his lips parted to meet mine. I leaned in to him, letting my lungs fill up with the smoke he was releasing into my body. And then we kissed. I wrapped my fingers around the jagged crook of his jawline, feeling a bit of stubble along his sideburn with my thumb. Greg's hand slipped around my waist to pull me closer. And then, as I released him from my grip . . . I felt nothing.

We looked quizzically at each other, knowing that what had just happened was somehow inevitable. It should have been a mind-blowing kiss, at least for me. Yet after all that sexual tension and endless waiting, it was pretty anticlimactic. As Greg turned up the stereo and lit two cigarettes, it was clear that neither of us felt much of anything special.

Greg handed me a cigarette and smiled. "I love you, David."

In a way I couldn't put my finger on, I was never so sure that Greg was my best friend. "I love you too."

"Did you give him the present?" yelled Raven, hopping into the back seat.

"Oh yeah! We got you this." Greg slipped me a small, tinfoil-wrapped square.

"It's white blotter. Good shit," added Raven, planting a bloodred kiss on my cheek. "For when Seguin starts to kill you."

I drove away at 5:45, knowing I'd be late but not really caring. In the rearview mirror I watched my friends load into Greg's car and thought about what their plans were for the weekend. I hadn't asked and didn't want to know. And although it hurt my heart a bit, it made me happy to think they'd probably have a great time without me.

An hour later, I pulled up to our quaint little house on the outskirts of town and lit a cigarette. I sat in my car and glared at the place, with its flower-filled window boxes, twenty-foot clothesline, and gravel driveway. On one side of the house was a field of dairy cattle; on the other, a Primitive Baptist ceme-tery. These were my new neighbors: bulge-eyed cows and baby corpses from the late 1800s. Five minutes later I finally willed myself to go inside.

"You're grounded!" snapped my mom, removing baked beans from the oven.

"What? I was in the driveway a few minutes ago!"

"You're late, mister," said Mike casually, strolling into the kitchen. "We have rules here. Rules that start *now*."

"But it was my last day and I was saying good-bye."

"Sorry, buddy. That's the way it goes," he said, shrugging his shoulders.

"Mom?" I whined.

"Honey, this is your first day here and you couldn't even get home on time!"

"But my friends—"

"The school only agreed to pass you because they knew you were leaving," she said. "It's a miracle you even passed your last exams!"

"But Mom—"

"Your history teacher didn't even know who you were!"

"But she only started a month ago—"

"David!" She shushed me. "Your mother loves you and ac-cepts your new gay identity, but . . ."

"Oh God, Mom. Stop with that!"

"Well, would you rather me be like your father?" she bel-lowed, slamming a pepper mill down on the counter. "I'm going to respect you and you're going to respect ME!"

My mother had never yelled like that before. I looked at her in her denim apron covered with little drawings of cows and chickens, standing over a boiling pot as her stepchildren set the table for dinner. This was who she was now: a homemaker with a husband and family. And I was an outsider who had never asked to be a part of it.

I stormed into my room: a large, carpeted, windowless cell in the center of the house. Mike had offered me other bedroom options, but I'd angrily insisted on that one.

"Who needs fucking windows anyway?" I'd said, hoping he'd see how miserable I was going to be. Mike, pulling out all the stops to ease my transition, agreed to redecorate the room any way I wanted. In a move that was both goth *and* gay, I demanded gray walls and track lighting. My furniture was made from cinder blocks I'd salvaged from Mike's work shed. My elbows and shins were already covered in nicks and scrapes from a week of accidental run-ins with my desk and shelving. I had designed a pretty mournful place for myself. A dark, windowless room full of sandpaper furniture lit by harsh spotlights did *not* make for a peaceful place of solitude.

Being in the center of the house meant sharing a wall with almost every room. I could hear it all: my mother humming in the kitchen, my stepsister singing along to the radio, and my brother playing video games. My new brother and sister were truly foreign creatures, their day-to-day lives full of banalities. I hadn't been around twelve-year-olds since I'd *been* a twelve-year-old. One day, after listening to constant scraping from Mickey's room, I went next door and found him hacking at a two-by-four with a pocketknife.

"Mickey, what are you doing?"

He looked up at me and shrugged as a cow from next door appeared in the window and let out a long, mournful "mooooo." *Is that what this place will do to me?* I thought. *How long until I'm sitting in silence alone on the floor of my room hacking at wood with a knife?* I sat in my gray room full of random noise and wrote these fears in a journal I named Claude, the only friend I had. My bedroom wasn't a place to sleep. It was a place to stew.

After two boring weeks in my cave, I had to get out of the house. I decided to drive down Highway 123 into Seguin, the actual town. Seguin proper was all very beige. And wooden. And concrete. Two facing strip malls seemed to house every business that anyone in town would ever dream of visiting, including Walmart. I smoked a bit of my last bag of weed and went inside the superstore. Surrounding me were men and women with teased hair and fanny packs, old people with melting faces riding electric wheelchairs, and dads with handlebar mustaches yelling at their kids. I could feel them watching me, sizing me up, recognizing me as an out-of-towner.

On my way home I passed the courthouse and pulled a U-turn to check out the famous giant pecan mounted in front. Looking at it closely, I could see that it was covered in deep pockmarks that revealed that it was actually a concrete sculpture and not, in fact, an actual two-foot-long nut. Passersby looked at me strangely, probably confused as to why anyone would take such an interest in their big counterfeit nut.

"Them ol' kids come on down and raise hell on dat thang!"

I turned to see an ancient woman in hot-pink lipstick. Her face looked to be made of saddle leather, and her spider-veined arms barely held her up on her walker. "Dagnabbit! Those hellions 'n' their shootin'."

"Excuse me, ma'am. What?"

"Those li'l sons-o'-bitches!" she groaned as her dentures slid down from behind her upper lip. "All summer they shoot at that-there pee-can wit' dare bee-bee guns!"

She continued to cuss as she strolled away from me, one of her pendulous breasts hanging six inches lower than the other beneath her Dallas Cowboys T-shirt. I tried to imagine what school here in the fall would be like, knowing that I'd probably never gel with high-schoolers who shot at fake legumes for fun.

That night I waited until everyone fell asleep and dropped my hit of white blotter. I stole myself a rum and Dr. Pepper and trudged to the Primitive Baptist cemetery with my journal and cigarettes. As the acid kicked in, I laid myself across the graves of a couple who had died on the same day in 1914. I lit a dozen tea candles and surrounded myself with them. I smoked and wrote for seven hours, drifting in and out of a coma-like nap as the sun came up. It was perhaps my gothest moment ever. And no one was there to see it.

Walking back to the house, I noticed a squirrel perched beneath a tree by the back door. It was standing perfectly still on its hind legs and staring at me intently, like it was going to say something. I crept toward it cautiously.

"Hey there, little guy. What are you doing?" I got closer and closer, ten feet, then eight feet, and then five feet. "Well, aren't you a brave little squirrel?"

His large black eyes stared into me, all-knowing. As I leaned down to him, I became convinced that he had something important to share.

"Do you have something to say to me? Who are you?"

"What the hell are you doing?" Mike yelled, shocking me off my feet. As I fell forward onto the squirrel, I could feel the hard, molded plastic of its artificial body mash into my face. I sat up quickly in an attempt to play it cool. But it was too late. Mike was convulsing in laughter. He slid down the screen door until he was on his haunches, covering his face and wheezing.

"You . . . thought . . . it . . . was . . . real . . ." he guffawed.

Mike was so entertained by this that he didn't even ask me why I was up at 6:30. He simply chuckled and patted me on the back. "You're weird, just like your mama."

I spent that day locked in my room, nursing a hangover and calling all my friends from San Antonio, none of whom answered. I read the deep and meaningful poetry I'd written the night before and had no idea what it was about.

Locked in Catatonia,
A place to build a black brick home
Where you calmly arrange
Aunt Laura's remains
On the entrance-hall wall
You peer through the sugarcane windows
To view the cadaverous children
Choking and gagging in the swampy mud
And clawing at the dying sun.
Covered by smoky funnel clouds
That cry on your black brick house
From tea to wine
All the time
Cutting clad crystal
In effervescent cultivation
Crawling up from pits of suicide contemplation

Where was Catatonia? What does it mean to "cut clad crystal"? Was "from tea to wine" a fancy way of saying "breakfast to dinner"? And, most important, who the hell was Aunt Laura? I didn't have an aunt Laura. Even if I did and she was dead, we didn't have an "entrance-hall wall" on which to display her remains.

Was Seguin sucking the creative spirit right out of me? What did this town, full of man-made replicas of nuts and animals, have to offer me? What did it mean that I'd wanted to kiss and touch Greg for so long, but that finally getting to had felt like nothing to me? I knew that something inside me was broken or defective. I didn't know who I was without my friends and my school and FX. I didn't know what role I played in this family or who I would be without my freedom.

I ran to my car after dinner and peeled out of the driveway. I drove past the strip malls, the Walmart, the fake nut; past the highway truck stop and farming-supply store and sewage-treatment plant. I drove until all the electric lights faded away, until it was just me and the moon and the road. I rolled the windows down and let in the wind. Out in the darkness I could hear the sound of toads and crickets and, somewhere, water. Soon I was entering New Braunfels. I didn't choose to drive there as much as gravity pulled me there. I thought I'd be able to locate the house unseen in the night. But as I drove down Max's street, he looked right into my eyes from the porch, watching me roll by at three miles an hour in my little blue car.

He sauntered over to my driver's-side window in unlaced Docs and a tight Guinness T-shirt. He leaned into the window with a grin. I could see his barely-there Mohawk, like a three-inch-wide landing strip on top of his head. As I greeted him with an outstretched hand, his baby-faced smile disappeared.

"Max, right?" I asked. "It's me. David."

"Yeah, I know."

"What's wrong?" I asked, my open hand still unshaken.

"You didn't eat a Vicks inhaler on the way over, did you?"

"No. I promise."

CHAPTER 23

I Like it Here—Can I Stay?

It's a love song when you really listen to it!" yelled Max.

"Huh?" I said, rolling down the window to let out a cloud of pot smoke.

"I said, IT'S A LOVE SONG!"

It was hard to hear him over the banging drums and sneering guitars erupting from his crappy car speakers. It sounded like noise to me, like most of the music Max played during our car trips. In two weeks of friendship, we'd established a ritual: I drove to New Braunfels around noon and met Max at his house. We spent the day together, until 6 p.m., when my newly watchful mother demanded I be home for dinner. Sometimes we spent the day visiting his friends. Other times we just drove around—through the golf course, to the abandoned train bridge, or in circles around the famous water park, Schlitterbahn.

During this time we engaged in a kind of musical show-and-tell. He played me the Misfits, Hüsker Dü, or Fugazi, and then I played him the Smiths, Soft Cell, or Peter Murphy. Slowly, we were compiling a playlist of songs we both learned to love. Between us in the car was a black vinyl case of "our cassettes": a growing collection of mixtapes that included the Lemonheads, New Order, the Sundays, Black Flag, and, surprisingly, Erasure.

I loved watching Max rock back and forth in the passenger seat with bloodshot eyes, screaming along to his favorite Erasure song, "Yahoo!," a jubilantly gay dance hymn about higher love. Watching his massive frame pound the dashboard to Andy Bell's sweet refrain, "find your way unto the Lord," made me laugh every time—not because I was mocking Max but because his joyous abandon was that infectious. Maybe it was weird for him too, watching me with painted nails and a turquoise nose ring scream Mission of Burma's, "That's when I reach for my revolver! That's when it all gets blown AWAY!"

The track du jour was "Ever," a raucous song by the Lemonheads that had reminded me of sound-check feedback the first time I heard it. But over time, it slowly revealed its layers of melody. Passing the joint to Max, I considered his thesis.

"It *is* a love song, isn't it?"

"Yeah," he wheezed before releasing a cloud of smoke. "It sounds raw, right? Like he's angry."

"Right. But the lyrics are so sweet," I sighed. "Like, he loves her so much."

Max handed the joint back to me and grinned. "I told you it was a love song."

An hour later we were at Sean's house. Sean was Max's best SHARP friend in New Braunfels. We'd met a few times, but he'd remained pretty icy toward me. Sean met us in the foyer, where he hugged Max and shook my hand, which always seemed less like a greeting and more like something I had to do to avoid being bludgeoned.

"What's up?" Sean asked, his white-blond hair cropped to the skin.

"What's up?" I replied, two octaves deeper than my actual voice. Sean walked ahead of us as Max, calling me out on my vocal machismo, mimed a squatting, orangutan-ish muscleman.

"Stop it," I whispered, backhanding his arm.

A dozen people, mostly SHARPs, milled around Sean's house. Each of them shook Max's hand as he towered above them; they greeted him in voices I would've sworn were also unnaturally deep. At the dining-room table, a SHARP ripped the cap off a bottle with his teeth while another passionately read some manifesto aloud from a book. In the living room, a short, shirtless skinhead was repeatedly lifting cinder blocks as a small cluster of guys counted. There wasn't a girl in sight. It was a penitentiary variant of my high school locker room.

Don't look down. Don't look down. Maintain eye contact.

"Max," I whispered in the kitchen, "don't these guys know that this is the hottest gay bar ever?"

"Hahaha! Crabb!" Max banged on the counter.

"I'm serious. They're like every boy I ever liked in a photo of a Joy Division concert, but on steroids!"

Max leaned his head back with his mouth wide open. Not a sound came out for five seconds. Then, suddenly, a deep, horn-like blast of laughter boomed out. "Haaa . . . Haaa . . . Haaa . . ."

"Don't any of these guys have girlfriends?" I asked, opening a soda.

"Dude," Max composed himself, "a lot of them are straight-edge."

"I know that means they can't get fucked up, but they can't have sex either?"

"Yep. But weren't rules made to be broken?" he said, flicking his tongue around the rim of his beer bottle. "Which one you want me to hook you up with, sexy?" Max started pretending to go down on the bottle. I tried to contain my laughter, fearing that Sean or one of his friends would walk in. "How about Sean?" he asked. Max turned to the counter and begin to hump it, slamming a drawer over and over again while moaning, "Oh, Sean. Fuck me harder!"

"What the fuck are you doing?" asked Sean, appearing suddenly in the kitchen doorway and visibly perplexed by the scene.

"Oh man, I can't find a bottle opener anywhere in here," said Max, fumbling through the drawer he'd just been fucking.

Sean looked at Max, and then at me, and then back at Max. "It's right there on the counter."

"Oh," Max said, holding up the opener and crossing his eyes. "Duh!"

"Come check something out," Sean asked Max.

"Okay. Come on, Dave."

"No. Just you," said Sean, glaring at me.

Max rolled his eyes and handed me his beer. "Okay. I guess this is top-secret SHARP business." He winked at me and followed Sean from the kitchen.

Five minutes into exploring the photos on Sean's fridge, I thought I saw Max over my shoulder. I turned to show him a funny picture of Sean as a baby. "Aw. He was so cute."

But it wasn't Max. It was two guys I'd never met.

"Oh, hey. I thought you were someone else." I could hear the pitch of my voice plummet so deep it sounded like a belch.

"Who the fuck are you?" asked the cinder block lifter.

"Oh, I'm friends with Sean. I mean—"

"You?" he asked incredulously. "Sean's friends with *you*?"

"Well, we're not, like, best friends forever." I heard the words come out of my mouth and imagined myself in their eyes as a thirteen-year-old girl with an armful of Beanie Babies.

"Well, we've never seen you around here before." They both took a step forward.

"Hey!" The deep baritone of Max's voice was like a foghorn. He stood in the doorway, with Sean dwarfed by his side. "What the fuck is going on?"

"Oh, we were just talking to this guy, Max," said one of them. The other nervously repeated, "Yeah, we were just talking."

"His name is David," said Max, adding sternly, "you two should introduce yourselves."

And then, in the most forced pleasantry I'd ever been party to, each of them shook my hand, their voices quivering. The cinder block lifter's hand shook in mine as I said, "Hello. I'm David."

As quickly as we'd met, they fled the kitchen, presumably to open more bottles with their teeth and weightlift lumber.

"David, come down here," said Max. "I gotta say bye to these guys."

I followed him down the hallway and into Sean's room, where half a dozen guys sat in a circle. In one of their hands was a small black gun. I'd seen rifles in person before, but never a pistol, like the ones cops had on TV shows. The boy holding it noticed me and quickly wrapped it in a small cloth.

"Who's he?" I heard him ask as Max said good-bye. I wasn't sure I wanted him to know.

When we got back to Max's house, the entire place smelled heavenly. His mother, Ruth, stood in the kitchen flipping burgers, her salt-and-pepper hair in a long ponytail.

"Well, hello, boys!"

"Hi, Ruth," I replied, noticing the dinner spread on her dining-room table.

"I was just cooking for me and the girls," she said as Max's two little sisters cut lettuce and tomatoes behind her. "But there's more than enough."

"Oh, I can't stay. My mom wants me home by six."

"But it's summertime. Is this some special dinner or something?"

"No, it's just . . . My mom is being a little . . ."

"Mom, David was a really bad kid last year," laughed Max.

"Shut up," I said, snapping him with a dinner napkin. "It's my curfew, and . . ."

"Nonsense," Ruth said, picking up the phone. "What's her number?"

"Ms. Fell, um . . . I can't—"

"Two. One. Oh . . ." Max interrupted, shooting me a smile as he recited my number.

Our mothers must have talked for half an hour as Max and I played cards at the dining-room table. I could hear my mom cracking jokes on the other end of the line.

"Uh, I think you're staying for dinner," said Max with a wink.

"You're actually staying overnight," said Ruth as she hung up the phone.

"But I can't, or my mom . . ."

"I told your mom that there are bars on all the windows and a moat around the house."

Max laughed loudly with a mouth full of hamburger and hugged his mom as he passed behind her. "You're a fucking riot, Mom."

Noticing my worried face, Ruth patted my hand. "Seriously, I told her that by the time we eat and watch a movie it'll be too late to drive. I also told her that I'm a single mom and could really use some help moving topsoil in the morning."

"See? She fucking puts you to work," yelled Max.

"Fuck this. Fuck that. Fuck him," replied Ruth. "Your mouth is like a fucking sewer, son."

They laughed together in a way that made me miss my own mom. After dinner, Max popped the Lemonheads cassette into the kitchen stereo and started cleaning up. The house felt full and warm, the sound of the TV clashing with the Lemonheads in the kitchen and Max's sisters giggling down the hall.

I was in someone else's home in a space I barely knew, but as Max leaned against the counter and smiled at me, it felt like exactly where I was supposed to be.

One thing I prided myself on during
my teens was my luxurious hair.
Sometimes I parted it on the left.
Sometimes I parted it on the right. I was
unpredictable like that. But it's styling,
for the most part, always followed the
hair choices of Depeche Mode's sexy
lead singer, Dave Gahan. On the left I
was sporting an over-gelled "Violator"-
era short-do. (In retrospect, it looks less
dangerous and more "Rick Astley.")
On the right I was into Depeche Mode's
more grungy "Songs of Faith and
Devotion" album, hence the Jesus-y
locks and sultry smizing.

CHAPTER 24

You're Gonna Need Someone on Your Side

My mother held the pillowcase from Sylvia's bed against her chest.

"It looks like Tammy Faye Bakker had a run-in with my linens!"

"Mom, quiet!" I whispered as Sylvia and Greg ate breakfast in the next room. "She'll hear you."

"I don't care if that girl hears me. She needs to wash her face before bed," she exclaimed, shaking the black-and-red-smeared pillowcase in front of her. "I think I'll have to *burn* this!"

Sylvia's morning face was such a mess that it looked like a demon was eating eggs in our living room: blood-smeared lips tore bacon in half as bloodshot eyeballs peered up from two charcoal-encrusted holes.

"Breakfast is great, Teri!" she yelled from the couch.

"See, Mom? She's trying to be nice," I insisted. What my mother didn't understand was that the sprawled-out girl watching *Lifestyles of the Rich and Famous* with a plate of food resting on her massive boobs was simply making herself at home. "She likes it here, Mom. She likes you."

"Well, she could have a bit more decorum."

"But Mom, we're all in our pajamas. We're just relaxing."

"Is 'relaxing' what you were doing out in the pasture until 3 a.m.?"

I could've answered honestly by saying, "No, Mother. Last night we were on ecstasy and Sylvia forced us to chase a cow she thought was a reincarnated shaman." But that wouldn't have gone over well. So I said, "Mom, we were just looking at the animals. Greg and Sylvia don't get out to the country much."

"Well, they're odd. And you know your mother loves odd people. But really . . ."

"Mom, you promised you'd be cool if I had some San Antonio friends visit."

"I am being cool," she said, aggressively setting the timer on the washing machine, "but I don't see why they can't be well-mannered like that Max."

"I know, Mom. You love Max. Geez . . ."

"He is delightful and polite," she said, dreamily holding a box of detergent to her chest. "He's so handsome and considerate. And his mother is a treasure."

Whenever my mother began to swoon over Max in relation to my San Antonio friends, a part of me wanted to interject with tales of Max stealing whiskey, and night-driving with the headlights off. He had the whole Eddie Haskell thing down. But whereas Eddie Haskell was a dick, Max was actually a great person. He just happened to have a penchant for hard drinking, whippit-huffing, and waking blackouts.

"Hello?" I heard Max say from the back door. My mom's face lit up as Sylvia zipped past us like a comet.

"Bitch, my face isn't on!" she screeched, locking herself in the bathroom.

"More like her face came off," whispered my mother, "all over my sheets."

I walked into the living room, where Max was standing with Greg, who looked up cautiously in his oversize sweatpants and giant New Order T-shirt.

"I've heard a lot about you, Greg. Glad we could meet."

Max towered over Greg in a way that made it look like they were different species. Greg readjusted his headband and tried to seem butch, which I was becoming an expert at. Seeing Greg attempt it with Max made me grin, wondering if I looked that hopeless when I tried.

"Hey bro," said Greg as they extended arms, his purple fingernails and assorted rings disappearing in the gargantuan catcher's mitt of Max's hand.

"Max!" sang my mom, throwing her arms around him. "Are you hungry, son?" she asked, her head barely coming up to his chest. "I swear he's a bottomless pit," she chirped with a smile to Greg, who had the fearful look of someone expecting to be sucker punched at any moment.

"Hey y'all," said Sylvia, turning the corner in a black smock, having put her full face on in record time. "Max! It's a pleasure to meet you," she cooed, peeking around newly platinum bangs.

Sylvia was in man mode—her voice huskier, boobs higher, and mascara even heavier than usual.

As my stepfather entered the room to greet everyone, I was struck by this odd collision: all these disparate people coming together in a tiny house off a dirt road in Seguin, Texas. Sylvia flirted with Max while Mike made coffee and Greg helped my mom clear the table. Things had been compartmentalized somehow, but right at that moment, every part of me seemed like they could coexist: Sylvia's drug buddy, Greg's gay copilot, my mother's son. And most of all, Max's best friend. He stood in the center of the room like a colossal lighthouse, shining a light that each person responded to; even Greg was starting to relax.

Six hours and a hit of acid each later, we were at Max's house in New Braunfels, greeting the arriving guests. My mom didn't know that Max's mother had taken his sisters out of town for a trip. As Greg's acid kicked in, I could sense his anxiety building over each shaved head that came through the front door.

"David, there are so many skinheads here," he said, looking around at thirty or so SHARPs as they milled around.

"Mama like!" purred Sylvia, gliding onto the couch beside us. "Girl! No wonder you hang out with these fellas, fagotron!"

"I'm mainly just friends with Max," I said.

"Well, duh, Crabb! Look at him!" Sylvia stared him down across the room. "I wanna climb him like a mountain! Girl, he's just so damn big!" I looked at Max through her eyes, at his broad shoulders and thick, strong neck. He wasn't all muscle, but he wasn't all fat. He was large, hard, and impenetrable, but dopey and soft too.

He noticed us looking and mouthed, "You doin' okay?"

"Hot damn!" whispered Sylvia, before mouthing "Just fine" to him with a wink. "David," she shuddered, "he makes me feel like a whore in church on Sunday."

"Sylvia," said Greg, his voice trembling, "I'm glad you feel secure enough to go into slut mode right now, but I'm fearing for my life."

"Oh gawd, bitch," moaned Sylvia, rolling her eyes, "we get it. You went through something. It was traumatic. Yada yada yada . . ."

"Greg, they're not racists, they're SHARPs," I said, explaining their entire manifesto to him as Sylvia and I shared a joint.

"Yeah, but they're not marching in pride parades, either," replied Greg, making a point I often overlooked. "Just because they're not racists doesn't mean they like gay people."

"Yeah, but none of them is going to do anything because I'm Max's best friend," I explained. Greg shot me a slightly hurt look. "Oh, come on, Greg. You know what I mean. I'm . . . protected, I guess."

"Damn, Gina," said Sylvia, lighting up a joint. "It's like you're Whitney Houston in *The Bodyguard*."

A few minutes later Max walked over with Sean, who was stern and joyless as usual.

"Hey," said Max, "this is my best friend, Sean." I heard him say *best friend* and realized how I'd just made Greg feel.

"I'm Sean," he said, and paused, midhandshake with Greg. "Oh fuck. I know you."

"Um . . ." Greg swiped his bangs behind his ear and looked down at the carpet.

"Dude," said Sean, "this is one of those kids from FX."

"What?" I asked, refusing to hear what I'd just heard.

"Oh shit," said Max. "I thought I remembered you, Greg. You're the blue-Docs guy."

We all froze. Sounds came from Greg's mouth—none of them words so much as slight, guttural hiccups. For a moment I reconsidered that familiar connection I'd felt with Max. Maybe there was no magic at work, just creepy synchronicity.

"Greg, I'm sorry." Max reached out to Greg with an open hand. "That was a long time ago. I was fucked up. But it's no excuse. I'm really, really sorry."

Sean chuckled to Max. "Dude, we were drunk. It's not the end of the world you beat up some—"

"Shut up," barked Max.

Sean closed his mouth and looked at the ceiling as Greg shook Max's hand. With sudden force, Max pulled Greg in close and hugged him. Greg looked at me, confused, his face smashed against Max's chest.

"I'm so fucking sorry, brother," said Max. "Apologize," he said to Sean, turning Greg to face him.

"But I was drunk and he was—"

"Fucking apologize." Max wasn't asking anymore.

Awkwardly and with visible resentment, Sean stammered, "I'm really . . . sorry."

"For what?" demanded Max.

"Geesh," sighed Sean. "I'm sorry we beat you up and took your boots. Okay?"

"Now shake hands," demanded Max. The two of them shook hands and Sean stomped off into the party. "I'm sorry that happened, Greg. It wasn't right."

"It's fine. It's over," said Greg as Max opened a tall boy and downed the whole thing in one gulp. After hugging and apologizing to Greg a few more times, Max walked back into the party, shaking his head and staring at the floor. I watched him shuffle away drunkenly, his big shoulders sadly sloped like a morose giant vanquished from a magic kingdom.

"One word, bitches: fuckable," said Sylvia.

"I think he crushed my shoulder blade," said Greg, bending his neck back and forth as Sylvia passed him the joint.

"Damn, Crabb," said Sylvia. "Are you sure he's straight?"

"What?" I said, her question taking me by surprise.

"What are you, deaf, Mizz Keller? I said, are you sure that fine piece of man meat is straight? Don't tell me you haven't tried. You spend all your time together. You never call me anymore. You go to parties with him and stay at his house all the time."

"So?" I asked.

"David," interjected Greg, "you're obviously into each other. Duh."

The two of them looked at me with the clearheaded certainty of someone telling a child, "The sky is blue." Maybe everything Max and I were feeling wasn't as simple as brotherhood. Although I knew Max was attracted to women, he'd never said he *wasn't* attracted to men. I looked at him across the room, tilting his head back and sucking the last drop of beer from his bottle. The kitchen light hit the back of his head in a way that made every striation of muscle in his neck visible. I watched the mound of his bicep flex as he lifted another bottle of beer to his mouth, his lips wrapping around the rim. I tried to keep my brain and libido from venturing to the place I quickly realized they were taking a trip to.

David, this is not an option.

My chest started to tighten as I realized how high I was. It felt like a weight was resting on my lungs. Greg and Sylvia were chatting too fast to each other in a language I couldn't understand. I slipped outside and walked into the front yard, looking up at the stars and trying to catch my breath. Squealing tires at the curb thirty feet away caught my attention. The doors of a maroon van all opened at once, each producing a skinhead.

"Hey faggot!" one of them yelled, advancing quickly. These weren't SHARPs. These were the skins Max had told me about. Each one was holding a baseball bat or a knife. More boys emerged from the van, like it was the most terrifying clown car ever.

"Get the fuck in here!" yelled Max.

I turned and ran toward the porch as the skinheads gained behind me, one of them screaming, "Get that little faggot!"

Max grabbed my hand and pulled me inside. Ten skinheads stood in a line in the front yard as everyone at the party gathered at the windows to look outside.

"Oh bitch," whispered Sylvia, her eyes darting back and forth. "I'm too high for this shit, Minerva."

"Oh fuck. Oh fuck. Oh fuck," repeated Greg.

"Give him to us!" I heard one of the skins yell.

This was it. All my fears about Max's social circle had come to fruition. I had interfered with a group dynamic I should've stayed out of. Even worse, I had dragged my friends along.

"Oh fuck, Max," I whispered. "I'm sorry."

"What the fuck are you talking about?" he asked, looking through the blinds.

"Well, if you have to surrender me," I answered.

"Dude, you're as high as I am drunk. They don't want you, David. They want him." Max pointed to the back of the kitchen, past thirty kids, where a gangly African American SHARP named Reggie cowered in the corner.

"Give him to us and we won't fucking destroy your house," yelled the skins' leader.

"Where's the gun?" I heard a SHARP whisper from the back of the room.

"No," I said, instinctively grabbing Max's shoulder.

"Who gives a fuck what you think?" said Sean, bouncing up and down with crazy eyes. "These guys are gonna fuck us up!"

I looked around the house and saw at least forty kids: mostly SHARPs, a few punks, maybe a goth or two. They reminded me of all our friends that night at FX when Greg was beaten up. I looked back outside at the ten skins in the front yard.

"There are so many more of us," I said to Max.

He looked at me and then over his shoulder at the party. "Yeah. Let's just all go outside." Max didn't look much more confident than I was, but the math was on our side. And whatever would keep the gun out of the equation seemed preferable.

"We're going outside," he said sternly to Sean, "without the gun."

"This shit is too intense for me, Minerva!" bawled Sylvia, her bloodshot eyes bouncing up and down in their sockets.

Max stood up and, with the intensity of General Patton, declared, "We're going outside. And we don't say anything." One by one and without question, each person stepped onto the porch. After all, Max was the mayor of freaks. A minute later, all of us were face-to-face with the group of skins, whose size and threat seemed puny by comparison.

"Where's the nigger?" yelled the leader, twisting the grip of the bat in his hand.

We stared at him in silence. He asked again and still wasn't answered. I could feel the heat of our collective glare intensify as we looked down from the porch on the group of intruders. Some of the skinheads started to retreat, their machismo disappearing as they realized how many of us there were. We all moved forward on the porch, up against the railing, the mass of us making the waterlogged wood creak and moan beneath our feet.

"Come on, man," said a skin to the leader as he jogged to the car. "This ain't good, man."

I felt powerful, seeing these guys twice my size retreat in fear. Five minutes later, the skins left and the party resumed, bigger and louder than before. In the living room we gathered around Reggie and toasted him. Then we lifted him above our heads and passed him through the party, almost cutting off his nose with a ceiling fan. Greg located the three goth girls in attendance and sat chatting with them about hair dye while Sylvia showed a group of SHARPs how to make a marijuana pipe out of an apple.

At 4 a.m. I sat tripping with Max in the front yard.

"No, you do it like this," he said, attempting to show me how to blow a blade of grass like a whistle.

"Like this?" I asked, attempting again but only making a flat fart sound. "I can't even whistle with my lips, Max. I suck at this. Maybe if—"

"Hey!" he slurred, covering my mouth with his hand. "I would never let a bunch of skins beat the shit out of you," he said, swaying as his drunken gaze roamed from my face to my shoulder. "Why would you think that?"

"Well, because you have to protect your friends."

"But you *are* my friend, you fucker," he said, grabbing my face and staring into my eyes. "Listen, I'm really sorry about Greg. I was different then. Please don't think I'm an asshole."

"Max, it's okay. We're really fucked up."

"I just want to be a good person," he said, making a clipped little whistle sound with his blade of grass. "I just want to be good."

"But you *are* good," I said, rubbing the back of his head.

"Please be my friend. Okay?"

"I *am* your friend, Max. I am."

He leaned forward and pressed his face against my shoulder, his hand falling onto the grass as he began to black out. I rested my cheek against the top of his head and inhaled, laughing to myself at how much the gargantuan beast in my arms smelled more like a newborn than anything else: mild, clean, like baby powder.

As Max moaned the satisfying rattle of a deeply tired person surrendering to sleep, I noticed Sean on the front porch twenty feet away, glaring at me with his narrow, deep-set eyes as he stamped out a cigarette on the railing.

David, this is not an option.

Here's Greg and me in my bedroom a few months after I moved to Seguin. Greg, unlike me, was wise enough not to style his hair into the shape of a mushroom. Greg had just helped me as any all-American boy would help his buddy: by building a small shrine to Keanu Reeves in his bedroom. We are presenting this against my newly white walls, which my mother had insisted I paint after getting spooked too many times while bringing in my laundry/going through my cinder-block shelving looking for drugs and cigarettes.

CHAPTER 25

This Is Not a Love Song

Hi, honey. Um . . . Okay, can you turn off that weird light that makes your teeth green?"

My mother stumbled through the black-light cave of my room with her arms full of laundry. "I wanted you to have clothes for Max's sleepover."

"It's not a sleepover, mom. I'm seventeen years old."

"Whatever you call it, then. A stay-over, or sleep-away, or . . . slumber party!"

"All of those are worse," I said, throwing my duffel bag over my shoulder. "Okay, Mom. I love you, but Max's expecting me."

"Of course he is. When are you going to bring him back over? It's been a month."

"Mom, no one wants to come to Seguin. What are we gonna do? Go cow tipping?"

"Honey, your attitude about Seguin has got to change," she

said. "Come September, you can't hang out in New Braunfels all the time, no matter how nice Max's mother is on the phone."

"Just let me enjoy the rest of summer before I become a hillbilly," I said, trying to evade my mom and get out of the house. "Just think, I could be hanging out with Sylvia."

My mother wrinkled her nose like I'd shoved a rotten egg in her face. "Oh God! That little blonde nightmare."

"I think it's lime-green now, actually."

"Green, pink, paisley, whatever. You know she called again today?"

Sylvia had been calling me for a month, but I had been too busy hanging out with Max to call her back. My mother would intercept the call, only to be wrangled into a twenty-minute conversation with Sylvia about her dating life or the kitten she'd found or a movie she'd seen.

"Honey, that girl keeps me on the phone forever. I love people from all walks of life, but I just can't handle her. She's a bad influence!"

"Well, Max isn't a bad influence, right? His mom is nice, and he only lives fifteen minutes away."

"His mother *is* really lovely," she said as I stepped over the threshold and into the hallway. "Please give her the recipes I tucked into your bag."

I paused in the doorway. "You went into my bag?"

"Well, yes. But it was empty. I was just . . ." She looked up dramatically and cleared her throat. "Okay, David. I need to tell you something."

"Oh God, Mom." I sighed and sat on the bed, preparing myself for an avalanche of confessional hand-holding and "feeling words."

"It'll be fast. I promise," she said, sitting on my bed. "Open and honest: I found your diary one day when I was arranging your sock drawer." She paused and stared at me in silence for a moment before admitting, "Okay! I'm lying. I was violating your private space, looking for cigarettes and drugs. Anyway, I found your diary and—"

"Mom! You did *not* read my journal?"

"Oh, right. It's a 'journal,' the 'masculine,' because you're a boy, well, a *man*, really. Anyway, I read in your journal about some of your . . . *feelings*." I got up instinctively, wanting to escape whatever was going to come from her mouth next. "Stay here, David. Let me finish. I know this is making you uncomfortable, but I'm your mother. I love you. We should be open with each other, open and honest. Now, your thoughts about Jake and his penis are nothing to feel bad about."

"Oh God! Mom!"

"Honey, sit down. We all have desires," she said, glancing to the parted bedroom door and whispering, "You know when Mother takes her 'long baths'?"

"Mom! You have to stop talking now!"

My mother stood and proudly raised her chin. "I have needs as well, honey. All of what you're experiencing is totally natural and nothing to feel ashamed about."

I grabbed my bag and headed for the door. "Mom, stop talking!"

"David! Come back here! I'm your mother and I love you just the way you are!"

My mom followed me to the car. As I started the ignition, she leaned into the window. "Honey, all I wanted to do is give you these." And with that, three boxes of condoms fell into my lap. "Max is lovely and in this day and age, even true love won't protect you from—"

"Mom! Max is just my friend. He likes girls!" I looked down at the variety of condoms in my lap and shoved them back into my mother's hands. "I'm only staying overnight. How much sex do you think I could even have in twenty-four hours?"

"Well, I had to get a variety because . . ." Unfortunately, I didn't drive away fast enough to miss the last part of her sentence. " . . . I have no idea what your penis is like."

In the rearview mirror I saw my mother in a cloud of dust, waving good-bye with boxes of condoms, yelling, "Think with the right head, sweetie!"

By 3 a.m., Max and I were sitting on Sean's kitchen counter, drunk.

"So, Max, where are Sean's parents?" I slurred as a party raged in the next room.

"Well, his mom's dead and his dad works nights at a jail," he said, popping open his umpteenth beer. "Just two of the reasons he's such a dick."

"You really think your best friend's a dick?"

"A. He's not my best friend. B. Yes. But most people are dicks, really."

"That's kind of a downer, isn't it?"

"Thinking that makes things easier for me, because if everyone's a dick then everyone's hurt. And if everyone's hurt, then everyone is . . . I don't know."

"Everyone is what?"

"Special, I guess," he said, polishing off the beer he'd opened a minute earlier. "Like, if you meet someone and they seem super nice, you just don't know the shitty parts yet. And the shitty parts are coming. Believe me. They always do."

Max filled my red plastic cup halfway with rum, tossed me a Coke, and continued. "But if I meet someone who's a total dick right off the bat, then things can only get better, right? You have something to look forward to."

"So I just haven't shown you my bad part yet, then, huh?"

"You're transparent," he said, taking a long swig off the rum bottle. "I can already promise you your bad part is a fraction as bad as— Goddamn!" he yelled, his face wrinkling at the taste of the warm well-brand rum. "How do you drink this shit?!"

"Well, the 'bad part' of me wants to tell you that you're a fucking moron for not putting it on ice with a mixer," I said with a smirk. "But since I'm so transparent and you're the Buddha, you probably know that."

Max smiled back and lit a cigarette. "You know what I mean, David. I know what you want, is all."

He leaned beside me and threw his arm around my neck, pulling me in close to him. The drunken weight of his body pressed me against the counter.

"See, Sean," he whispered in my ear, pointing over the kitchen bar into the crowded living room. "He wants discord. He likes problems. But once you get to know him, you realize that what he really likes is solving problems. He's just so fucking bored and uninspired in this bullshit town that he has to make problems to have anything to do."

Max leaned his head against mine, slurring with half-closed eyes. "And Jennifer," he said, pointing to a girl with a shaved head on the sofa. "She's a slut because her mom was a slut and her older sister was a slut. She wants someone to love her, but she doesn't understand that you can't fuck your way to that kind of comfort. And Rocky," he whispered, pointing to a tiny fourteen-year-old skinhead with freckles and ginger hair. "He acts all tough and is always coming to these SHARP parties trying to be cool. He's not actually one of us yet. He just wants a brother, I think. Wait . . . is his name Rocky?"

Max reached up and rubbed his head in thought, his fingertips grazing my head, which rested against his. As I looked up at his face, the rest of the party receded into a black hole; every voice turned down and every light faded. Everything behind Max slipped into a blur when he looked into my eyes. For a moment, I couldn't see past him.

Just then, a beer bottle shattered. In the living room, the little redheaded wannabe-SHARP was cutting his chest with a broken Heineken bottle, an attempt to flirt with Jennifer, who watched with come-hither eyes from the torn, dirty couch.

"See?" said Max, releasing me and letting out a huge belch. "I think that's our cue."

Max stumbled behind me through the front door as Sean looked on.

"You boys leaving already?" he asked, placing particular emphasis on the lispy *S* in *boys*.

"Fuck you and good night," exclaimed Max with barely open eyes.

Sean looked at him and laughed, immediately charmed out of saying whatever homophobic slur was coming next.

"Good night, Sean," I said, smiling as I left. Sean shifted his focus to me and scowled, shaking his head, as if to say, *How dare you?*

That night I lay in Max's bed about to go to sleep when he wandered in with a Guinness and an aerosol can.

"Max, don't you want to go to sleep? We're pretty fucked up."

"Dave, it's only midnight. Come on, dude."

He sat on the floor Indian-style and gulped the beer, half of which spilled onto his shirt. "Wanna do some Scotchgard?"

"That spray stuff you put on couches and leather jackets? How?"

"Like this," he said, spraying the Scotchgard onto the bottom of his T-shirt and covering his face with it. He took a deep inhale and leaned back against his bed. "Do it, Dave," he said, his eyes closing as his mouth slackened.

After a year of friendship with Sylvia, getting high this way seemed downright pedestrian. I sprayed the edge of the bedspread with Scotchgard, not wanting to stain my favorite Violent Femmes shirt or reveal any part of my naked torso to Max. I took a deep breath and immediately felt a numbing rush slip behind my eyes. The white noise of the room began to pulse in superstereo; a crashing wave of wah-wahs sped through my brain. VHS head cleaner had nothing on fabric and upholstery protector.

"David. Wake up."

Max was shaking the back of my head. I had face-planted in the carpet and was drooling on his thigh.

"What? Shit . . . Did I pass out?"

"Yeah," he said, a huge smile plastered on his face. "It happens. We should watch each other, okay?" He sprayed more Scotchgard onto his shirt.

"Max, you're going to do more?"

"Yeah. Sean and me do this back and forth for half an hour. It's total fucking euphoria. But if I pass out, you gotta wake me

up in a couple minutes. Just to make sure I don't have an adren-
aline overdose and then a heart attack."

"A heart attack?" I asked, dreary-eyed.

A million fairies were whizzing through my brain as the reggae music warped in and out of my aural field. I wanted to be
concerned about Max's possibly having a heart attack, but my
body felt too good to care.

"What is this reggae music you're playing?" I asked, the bass
line twisting through my spine.

"It's nah raggah, iss duhhh," Max moaned through his shirt.

"What?" I started to laugh. "I can't fucking hear you."

"It's not reggae. It's dub!" he yelled louder through his shirt
and laughed. Then he went silent, still upright but swaying with
his eyes closed. His hands held the shirt up over his face, exposing his soft, tan belly and chest. I wanted to reach out and touch
him; to wrap my arms around his body and hold him as tight as
I could. He fell forward onto my crotch with a thud. His big,
bald head rested right in between my legs. He murmured something and turned his head to the side. His shoulders pushed back
against my thighs with each long, unconscious breath. Carefully, I reached down and placed my open palm against the back
of his neck. I ran my fingers in circles on his scalp, which was
soft yet sandpapery. I leaned down and ran my cheek along the
side of his face, my ear grazing his. I always thought of Max as
having brown hair, but this close to his skin I could see hundreds
of fine blond hairs, like a smattering of gold dust across his skin.

Wait. Is he breathing?

I started shaking him violently, yelling, "Wake up!"

Max sprung up on his feet with such intensity that he smashed
the top of his head on the ceiling.

"Oh God, Max! I thought you were dead!"

"Jesus Christ," he said, rubbing his bruised scalp. "You have to be asleep for a long time!"

"But you were," I said. Max looked at me doubtfully. "I think."

Max delicately pushed me against the side of the bed, with his foot against my chest. "You fucker," he grinned. "I'm going to get ice."

After Max walked out, I crawled into his bed from the floor. I stared up at the slowly rotating ceiling fan, one of its four blades slightly askew. My temples were warm and pulsing in time with my heartbeat. All I could smell was Max, and I curled up in his comforter.

"Dude, you're not passing out," said Max, walking in with a plastic bag of ice on his head. He grabbed the Scotchgard and sat on the bed next to me. "We've got a long night ahead of us."

"More? How much of this stuff can you do at once?"

"I don't know," he winked at me. "Let's find out."

We lay in his bed groggily, laughing and trancing out on the music for a while, occasionally shaking each other awake from a puddle of drool. Eventually the conversation turned to our families.

"So you're in this shithole because your dad flaked on you?"

"He didn't flake," I replied. "I fucked him over."

"So you think he doesn't love you?" Max asked, spraying the last bit of Scotchgard onto his shirt.

"Not like he used to."

"He will again, Dave," Max said, covering my mouth with part of his shirt. "Take the last huff."

As my brain became goo and my extremities went numb, I asked, "What happened to your dad?"

"You have really beautiful eyes," he said, his face a foot from mine.

The last thing I remembered before passing out was Max saying that he knew what I wanted. I really hoped he didn't.

As the summer continued, my feelings for Max became more intense, but I didn't know how to process them because I wasn't sure what they were. When Greg and I would go to the Bonham Exchange and watch strippers or check out guys at after-parties, I had a very clear idea of what I wanted from them. I built a small shrine to Keanu Reeves after seeing *My Own Private Idaho*, imagining him to be a delicate lover and an ideal long-term companion. Our fantasy relationship involved a lot of wine, poetry, and travel. Marky Mark would be my closeted booty call. It would only happen once a month, when he came through town, and I'd keep it a secret if I knew what was good for me. I could project myself into a myriad of sexual scenarios with the models from the *International Male* catalog, most of which took place to a sound track by Nine Inch Nails.

When I'd been Greg's best friend, not being able to kiss him had felt like a constant thorn in my side, to the point that being in his presence sometimes felt like torture. But Max was different. I would miss him and ache to hear the sound of his voice, but as soon as I was in his presence, any negative feeling subsided. It wasn't so much that I needed to touch him. I just needed to know that he was close enough that I *could*.

Wanting to be near him was fine, but I kept thinking that I should be wanting less and *doing* more. I was a gay seventeen-year-old who'd just come out to his family. I was supposed to be meeting guys and flirting with them and . . . other stuff. Being an adult gay male surely meant having lots of sex, everywhere, all the time: in beds, on couches, in backyards, in club restrooms, in the backseats of cars. But instead of going to the Bonham with Sylvia or tracking down my gay friends in San Antonio, I was constantly hanging out with a heterosexual skinhead in a tiny town surrounded by aggressive straight guys, males who were so suspicious of my presence that Max had to be my bodyguard. That couldn't be good for my burgeoning sexual identity.

What did it mean that kissing and touching Greg had felt like nothing, yet just being at arm's length from this utterly unattainable boy made me feel like my head was spinning? And as unlikely a lover as Max seemed, why was he hanging out with a tiny goth gay boy? He laughed at all my jokes, hugged me every ten minutes, and had me practically living in his bedroom for half the summer. He told me I had beautiful eyes, for Christ's sake! What heterosexual boy tells a homosexual boy that he has beautiful eyes while lying in bed with him? (Well, maybe one who'd been huffing furniture protector every night since the summer started.)

After that night, I felt an increasing discomfort. Over the next few weeks with Max I became distant: watching myself watch Max, doubting my intention when patting him on the back after he cracked a joke, scanning the room of SHARPs to make sure no one had seen me looking at Max's lips or hands or butt while he talked to someone else. Sylvia sensed it. Sean seemed suspicious. My own mother forced condoms on me simply because I was going to Max's house. It was that obvious. And I had to make sense of it all somehow.

It was the end of July. In a month, school would start. Max was driving me into the sunset with the Lemonheads playing as I processed all these thoughts over and over again in a loop.

"What's wrong, my little Sequined Matador?" Max asked. He rested his hand on my shoulder and it felt like it was burning through my shirt. I leaned forward and turned down the stereo so that his hand would slip away. I had reached a threshold with the amount of physical contact I could receive from him.

"Max, do you like me?"

I could feel my heartbeat begin to race as he leaned forward to turn off the stereo.

"Well, hmmm . . ." Max scratched the little bit of hair on his chin and cleared his throat. "There's a few things," he began slowly while staring ahead, like someone delivering a book report from memory. "No one makes me laugh as much as you do. And I wish you were part of my family. Like, my mom really likes you, and, uh . . ." Max grinned at me and quickly looked away, squirming in his seat a bit. "I guess what I'm saying is, if I *was* gay that would be awesome. Like, I would be your, uh . . . boyfriend for sure, but . . . I'm not," he said with a nervous smile, each cheek dimpling as he morphed into my big toddler skinhead. "I just really like you."

Then he reached out, turned up the stereo, and, in a tuneless baritone, sang the entirety of the Lemonheads' *Lick* album to me.

I had my answer. I could breathe. After weeks of confusion and mixed signals, Max had alleviated all my fears and doubts. I could finally relax, knowing nothing was ever going to happen between us. And in that clearheaded moment following his answer, I looked at his sunlit face singing to the road ahead of us and thought, *Oh, wow. I am so in love with you.*

Warm leatherette:

Here I am in my 1987 baby blue Mercury Lynx. Or as Sylvia called it, "A poor man's Ford Escort."

CHAPTER 26

This ~~Beautiful~~ Creature Must Die

Davis! You have to phone that girl!" My mother had been deflecting Sylvia's calls for weeks. "Honey, your mother cannot handle another desperate call from her. I've given her advice about her brassieres and ingrown toenails and counseled her through a breakup with a bisexual man named Linus," she complained. "Call her, if only to say, 'Leave my poor, sweet mother alone!'"

I called Sylvia that afternoon to catch up. She was broke, single, and lonely. I knew this was all her own doing, but I still felt bad for her. I couldn't find it in my heart to deny her invitation to visit, especially since she still didn't have a car.

"Mom," I asked, "can I go visit Sylvia for just one night?"

"School starts in two weeks and you've been well-behaved all summer. So I'll let you have this one last hurrah."

I didn't tell my mom that the reason I seemed so well-behaved was the chemical stupor I was in from my daily huffing of household products, but I took her up on her offer and drove to San Antonio that night. It would be a relaxing evening in, catching up with an old friend. A night away from my brother-friend-husband-roommate, Max, might help me work out the increasingly tight knot in my heart.

"It's ninety-nine degrees, bitch," said Sylvia as she handed me a Dr. Pepper. "You look like you just jumped out of the river."

"My AC broke," I said, gulping down half the soda before holding it against my sweat-soaked chest.

"Girl, you are just simple white trash with no AC," she said, curling up on a tan recliner covered in cat hair.

"It's probably broken because you sucked all the Freon out."

"At least Ryan has central air-conditioning here."

"Well, Sylvia. At least I have my own car," I replied, chugging the rest of the Dr. Pepper.

Sylvia had been sleeping at her friend Ryan's apartment for a week, ever since Ray-Ray had kicked her out.

"Yeah, girl," she said, with Voltaire in her lap. "He passed out at a party one night, so I took out a Sharpie and wrote all over the bitch. 'MISS THANG' on his forehead and pentagrams on his ass cheeks. He was *not* happy!"

"Sylvia, that's horrible," I said, trying to stifle my laughter at the thought of Ray-Ray's frightful reflection greeting him the next morning.

"I know, Minerva. But I was just havin' a little fun," she said, getting up to pour herself a vodka tonic. "So he lost a few days of work at Dairy Queen! They should loosen up their dress code.

Who's to say it wouldn't be a treat to order a Blizzard from a queen with penises scrawled on his cheeks?" Sylvia almost toppled over laughing at her little prank.

"Sylvia, are we the only ones here tonight?"

"Yep," she sighed, plopping down in her chair/recliner/bed.

"Oh, great. Then we can just bring home burgers from Wendy's and hang out!"

"Bitch, are you crazy?" she said. "We're going out tonight, Minerva!"

"But Sylvia . . ."

"Don't give me no lip, bitchface!" she demanded, stamping out her cigarette so hard that the ashtray spilled over the arm of the chair. "Goddammit! See what my life has been like? Just one bad thing after another! No job. No place of my own. No man and no friends!"

"Well, what about Greg?" I asked. "He hasn't answered his phone in weeks. I assumed y'all were going out and having fun."

"Fun?" she hissed, scooping the butts off the carpet. "I heard Greg went to rehab."

"Greg went to *rehab*?"

"Bitch, are you serious? It was almost two months ago!" she barked, furiously scrubbing the carpet. "Shit went down while you were off in Hicksville with your new daddy."

"He's not my boyfriend."

"Look!" Sylvia was wild-eyed and angry. "You've been MIA. Greg's parents moved him to Alamo Heights High School, and he's a . . . Well, he's a . . ."

"He's a what?"

Sylvia clutched the invisible pearls around her neck. "He's a 'prep' now."

"No!"

"Yes, Minerva," she sighed, as if he'd been murdered. "I saw him in Alamo Heights the other day in a car full of Bowheads listening to Celine Dion. It was awful, David!"

"Oh Sylvia, that's horrible."

"That's what happens when you leave your friends high and dry, Crabb," she said, stomping to the kitchen to refill her vodka. "So we *are* going out tonight. *Capisce?*"

"But I wanted to catch up and just chill."

Sylvia stared at me from the kitchen counter as a fiendish smile spread across her face.

"What? What is it?" I asked. Slowly, she lifted her finger to point at the empty Dr. Pepper bottle beside me. "No," I said. "You didn't."

"You ain't gonna chill tonight. I spiked that Dr. Pepper with two hits of Golden Purse acid!" she exclaimed excitedly, the way you'd wish a five-year-old "Happy Birthday!"

The next few hours were a speedy blur. Golden Purse sounded like a fairly benign name for a hit of acid. Unfortunately, my golden purse was full of nightmares and razor blades. Something foreign and insidious loomed around every corner of Ryan's dark apartment. As I begin to peak, every synaptic center of my brain shut down, as if I was checking out of my own consciousness. I became an emotion-free robot: superfocused, task-oriented, and humorless. I moved quickly through each action like it was part of my programming, like my mind was simply following my body through an endless list of small activities without free will.

Pour a glass of water. Drink the water. The walls seem to be moving. The cigarette between your fingers is growing longer. Your hands

look strange. Look into the mirror. You are hideous. Allow Sylvia
to apply concealer, blush, and mascara to your broken face. You are
now wearing the mask of a gorgeous stranger with lips that sparkle.
Each of Sylvia's breasts has a giant pink eye that will always know if
you're lying. So you will allow her to dress you in her clothes. Now you
are driving her in your car. The roads are full of radioactive snakes
and assorted vermin. The convenience-store cashier has a harelip and
might be Jesus. He knows you're a liar, but he loves you anyway.
Where is your bracelet? Has anyone seen your bracelet? It was just
on your wrist. Harelip doesn't like that you're crying now. Leave. Get
out. Drive some more. Drive farther. You love this song. BUT WHY
IS THIS SONG SO LOUD? The streetlights strobe through the
car's interior as we pass beneath them. Sylvia is beautiful then hid-
eous, beautiful then hideous, beautiful then hideous. She looks like
the angel of death. But in a nice way. You know what? You never
actually liked that bracelet. You can't feel anything. You can feel ev-
erything. How did gum get in your mouth? When will you die? How
will you die? Why will you die?

Let's drive to Waco!

Driving, driving, driving . . .

Sylvia directed me off the highway and down a gravel road.
The moon was beginning to set behind an airplane hangar–
sized warehouse. We parked the car and walked into the tiny
office attached to the front. From up a dark staircase in a thick
Hill County drawl we heard, "How y'all doin'? Come on up!"
As we ascended the staircase, I heard a deep, moaning hum. The
rank, fetid odor of feces and something rotten filled my nostrils.
A sixty-year-old man with a white handlebar mustache wearing
a white ten-gallon cowboy hat welcomed us. He wore a crisp
white suit and looked like the Weight Watchers' "after" photo of

Boss Hogg. He spread his arms like an angel inviting us into an unimaginable Elysium.

"Howdy, y'all! My name is Hank. What brings y'all to the Glendale Slaughterhouse this morning?"

I gripped the balcony and looked out over the endless expanse of cattle. Hundreds of cows were shoved against one another in a massive industrial barn. The hairs on my arm stood up as I thought, *That's just one huge animal in the shape of a big, flat, hairy blanket and it's going to grow larger and soon the whole world will be covered in beady brown eyes and pendulous, drooping udders and we will all be a part of one grotesque, bovine amoeba!*

I could feel my face swell as I turned to Hank. The brim of his cowboy hat was moving in time with his lips as he tried to make awkward conversation. "It's pretty early for y'all to be here on a Sunday, ain't it?" he stammered, the stark white brim of his hat flopping up and down. "What can I do ya for?"

I know what's going on. Hank's hat is really who we're dealing with here. Hank's hat is the ventriloquist, the mastermind behind his entire identity. Hank is just a dummy!

I could tell that Hank's hat psychically perceived my realization as it began to move more violently atop his head. I wanted to scream, *Hank, look out! Your hat is eating your head!*

As Hank stared at us, it occurred to me that I'd been thinking for quite a while. Neither Sylvia nor I had actually been answering Hank's questions. I wanted to say something, but no words came out of my mouth. I looked to Sylvia for help and saw her staring blankly down at the ground, biting her pinky nail and humming. I felt a sharp pain and realized that I'd just hit my pelvis with my fist, trying to beat a response out of my own body. Above me I saw the Glendale Slaughterhouse logo paint-ed on a corrugated metal wall: an image of a grinning, upright-standing cow offering forth a juicy rib eye on a silver platter with its hoofed hand. I thought, *Oh my God. Does that cow know what it is? Does it understand what it's serving? Is that cow a cannibal?*

I turned to Sylvia in a panic. "Sylvia! Am *I* a cannibal?"

Sylvia turned to me like a deer caught in headlights, her face a throbbing psychedelic explosion of black and silver and red. Her mascara-clumped eyelashes looked like the legs of a dozen tarantulas. I realized that she'd brought us there with no game plan. My tour guide down the rabbit hole had become lost in the terrifying field trip of her own making.

Sylvia tried to answer Hank, fumbling with her purse as she piecemealed her story together in real time. "Uh . . . This is my brother and . . . uh, he's in the 4-H Club and, well . . ." Sylvia dug deeper into her purse as key chains jingled and zippers un-zipped. "Well, I'm . . . Uh . . . Oh! I'm buying him a COW!" As she pulled out her empty checkbook, an impossible number of tampons exploded from her purse, like some kind of femi-nine hygiene fireworks display. No fewer than twenty of them rocketed through the air before landing on the metal-grate floor between Hank and us.

Hank stared at us like he was considering drawing his weap-on. It occurred to me that he must have been really confused as to what two people like Sylvia and I were doing at the Glendale Slaughterhouse at the crack of dawn on a Sunday. How many boys with a future in agriculture wear rhinestone brooches and "Perfectly Pink" MAC lip balm?

"MOOOOOO!"

We looked over the balcony at a swollen, pregnant cow lying

on her side with a pool of blood coming from her back end. I could feel the strychnine in the acid tighten and shrink my guts into a knot the size of a tennis ball. The cow looked up at me with big, wet, tired eyes and let out a long, exhausted groan, as if to say, *There are days . . . and there are days.*

"Oh. Uh, sorry," Hank said as he ran down the stairs. "Y'all wait here for a minute!"

As soon as he left, Sylvia threw her arms around me and began to sob.

"This is too much, girl! I can't handle it. I'm gonna have a conniption fit or a seizure or something!"

Just then, Hank appeared below us with a rifle. "Y'all might wanna turn away!"

I stared transfixed into the cow's eyes and for a brief, chemical-induced moment thought I could feel her psychically invade my mind. I could feel the pain of her long, confined life and empathize with what she'd endured and was about to experience. I wanted to look away, but I couldn't, hypnotized by the car crash but also feeling like I owed it to her to bear witness to this final humiliation.

I am a superfocused, task-oriented robot, and this is part of my program tonight.

The bang of Hank's gun was so loud that it muted every sound after it. I was suddenly running—over the metal grating, down the stairs, through the gravel parking lot. I sprinted to my baby-blue '87 Mercury Lynx and jumped inside. As I shifted the car into reverse, I felt a combination of terror and elation that I had been born into the body of a human and not a cow. I was peeling out of the lot when I heard a familiar shriek and realized I'd forgotten something: Sylvia. In the rearview mirror I saw her trip and fall in her four-inch heels. She became a whirling dervish of black gauze, spinning and struggling to regain her composure like Leatherface in that final, iconic scene from *The Texas Chainsaw Massacre*.

"Go!" she screamed, slamming the car door shut. "GOOOO!!!"

Twenty minutes later we silently shuffled back into Ryan's house, covered in a fine mist of sweat and dust, like zombies who'd been working construction jobs.

"I need to be alone," said Sylvia, staring blankly at a spot on my chest through tear-filled eyes. "I'll be in my room for . . . forever."

Down the hall, I heard Sylvia lock Ryan's bedroom door. I lay down on the couch, but my eyelids were superglued open. My guts were churning and my jaw was clenched so tightly that I thought my bite would shatter my teeth. I surveyed the living room, full of old pizza boxes and overflowing ashtrays. A water bong was knocked over in the corner and a pool of stinking pot-water had soaked into the carpeting around it. Fruit flies buzzed over a kitchen sink full of dirty dishes. Everything was covered in cat hair and dust and smelled like musty tobacco.

Outside, I heard voices. I ran to the venetian blinds and cautiously peeked out, like someone in a crack house expecting a raid. Across the street, a husband and wife in their midthirties were walking down their sidewalk with their kids, a boy about three and a girl around seven. They were the picture of nuclear, suburban bliss. They looked fit and tan and well-rested. The kids giggled as their mom helped them into the backseat of their car. She was slender and petite, with long blond hair and a knee-length floral dress fitted at the waist. Her husband helped her into the passenger's seat, kissed her on the cheek, and shut the door. He walked around the SUV to the driver's side while swinging his keys on his finger and whistling. He looked so boring in his stupid slacks. He was clean-shaven and wore a styled newscaster helmet of brown hair. I smirked and thought, *Wow. I will* never *be that boring. I will* never *be like them.*

To my right, I caught a glimpse of myself in the mirror over the couch. My stomach did another somersault as Dick and Jane started their car across the street. Looking at my reflection, I saw that my hair had become completely mashed to the left side of my head. I was covered in a glistening sheen of sweat that had washed away the powder on my face. A horrible, subterranean zit had begun to swell on my right cheek. Sylvia's thick application of eyeliner had run down both of my cheeks. I looked like a dandy teenage coal miner in a heat wave.

Everything was crooked, dripping, misplaced, and sad. As the happy family outside zoomed away, my reflection reminded me, *You will never be like them.*

Sometime later I woke up to a clock that read 7:37. It meant nothing to me. I'd slept for either thirty minutes or twelve hours. I knocked on Sylvia's locked bedroom door, but she didn't answer. I slipped on my shoes and walked to the driveway. Observing the quality of light outdoors still didn't help me figure out the time. So I sat in my car and smoked for twenty minutes until I could tell that the sky was getting darker, not brighter. I'd been asleep on the couch for half a day.

I drove with the windows down, letting the warm August wind blow through my hair. I bought a pack of gum, a Slurpee, and Marlboro Ultra Lights with my last eight dollars. The pregnant, 7-Eleven clerk looked at me fearfully throughout our exchange, keeping one of her hands out of sight behind the counter. In the car, I looked at myself in the mirror. I was a paler, more corpsey-looking version of the person I'd been that morning, the creep who'd watched that family through the window like a junkie sniper.

As the sun disappeared and the stars came out, I drove, and drove, and drove.

CHAPTER 27

It All Gets Blown Away

Greg had disappeared. Sylvia was too much. San Antonio was no more a home to me than Seguin, where I was starting my senior year. I toned down my look for the first day and wore a vest over a T-shirt and blue jeans with combat boots. I wore my hair down and shaggy, and not a drop of makeup. Unfortunately, the day before I'd gotten baked and overplucked my eyebrows to within an inch of their lives.

"Honey, what's wrong?" my mother asked at dinner. "You look worried . . . or suspicious . . . Are you surprised?"

The next day at school, I felt like an alien. In spite of my toned-down clothing, some of the kids were still perplexed by me. By midweek I had the nickname "RuPaul," which reminded me how far from the real world I was. Seguin kids were so taken aback by me that their nearest cultural reference point was a seven-foot-tall, black drag queen.

That first week of school was the longest I'd been away from Max. On Friday morning I put my weekend bag in the trunk of my car and slogged through the day, which was full of atrocities. I met one of the "alternative" kids in first period, but he'd somehow never heard of the Violent Femmes. At lunch I was forced to tuck in my T-shirt by a one-hundred-year-old science teacher with a tracheotomy. After English class I watched a hallway fight between two Hispanic girls, who were coating their faces with Vaseline between blows.

"Why do they do that?" I asked a girl with a long braided ponytail under her cowboy hat.

"Aw, hell, RuPaul. Don't you know nothin'?" she replied. "Keeps their faces from gettin' scratched. Those wetbacks are smart!"

I couldn't leave fast enough when the 3 p.m. bell rang. Max's mother was the only person home when I got to their house. We sat on the couch in silence, watching television.

"Have you talked to Max today?" she finally asked.

"No. Why?" I asked, eating a bag of Cool Ranch Doritos she'd given me.

"No reason. How is school going? As awful as you'd thought?"

"It's pretty crappy. I can't believe my mom moved us to that town."

"Your mom does the best she can," Ruth said sharply. "It's hard."

"Oh. Sorry," I said, realizing I'd upset her. "I didn't mean anything. I just . . ."

"No, I'm sorry," she said, patting my leg and getting up. "I had a long night."

The front door opened and Ruth went to the foyer. I could hear her and Max exchanging heated words.

"You call next time, dammit," she said, storming down the hall to her bedroom.

"Hey, mister," said Max behind me as he grabbed my shoulders. I looked up from the couch and saw his upside-down face smiling at me. "How's my little Sequined Matador?"

In Max's room, we sat against his bed. He let out a long, tired sigh and pulled out a can of Scotchgard from beneath his bed.

"Max, I can't," I said, placing my hand over his on the canister.

"Aww, come on, man."

"No. I just don't want to get fucked up for a while," I said, still reeling from the slaughterhouse trip with Sylvia.

He slid the Scotchgard back under the bed and told me about his first week at school, mentioning a bunch of names I'd never heard before. He seemed jumpy and preoccupied, getting up every fifteen minutes to take a phone call.

"So we're going to my friend Jamie's party tonight."

"Cool," I shrugged. "Who's Jamie?"

"She's this girl I used to date," Max answered, beckoning me into the kitchen. "It'll be cool," he said, taking out two thermoses and looking down the hall to make sure Ruth wasn't coming. "Mom's pissed at me because I stayed out last night."

"Like, all night?"

"Yeah, but I was just with Sean," he said, pouring me a rum and Coke and tightening the lid. "She didn't have to freak out so much."

"Well, she was probably worried about you."

Max stopped pouring and stared at me like I'd challenged him.

"What?" I asked. "I'd be worried about you too."

In his car we shared a joint. As the interior filled with smoke and the sun set, his dimples came out and everything started to feel right. I told him about the crazed, Vaseline-faced girls of Seguin High School and he detailed all Sean's dumb, macho antics at the previous night's party. I pulled out our case of mixtapes and popped one in the cassette player. We tooled through New Braunfels for an hour, laughing and singing, driving nowhere in particular.

"Hey, I need to make a pit stop," Max said, popping in a different mixtape and pressing "play." We pulled off the road and drove through a grove of trees as "That's When I Reach for My Revolver" blasted through the speakers. Bleary-eyed and baked, we screamed the song out the windows. Each beat of the drum hit like a sledgehammer crashing down on the lonely, Max-less week that had preceded this night. At the end of a dirt road we arrived at a small pond. Three cars were parked in a circle with their hazard lights blinking. A group of a dozen or so SHARPs sat on the cars' hoods and bumpers, drinking beers and smoking cigarettes.

"Stay here," said Max as he parked the car. "I'll be right back."

I grabbed the door handle, starting to get out. "Well, I can go if—"

"No!" he barked. "Stay here!"

Max walked toward the group and greeted them. He shook hands and hugged some of the guys in that awkward masculine way, making sure their torsos didn't touch while aggressively patting each other's backs. I recognized Sean and a few other guys, but most of them were older SHARPs I'd never seen.

Slowly the group started to walk in a circle, like roosters—

the way they had that night at Club FX two years earlier. As the SHARPs marched and thrashed their heads, clouds of dust rose from the ground and hovered in the orange light of the blinking flashers. In the spaces between their pacing bodies I noticed a boy, around fourteen. Through the haze I realized it was Rocky, the little, ginger-headed kid with freckles I'd seen at SHARP parties before. One by one, the SHARPs began taunting Rocky and smacking his head, pushing him back and forth across the circle between them like a beach ball. The kid took the abuse for a while, his fists clenched at his sides. He sneered at them to seem threatening, but he looked like a frightened kid in his older brother's oversize, big-boy clothes. As they called him a pussy, a little bitch, and a faggot, my body slid deeper into the passenger seat. I was becoming small. I wanted to disappear.

It wasn't until one of the SHARPs spit in Rocky's face that the kid reacted, spinning and screaming as he punched blindly anywhere he could, like an angry dreidel. His reaction was immediately crushed by a dozen angry SHARPs, all punching, kicking, and beating him at once. As a great, flashing cloud of dust enveloped them, I could hear the kid scream and cough, but he never yelled, "Stop!"

In the blinking hazard lights I caught glimpses of Max's face—a sneer of teeth and saliva, an open, screaming mouth, a tightened, swinging fist. After a few moments the group stopped. As the cloud of dust around them dissipated, I could see them standing in a circle and looking down.

"Get up," yelled Max.

Rocky stayed on the ground in a ball, covering his head and begging, "Please, please, please . . ."

As Max reached down and helped the boy up, I thought I saw a trace of the friend I knew. Max threw Rocky's arm around his shoulder and helped him limp to a car, where he leaned against the hood. The kid's bottom lip was broken in the middle, oozing a solid crimson line of blood that ran down the center of his chin, neck, and chest. A mound of swelling flesh surrounded his eye. Max smiled flatly, rubbed Rocky's head, and embraced him. And then they all did. The fight club morphed into an agro love-in as the boys started hugging and shaking hands and passing each other beers.

In the blinking lights I caught Sean looking in my direction. The smile evaporated from his face as he realized I was there.

"What the fuck?" he asked Max, pointing at me. "You brought him?"

"Yeah. So what?" Max replied.

"That's not fucking cool, man." Sean marched to the passenger door and kicked it, glaring at me. "This shit isn't *for* him."

"Calm the fuck down," Max said. "He's cool."

"Oh yeah?" replied Sean, shoving his index finger in Max's chest. "Who says?"

"I SAY!" said Max, his voice bellowing through the trees.

Sean smirked at me through the car window and knocked on the glass, saying, "Hey Davey. Why don't you roll down the window?"

I reached for the window crank before Max barked, "Do *not* roll it down!"

"I said roll down the fucking window!" Sean screamed. Slowly I rolled it down, my hands shaking as the other SHARPs began to circle the car. "So Davey," Sean said with a huge, mocking grin as he leaned through the open window, "wanna join the club?"

"Come the fuck on, Sean," said Max. "Leave him alone."

"Let's make him a SHARP, Max! He's your best fucking friend, right?"

The SHARPs surrounded the car now, each of them still breathing hard from the beatdown they'd just given Rocky. As they glared at me through the windshield, it occurred to me that they weren't worn out but warmed up. All I could think about was the gun.

Did the gun belong to one of them, or was it one of their dads'? Was I just really messed up that night and only thought I saw a gun? If the gun belonged to one of them, did they have it on their person? Was Sean about to grin a little bigger at me and tap the shiny, black tip of that gun on the windshield?

"Get out!" yelled Sean as he reached out and opened the door. Max jumped in front of him and slammed it, grabbing Sean's shirt and shoving him away. The other SHARPs looked at the two of them, and then at one another. Instead of retreating, they each took a few steps closer to the car. It was the first time I'd seen Max's authority met with anything other than immediate obedience. He was the only person in my corner, and he couldn't protect me alone. In the rearview mirror I saw two guys standing by the trunk. Another with a bullring in his nose leaned down to stare at me through the driver's-side window. Through the settling dust ahead of me I could see Rocky limping forward with a glimmer in his eye, a look that suggested that he wanted to beat me more than anyone. And who could blame him? By beating me *with* them, he could really commune with this club he'd just joined. I was the guy they could *all* get their rocks off on by pulverizing. There wouldn't be limits with me. They wouldn't have to be careful. It wasn't a beat-in or an initiation. I was an outsider. And I was in the wrong place.

In the tension of the standoff I felt like my senses were heightened. I could hear the distant hum of traffic on I-35, the Doppler waves of crickets in the woods, the mechanical click of the car stereo turning the cassette over.

Click.

Suddenly, and with overwhelming volume, Erasure's "Oh L'Amour" began to pulse from the car stereo. I sat still, too afraid to move, worried that reaching to mute the sound system would be perceived as gayer than the sound of the song itself. So I sat there, with my Patty Duke bob and my rum and Coke, surrounded by skinheads, as Andy Bell longingly wailed, *"Mon amour. What's a boy in love supposed to do?"*

It was as if time stopped, like they were all too stunned by the sheer queerness of the song to care as Max slid into the driver's seat. The plaintive, fey cry of the lisping vocalist was too shocking for them to process as Max started the car. The propulsive twinkle of synthetic harpsichords was such a diversion that all they could do was stand there as we drove away.

In actuality, the sweet, giddy sound of Erasure probably didn't hypnotize anyone. I think it enraged them so much that allowing Max to leave was the only way they could be sure they wouldn't kill me.

We emerged from the grove of trees and onto the highway as a fine mist of rain coated the windshield. We didn't speak. I felt like I should appreciate Max in that moment, as if I should've been thankful to him for getting me out of there. But what I couldn't stop thinking about was that *he* was the one who had brought me. Max, like Sylvia before him, was the one who exposed me to the very danger he saved me from. So I didn't feel protected. I wasn't impressed or turned on. I was disappointed. Half an hour ago I'd been with my best friend. But now I was in the car with a sadistic, macho shithead, one of those monsters from the dance floor two years ago. My *new* best friend had just become nothing more than the guy who had beaten up my *old* best friend.

"Look, that was just an initiation, okay?" he said after a long spell of silence. "Will you fucking talk to me?"

"What do you want me to say?"

"I don't just go out and beat people up, okay? I used to, but not anymore."

"Well, Sean does, I bet."

"I'm not Sean," yelled Max. "He enjoys it too much. It's not supposed to be fun."

"Then what's the fucking point of it?" I yelled at him, for the first time. "Why would you want to do that to someone? To anyone?"

"What?" Max said, looking at me with genuine bewilderment.

"Why would you do that if it doesn't make anyone feel good?"

"You don't understand, David."

But I did understand. And I knew it was beneath Max. And I couldn't shake the feeling that my watching it happen had sullied our friendship. "Why would you fucking bring me to that?"

"Why shouldn't you be able to go?" he sneered.

"Because I'm not like you," I murmured, more aware of it than I'd ever been. "And I don't want to be." I stared in silence at the road the rest of the way home, knowing that I couldn't take back what I'd just said.

At 4 a.m. I woke up in Max's room, and he was gone. I crept to the living room and saw him sitting alone on the couch, cycling through cable channels, watching nothing on a loop and clicking the remote every fifteen seconds. I wanted to talk about what had happened, but a part of me didn't care what Max was thinking. A certain feeling I'd had for him was no longer there. Looking at the back of his stubbly head and thick neck, silhouetted by the big-screen TV, I wondered if I hadn't misinterpreted that "familiar feeling" I'd always had for Max. Perhaps I felt so close to him for all the wrong reasons. He wasn't a kindred spirit; he was a repressed memory.

The next morning I woke up under a blanket on the floor. Max was asleep in his bed. I got dressed, grabbed my bag, and quietly headed down the hall to leave.

"David?" I heard Ruth say. I turned to see her in the kitchen, making breakfast. "Where are you off to so early?"

"I have to get back home."

"But it's Saturday morning. You boys have the whole weekend."

"Sorry, I just need to get home."

"Oh," she said. She wiped her hands on a dish towel and walked up to me, taking my hands in hers. There was a frailty in her eyes that I'd never seen before. She had always been affectionate and sensitive, but there was something else there now—something damaged, tired, and a little bit broken.

"David, you know how much Max loves you?"

"Um," I replied, taken aback.

"Well, I do too," she said. "It's nice to have you around. You're a good influence."

She looked into my eyes for a long time, like she was going to say something else. But all that came out was, "Thank you."

On the drive home I couldn't stop thinking about what Ruth had said. How was I anyone's "good influence"? I was a queer, moody, drug-taking, school-skipping brat. I'd cost my father thousands of dollars and then broken his heart, and abandoned my mother when she needed me most. I thought about my own mom, and how Max played the same "good influence" role for her. How could two such bad kids be good for anyone, let alone each other?

In the kitchen at home, my mother was cooking herself lunch.

"Honey, you're home!" she said, surprised to see me. "Mike took the kids to see their mom today, and I wasn't expecting you."

"Yeah," I replied, "I was feeling sick and decided to come back."

"Well, let me feel your forehead," she said, bending my face down to her cheek. "Oh, you're a little warm."

I've probably been "warm" for an entire year, I thought.

"How about we stay in and watch a movie?" she asked, handing me a cold washcloth for my head. "Your mother hasn't watched a scary movie with you in ages."

Ten minutes later we were curled up on the couch with bowls of soup, watching *Rosemary's Baby*. I'd taken a cold shower and put on comfortable clothes: gym shorts, ankle socks, and a huge shirt with a leprechaun on it.

"I'm sorry. But when a neighbor you barely know whose niece just committed suicide brings you a chalky mousse to eat, you do not eat it!" declared my mom. "*Especially* in New York City. This Rosemary is not the brightest star in the sky."

An hour into the movie, I started to fall asleep. I felt my mother's lips kiss my forehead and heard the delicate tinkling of spoons in bowls as she took our dirty dishes into the kitchen. I could feel my body sinking deeper into the couch, and I wasn't fighting it. I felt tired and toxic. And as a screaming Mia Farrow was impregnated with the spawn of the devil on a black silk bed, I felt something I hadn't felt in a long time. I felt like I was home.

The Moby Dick of oversized sculptures of legume replicas: Seguin's giant pecan.

CHAPTER 28

Being Boring

My senior year was going to be the year I became a "teenager." I surrendered: to my family, to school, to Seguin. I no longer saw the three people who'd meant the most to me: Greg, Sylvia, and Max. I'd lost Greg somewhere in San Antonio to a new crew who wore loafers and went to Glee Club. Sylvia was probably waiting somewhere in a clown mask with a bag of PCP-laced cat turds. And Max, he just didn't call anymore. It was like we both knew something had splintered and we agreed, without words, to let it stay that way. I wanted new friends—friends who wouldn't get me beat up or trick me into smoking crack or enter my body with produce. I wanted to feel what *normal* felt like. And I assumed it was somewhere on the spectrum between being a khaki-wearing wallflower and a Freon-huffing slaughterhouse creeper.

I made a concerted effort to settle into life in Seguin. I sanded down my rough edges a bit and chopped off most of my hair. In the country it was easier to find open spaces to feel alone in, Primitive Baptist cemeteries not included. Each day after school I'd drive down a long dirt road ten minutes from our house. I'd park my little blue car by an open field with an abandoned shed in it. I would take my shirt off and lie in the grass, reading my first-semester English assignment, *Brave New World*, over and over again. By October I had an honest-to-God tan. I had never known that my skin could gain, let alone maintain, actual pigment. A thing called *grunge* was screaming its way onto mainstream radio, which I inadvertently familiarized myself with thanks to the thin wall between my and my little brother's bedrooms. Before bed, I'd listen to a muffled Eddie Vedder screaming as I sketched, which I hadn't done since I was a little kid.

The strangest part of my life during the fall of 1992 was really just the act of going to class. The routine of it felt like such a novelty. But it really wasn't so bad once I got used to the rhythm of it. I even decided to involve myself in a thing called an "extra-curricular activity," which my guidance counselor had suggested would help me "get into college." Somehow, I managed to hold in my guffaw at her suggestion.

Since I was drawing again and had always been interested in theater, I decided to join the set-design crew for the Seguin High School production of *Into the Woods*. The job itself was fine, but I'd overlooked one very troubling part of it: being around "theater people." Loud, jubilant girls and flaming, overenunciating boys surrounded me every day after school. For the first few weeks I wanted to turn the nail gun on myself. Then I imagined turning it on the cast as Ministry's "Stigmata" roared over the PA.

Then I'd take a deep breath and remind myself, *David, this is part of the process. And you're on their turf, not the other way around.*

One afternoon I noticed some girls rehearsing onstage. One of them was a big, blond, cheery girl with sunlight virtually blasting out of her face. She had bright-blue eyes and massive, orblike boobs. She was playing one of Cinderella's evil stepsisters.

"I wish to go the festival. The festival? The festival!"

It should have driven me to nail-gun my ears closed. But this one girl's booming presence and incredible voice made it all okay. Every day, she cracked me up. I'd howl with laughter from the back of the auditorium while gluing sequins onto a wooden cow or spray-painting cornstalks onto a curtain. No one else seemed to pay attention to rehearsals, too involved in school gossip or Sadie Hawkins Dance planning to notice the incredible talent in acid-washed jeans singing before them.

Her name was Molly O'Brien. She noticed my laughter and eventually started playing to the back of the house, looking directly at me from the stage. I was her one-man audience—her audient, if you will. When we finally met I was nervous, like I was meeting someone I'd seen a lot on television. Ten minutes later I felt like I knew everything about her. Molly loved the beach and sweet cocktails and Janet Jackson. She sang in choir and was always busting out in huge explosions of song. She was the bizarro Sylvia. If Max was the mayor of freaks in New Braunfels, Molly was the queen of pep in Seguin.

She introduced me to her social clique, and soon my circle of friends consisted of girls in Daisy Dukes with spiral perms and boys on the basketball team who wore flannel shirts and loved Stone Temple Pilots. I felt like Jane Goodall, observing myself in an exotic locale while thinking, *I can't let them know I'm* not *one of them.*

My being gay was a novelty for about a week. And then I was just . . . Dave.

The structure of my social life became vastly different. A year earlier, I'd been snorting poppers with Sylvia and driving downtown to watch transsexual hookers fight behind the Alamo. But now I was riding in the back of someone's mom's Geo Metro squeezed tight with six people going to football games, cheering with a bunch of bros and blondes as the Sequined Matadors burst through a giant piece of craft paper onto the field. My new friends had curfews and part-time jobs, and so did I. By Christmas I'd moved from my dishwashing job at the Holiday Inn to a retail job at Seguin's only music store, Hastings. I hated wearing the green apron and the price-gun belt, but the position made me significantly cooler to my new group of friends, whom Molly had named the Freedom Club, after George Michael's 1992 hit song.

The Freedom Club was a far cry from my former life, and I could sometimes hear Sylvia's running monologue in response to our tame escapades. When we adorned Molly's dad's old VW van with rainbow colors and painted *Freedom Van* on the side, I could imagine Sylvia turning up her nose and shrieking, *Minerva! Get me away from these Goody-fuckin'-Two-Shoes before I get a cavity!*

I imagined her on our spring-break trip to the beach, when our friend Cindy told us that she'd snuck something "crazy" into her purse and wanted to "party." I braced myself for Sylvia's brand of "crazy" and "party." I thought, *Well, I am eighteen now. Maybe it's time I tried mainlining heroin through a syringe that someone stole from their diabetic father. After all, it is spring break.* Then Cindy pulled a tiny bottle of grape liqueur from her Liz Claiborne purse and erupted into giggles. As I hooted and chanted "Party!" with everyone else in the van, I felt like the Johnny Depp character in *21 Jump Street*. I'd become a narc, a twenty-six-year-old undercover police officer with a very youthful complexion who was *this* close to busting a high school dope ring.

That duplicitous feeling was entirely gone by the time we graduated. It had taken a year, but I didn't feel like an impostor anymore. I'd become . . . a teenager. And just in time.

On graduation day, a hundred of us stood in the town square wearing our mustard-yellow gowns. We were arranged alphabetically before walking onstage, and I could barely see the members of the Freedom Club through the mass of seniors. After walking across the stage, I opened my rolled-up "degree" to see that it was, as we'd been told, just a blank piece of paper. I laughed to myself at how appropriate this seemed, but I wasn't sure why.

Afterward, Molly bounced toward me through the crowd and threw her arms around my neck. She took my hand in hers and with a giant, sunny smile, asked, "Are you excited?!"

Just then I noticed that ridiculous pecan on its pedestal behind her. Much of its outer layer was gone now. It looked like a giant ball of chalk that someone had clumsily poured chocolate malt over. It was defeated and broken, a piece of sculptural trash that no one wanted. I felt bad for the big pecan, the way I'd felt bad for Charlie Brown's sad Christmas tree as a kid. I wondered why saving it wasn't a priority for anyone.

"David," Molly said, rubbing my hands in hers, "I'm so glad you came here and we got to know each other."

"Yeah. Me too," I said as we hugged.

Over her shoulder I noticed something. There was a paper sign blowing in the breeze beneath Seguin's famous giant pecan. It had been bright yellow once, but now it was a pale tan from exposure to sunlight and moisture. I squinted to make out the bleeding text under the thin laminate cover.

Restoration Coming Summer of 1993!

A week later, a new nut was unveiled. It was a ten-foot oblong balloon painted to look like a pecan. It wasn't exactly a restoration. I had no earthly idea who'd thought this would solve the whole shooting problem, but it felt like good news. It sat in the scorching sun behind a chain-link fence in an ugly part of town.

"It's not exactly charming, is it?" said my mother, making a face at it and wiping her brow with a tissue. "Good Lord, son. Let's get your mother a cold Coke!"

When we got home from seeing the pecan, my acceptance letter to Southwest Texas State University was in the mail. It was a school about twenty minutes down the road in a big college town called San Marcos. My mother jumped around the kitchen like a maniac, calling all her friends while digging through her Tupperware crafting tub for a frame to mount the letter in. I felt strangely suspicious of it, thinking, *Their automated mailing system must be on the fritz. This must be a mistake. What is wrong with this institution that they would have me attend it?*

I shared these concerns with my mom as she hung laundry outside.

"David. Don't question it! Just start class!"

"But I don't even know what I want to study."

"Honey, just soak up the experience! You'll love college. There will be so many boys there. And a lot of them will be like you . . . homosexuals!"

"God, Mom. Please don't—"

"No, David. Look at your mother. You've got to learn to own that word! Just think," she said, holding a wet towel over her heart as tears welled in her eyes, "you can bring home a boyfriend to meet your mother!"

"But it's not the end of the world if I don't meet anyone."

"Hush with that! You're going to meet someone special! Maybe someone with an 'athletic build.' You like 'jocks,' right, honey? You call them 'jocks'?"

"Why are we talking about this?" I said, trying to shield myself behind a hanging sheet.

"Open and honest," she sighed, her warning cue for oversharing, "I didn't hang up the phone the other day when you were on with Molly talking about your 'type.'"

"Mom!"

"I just want you to be happy," she said, taking my hand. "You can bring home anyone, and if you love him, so will we. He could be black or Asian or even . . . handicapped!" she shouted with glee. "Your stepfather will build a ramp into this house if that's what it takes for you to have the love you deserve!" She dropped her laundry basket and threw her arms around my neck. "And he can be in family portraits with us! We'll have professional photos done at Montgomery Ward by *someone* in this town who isn't a bigot!" she railed. "Fight the power, honey! You're here! You're queer! I'm USED to it!"

The PFLAG brochures arrived a few days later.

My dad and I were still dancing around what he called my *issue*, but he was proud of me for getting into college. I think he was also simply happy I was alive. During a brief senior-year spell of family therapy with a woman named Barbara Battle, I had admitted almost every infraction: the lies, the sneaking around, and the drug use. Spending an hour in a small room with an older woman while his queer son explained how LSD made him feel was a lot for my dad. He'd leave the sessions pale and tired. Afterward, at dinner, he'd be listless, staring blankly at his plate of enchiladas. Three weeks into our sessions I went on a very long tangent, explaining the time I wore a corset and heels to *The Rocky Horror Picture Show*.

"How did that make you feel?" asked Barbara.

"Alive!" I responded. "And everyone told me I looked great!"

That was our last session. Thank God I never brought up the pickles.

At least he stopped asking me in his clinical way about being a "homosexual." As many hurdles as we'd jumped, it was still awkward when anything remotely gay came up in his presence. When we were on our way to buy textbooks a week before my freshman year of college started, a story came on the car radio about how Greg Louganis, the famous Olympic diver, had just come out of the closet. The word *gay* kept repeating through the speakers.

"Gay—blah blah blah—homosexual tendencies—blah blah blah—queer identity—blah blah blah . . . sex with other men . . ."

It was like that horrible moment when you're watching a movie with your family and you realize too late that it's full of explicit language and graphic sex. The next thing you know, you're in full rigor mortis beside your ninety-eight-year-old aunt Ruby, thinking, *Dear God. When will this rape scene in real time be OVER?*

At the end of the segment they played a clip of Greg Louganis being interviewed about his sexuality and HIV-positive status. At first I was embarrassed for him, saying these things out loud. The feelings he was expressing belonged hidden in notebooks and behind the locked doors of therapists' offices, not on National Public Radio. Shouldn't he be ashamed? And shouldn't I be ashamed? As he spoke, his voice began to crack and wane. In the silences between his words I could hear the sound of a man trying to compose himself, trying his best to focus on the message at hand and not his feelings. As the segment came to an end, he talked about the rejection he felt from his friends and family, especially his father. His emotions overcame him, and the silence between his words was suddenly filled with quiet weeping.

"What an asshole," I said, not meaning to express what I felt out loud, something I usually excelled at in my father's presence.

It was quiet for a moment. And then my dad smiled at me.

"I don't understand why parents would love their kids less because of that," he said, his lip trembling a bit. "Seems to me like it's the reason you have to love 'em even more."

As we turned into the bookstore parking lot, I wished I hadn't made fatherhood so hard for my dad. I wished I hadn't tried to keep so many parts of myself a secret from him. And I wished I hadn't thrown out that greeting card.

That night, I walked into a house party in Seguin and immediately heard him.

"DUDE!"

Max stood at the opposite side of the apartment through a crowd of forty people. He rushed toward me and picked me up off the ground, hugging me for so long I had to say, "Max, you're hurting me."

"David! Oh man, I've missed you," he said, flashing his dimples and rubbing the top of my head. "My little Sequined Matador!"

His hair had grown in, and he was a bit stockier. He was still wearing his big black boots, but the tiny suspenders were gone. He introduced me to a petite, demure girl with pink bangs and oxblood boots.

"Max has told me so much about you," she said, shaking my hand with the strength of a light breeze.

"This is Lori," he beamed, handing me a rum and Coke. "She's my girlfriend."

Max grabbed a six-pack of beer, and the three of us sat on the grass in the front yard. Max told me how his mom was doing and what his senior year had been like. He caught me up on his sisters and told me about the part-time job he'd gotten at a video store.

"How shitty has Seguin been?" he asked.

"Actually, it turned out okay," I said, passing him another beer. "Once I found the right people it was nice, actually."

"The right people make everything okay," said Lori, grabbing Max's hand and looking at him intently, clearly in love, like she couldn't see past him. For a moment I thought I saw him blush, which I'd never seen before.

"How's New Braunfels?" I asked him.

"It's kind of lame there now. But I'm starting college in San Marcos soon."

"Wait," I said, "I'm starting college there too!"

"Oh, dude! We can party together!" yelled Max, toasting me with his can of Foster's and downing it in one giant slurp.

We caught up on music we loved, ranted about social injustices, laughed about our weird-ass parents, and complained about politicians and small towns and our minimum-wage jobs. We talked until 3 a.m. about whether our classes were near each other's and when I'd be able to visit his mom and how he wanted me to crash over at his place soon.

"It's gonna be awesome," Max said as he hugged me good night. I held on to him a little too long, remembering how large he was and how his body always felt warmer than anyone else's, like it was on high heat. I'd forgotten the way he smelled and hadn't realized how much I'd missed it. As we let go of each other, I remembered something.

"Max! Remind me I still have your shirt."

"My shirt?"

"The one you gave me when I puked all over myself the first night we met."

"My big leprechaun shirt?" he exclaimed, grabbing me by the shoulders and grinning. "Awww, man! I missed that shirt." He pulled me in and joyfully crushed me in a too-tight bear hug. "And I missed you too."

"Come on, drunky," said Sarah, smiling as she pulled him toward her car. "He doesn't know his own strength," she whispered, winking at me as she led him away.

I started my car and pulled away a few minutes later. Twenty feet down the street, Max jumped in the middle of the road, flagging me down to stop. Sarah stood by her parked car, rolling her eyes and mouthing, "Sorry, David."

Max gestured for me to roll down the window and leaned inside the car.

"Hey," he mumbled, his drunken gaze slipping from my eyes to my shoulder as he spoke, "listen to this!"

He handed me a Memorex cassette. The case was covered in both of our handwriting.

"This one is my favorite. I still listen to it all the time."

"Thanks, Max. You still have these?"

"You got my shirt in the breakup. And I got the tapes," he said, resting his chin on the window ledge of the door. "Hey, man. Um, I just need to say something."

"Max, you don't have to say—"

"Shhh," he said, reaching down with his fumbling hand to hush my mouth but accidentally covering my entire face. "No, it's just . . . I'm sorry."

"I am too, Max."

"You?" he asked. "Why are you sorry?"

A car behind us honked as Sarah skipped into the road to grab Max.

"Baby, let's get you out of the road and home. You're drunk."

"Okay, uh . . ." The rest of his sentence faded away as they walked back to Sarah's car.

As she stopped him from tripping over the curb and helped him into her car, I popped the tape into the jam box in the passenger seat. He waved good-bye with a huge grin as I pulled away, our favorite song thundering through my cheap, tinny speakers.

She tuned the radio 'til music was around us
A rushing calm around my heart I knew had found us

Some of the friends I'd made in Seguin were nice enough to invite me to hang out after prom. I was dateless and didn't actually attend. But they picked me up in a limo afterward. Because it was a special occasion I blew out my hair and put on a paisley tie. This is one of those moments during which I was overtaken by the feeling that I was supposed to be somewhere else, in spite of how much fun I was having. I think my hands nervously picking at my jeans and the far-off gaze out the limousine window say it all.

My Seguin friends
called themselves
the Freedom Club.
Here we are with the
Freedom Van.

CHAPTER 29

Here's Where the Story Ends

I was supposed to be in my art history class. I loved that class. I liked sitting in the stadium seats of that cold, dark room, looking at slides of famous works of art. It was almost Thanksgiving and we'd moved into pop art, my favorite period, full of romanticized representations of Coke bottles, comic-book panels, and vacuum cleaners, ordinary stuff that someone turned into "art" by placing it on a pedestal or under a glass box. I wanted to be there that day, shivering in the hyperactive air-conditioning, looking at a stack of soup cans that transcended themselves because someone loved them so much. I was supposed to be in that classroom, not standing in a black suit in the rain.

The minister finished his sermon and a few members of the family approached the casket, placing their hands on it or whispering to it, as if the dead person inside could hear them. I hadn't expected so many people to be there, so many kids I hadn't seen in ages, wearing makeshift, not-quite-matching black suits and baby-doll dresses carefully tailored into tasteful funeral attire. Nose rings had been taken out, and Mohawks were combed over and gelled flat for the ceremony. Some of the kids I'd remembered didn't look like kids anymore. They'd gotten chubby, or cut their long hair, or had bags under their eyes, like they'd aged ten years in a little over one. A couple of girls I'd remembered in dog collars and fishnet gloves were now wearing sensible, knee-length skirts, sobbing over the tiny babies they held in their arms.

By the time the casket was lowered into the ground, we were all soaking wet, two hundred people beneath a slate-gray sky, looking like drowned rats. The ones who'd retained their goth/ punk aesthetic post–high school looked especially pathetic, streaks of black tears and dripping hair dye in the rain, like those clammy kids in the crosswalk I'd seen years earlier. We paced through the mud toward the tent to pay our respects and greet the family. I got in line and made my way forward, wanting to be out of the rain and under the tent but not looking forward to hugging Ruth, not like this. As I got closer to her I started to think about all the things I wanted to say. I wanted to tell her how much I loved her son, how he saved me from being completely alone, how the times she'd let me into her home were so special to me. She was my summer mom.

I nodded to Max's sisters, whose faces looked gray and hard, like stones. Ruth looked exhausted too, but she was managing to put on a smile as each kid broke into tears and hugged her. She comforted each one of them, stuck in the role of mom even at her own son's funeral.

I told myself I wasn't going to break down or freak out. I was going to be strong and mature. I was going to say something substantial and honest that was meaningful and true. As I faced her and smiled, she tilted her head to the side, her bottom lip quivering a bit. I threw my arms around her and we held each other for a moment.

"Hi, David," she whispered, rubbing my back.

"Hi, Ruth. I'm sorry, I . . ." I stammered, suddenly at a loss for words. I always managed to say so much in the moments when I didn't mean to, but now I was coming up dry when it mattered.

"You, uh . . ." I stuttered, "you smell so good."

That was what I said to her before she started to cry on my shoulder.

You smell good.

We held each other for another moment, before the outside world around us interrupted our embrace. A line of a hundred people was waiting behind me. Ruth had to do this another hundred times, hopefully with people who could muster something more meaningful than complimenting her perfume.

"Thank you," she said, taking my hands.

"Sorry," I stammered. "I'm sorry, Ruth. I'm sorry . . ."

"I know," she said, smiling and patting my cheek.

I walked through the mud back to my car, where I sat in the driver's seat and watched people leave the cemetery. Sean noticed me from the driver's seat of his brown truck and nodded solemnly, a gesture that, coming from him, felt like a tearful embrace. An hour later everyone had left and a small crew of men arrived to shovel dirt into the hole on top of Max's coffin. By the time they finished and left with the tent, it was a full-on rainstorm outside. I got out of my car and walked back across the field to Max's grave, which now looked like a work site. Orange tape and wooden pegs in the ground surrounded the area. A few two-by-two-foot flats of soiled grass sat stacked in a small wheelbarrow beside two shovels that stuck up from the ground. Max was down there, somewhere underneath a small hill of mud. Alone.

"I'm sorry," I said, and finally had the opportunity to put my feelings into words.

Fifteen minutes later I was driving down I-35, not knowing where to go. I drove around New Braunfels, past the places Max and had I spent time together, all of which felt empty and transformed without him. I drove to Seguin past the Primitive Baptist cemetery, thinking of all the stupid poetry I'd written there. I stared past the flower box into the window of our little country house, at my mother washing dishes, and knew I couldn't go inside. So I drove to San Antonio.

I pulled up at Greg's house and walked halfway up the sidewalk before I noticed the silence. There were no twinkling chimes to welcome me up to the front door. Behind me I noticed a FOR SALE sign sticking out of the grass. I walked behind the house to the office window, which had always had a broken lock. Inside the house was nothing. The electricity had been turned off. It felt like a tomb. I illuminated my way through with a Bic lighter. Absentmindedly I called Greg's name, as if he would pop out from the kitchen in a Morrissey shirt with a tray of defrosted egg-roll bites. I walked down the corridor to his room, which, of course, was empty. I stayed in the room and smoked for a while, lying in different spots on the floor where I approximated that my twin bed had been.

And then I drove, and drove, and drove . . .

Sylvia was surprised to see me. I was surprised that her phone number was listed, let alone still connected. She answered the door in a long Betty Boop T-shirt and jeans. Her brown hair was pulled back under a pastel headband. She had almost no makeup on. She looked prettier than I'd ever seen her. She welcomed me into her apartment, which was, strangely, in the same complex where I'd lived with my father.

"Girl, I always loved this complex," she said, giving me a kiss on the cheek. "Reminds me of good times."

Walking into the living room, I was greeted by a motley crew of small animals.

"Meet my children," she grinned, pointing at each of the four dogs and cats as she listed their names. She poured me a glass of water and caught me up on the last year and a half of her life.

"Well, Minerva, I *was* doin' phone sex for a while but this creep kept callin', begging me to make him jerk off with chunky peanut butter. Ooh! That bitch would scream!" she sighed, lighting a cigarette off the stove. "So now I just do telemarketing. Which is a different kind of phone-torture."

"What are all those?" I asked, noticing that her refrigerator was covered in magnets and calendars for PETA and the ASPCA.

"Oh girl, I'm a vegetarian now," she said with a smirk. "Sorry if I ruined you on burgers."

Around her apartment I noticed odd details: things that suggested responsibility. In the kitchen hung a big marked-up calendar. By the front door was a wall-mounted key-ring holder. In the hallway there was a little slotted shelf that said MAIL on it. Even the simple clock hanging by her patio door suggested something too pedestrian. Since when did Sylvia care about time? How could Sylvia possibly have anywhere to go?

We sat down on the couch and paused the *Friends* DVD she had been watching.

"You watch *Friends*?" I asked, surprised that she watched such a mainstream show.

"Girl, I just love me some Ross. I could eat that Jew's cookies!" she snickered, exhaling an endless plume of smoke. The idea of Sylvia liking a bumbling, uptight Jewish professional seemed out of sync with her usual tatted-up, angry poet type.

"Do you have a roommate, Sylvia?"

"Roommate?" she exclaimed. "Hell no, bitch. I'm a grown-ass woman with my own jobby-job, thank you very much."

I looked around her apartment, and it was indeed her own: full of her own thrift-store furniture and stacks of fashion magazines and framed photos of friends. Her animals napped on every surface as we talked about Greg and Raven and Ray-Ray and the Bonham Exchange, remembering insane nights out, filling in the drug-induced blanks for each other as we went along.

"Guess what, Sylvia? I'm going to college in San Marcos now."

"Bitch! College? That's so great," she said, bouncing up and down on the couch like I'd just told her an eight ball was on the way. "Your mom must be so proud!"

"You know her. She's over the fucking moon."

"Oh, I miss your mama. But truth be told, she is a talker. Dear Lord, she could keep a bitch on the phone for hours! I had to fake a kitchen fire once just to hang up."

I chuckled to myself at how incredulous my mother would be.

"So you like your job?" I asked.

"Hell no! I'm gonna save up my money, buy some real nice

clothes, and get an internship working for a magazine in New York City. They won't pay shit, but I can shack up with a bunch of weirdos in the ass end of Brooklyn. I don't care if my bathtub's in the motherfuckin' kitchen. I can douche and boil ramen at the same time!" she snickered.

"Do you have a boyfriend?"

"No, ma'am. Know why? 'Cause ain't no man good enough! I locked up the goodies until I get to the Big Apple. Cla-clink!" she cackled, miming a chastity belt locking between her legs and throwing the invisible key over her shoulder. "What about you, Minerva?"

"No. Um, I'm not seeing anyone."

"Oh, stick-in-the-mud, are you still livin' like a nun? What about that big old skinhead, girl? Have you knocked boots with Mr. Clean or what?"

I wanted to tell her where I'd just come from. But nothing came out.

"Hey, you," she said, touching my hand, "what's wrong?"

"Well," I paused, worried that once I started, I wouldn't be able to stop. "A week ago, Max was driving alone at night along the highway. They're not sure what happened, but . . . He lost control of the car and flipped it. It was late, so he didn't hit any other cars, but he crashed upside down in the emergency lane. They think . . . They think he hung upside down like that for a while, suspended by the seatbelt. Maybe he was unconscious for part of it, maybe not. He eventually freed himself and barged the door open, but . . ."

"It's okay," Sylvia said, gripping my hand tighter as the tears came.

"But he fell out of the car just as another car was passing and it . . . hit him. They say he died instantly, that he didn't feel any pain. But I don't know how long he was in there. How long was he alone and conscious? I keep thinking about how scared he must have been, waking up like that. And was his body hurt? Was something broken or cut before that? Was he bleeding? Did he call out for someone? Was he scared?"

I covered my face in my hands and kept talking, my mouth like a gaping wound now, pouring everything out in a way I wanted to stop but couldn't.

"I was just at the funeral surrounded by all these people, all his friends. Some of them were people I used to know. I thought it would make me feel better, but without him there I felt like . . . no one. Like I didn't know any of those people. And I thought when I saw them or hugged his mom that I would . . . feel something. Like I would feel . . . him. Like a presence or a spirit or something."

The sounds of the words I was saying reverberated back at me and pushed out more tears and spit and mucus. I felt messy and ugly and full of imperfections. I wanted to shut up, to be mute, to simply disappear. But I couldn't.

"I started to panic because I knew Max really wasn't there. So I went to his grave later and said all this stuff to him. Stuff I'd meant to say but was either too scared or lazy or dumb to have said before. And I waited, thinking he would . . . But . . . I couldn't . . . I couldn't feel him, Sylvia. You know? I had not even just a little sense that he was there, because he's gone. Not gone the way you've been gone or Greg is gone, but really gone. I'd just seen him a few months ago and we were going to be friends. But our classes were on different days and I met other new people and he was dating this nice girl and we . . . We just . . ."

I looked through my fingers at the coffee table, noticing the interlocking rings of drinking-glass stains in the wood.

"Me and him . . . We were gonna be friends again."

The silence between us was cut by a sound, a bubbly, rumbling hum. I uncovered my face and looked at Sylvia, who was holding, as if it had materialized from thin air, the biggest water bong I'd ever seen. It was two feet long and flesh-colored, streaked with small pink lines. She held it by its base, a pair of darkened lavender orbs full of percolating water. She drew her lips away from the dark-pink, spherical mouthpiece atop the chamber shaft.

Sylvia was smoking weed from the hollow mold of a two-foot-long, erect penis.

"Bitch, that is the saddest shit I ever heard," she sobbed, blowing out a massive cloud of smoke as I looked on, shocked out of my state by her magically appearing dong-bong.

"What?" she asked, seeing the appalled expression on my face.

"What the fuck is that?"

"Oh. It's just a little purple haze," she said, handing me the huge dick. I paused with it in my arms and shot her a look of concern, doubting the bowl's contents.

"Okay, Minerva," she blushed, "you got me. I put a little cat-nip in there too. Just tryin' somethin' new."

I put my lips on the bong and inhaled, letting the thick, warm funk fill my lungs and take me somewhere else.

"I missed you," she said. "And I'm sorry. About everything."

"Me too," I choked out, holding a giant cloud of smoke inside my chest.

"I'm glad you're here, David."

Sylvia let go of my hand and got up. I could feel the damp moisture on our palms as they grazed each other. I lit a cigarette as she walked across the living room and pressed play on the CD player, filling the apartment with the sound of a song. It was a song I knew and loved but couldn't name. In the glass of a frame across the room I caught my reflection, dressed in all black again, but for a different reason. Behind the glass is a photo. In it, most of my friends are on a dance floor, probably FX, but maybe not. Sylvia is there in a black smock throwing a shady look to Raven and Carla, who are wearing dog collars and sticking their tongues out while dry-humping each other. Hector is there in his torn blazer with the words "I am human and I need to be loved" scrawled across the lapel. Daphne is in the back, sipping from a plastic cup, looking bored and staring off with glowing red eyes. Jake is shirtless and covered in sweat, head back and eyes closed, fully surrendered to the music playing. Greg is in the foreground with his perfect bangs, reaching toward the lens. He's gesturing to whoever's taking the photo, his index finger wagging them toward him. His mouth is frozen midword, probably saying something like, "Come on! Come dance with me!"

The flash is unflattering; the harsh truth of the camera eye reveals every zit, pore, and smeared eyebrow. They're clumpy and drippy and torn, trying to come off world-weary and sexy but failing in the most charming way. Collectively, they think they're almost there, standing at the threshold of becoming who they're going to be for the rest of their lives, not knowing that they've, thankfully, just begun.

They're brash, flighty, messy kids. But in that frame beneath a pane of glass, they transcend all that. They're special, preserved, and perfect. I look at the picture and try to imagine having known anyone else, but I can't. Because when I look at the picture, all I can think is, *I am just like them.*

I pressed myself back into the couch, feeling the cool fabric of the upholstery against my arms and neck. I let out a long sigh and smiled as Sylvia turned from the stereo to look at me.

"What?" she asked, flashing me a smile I'd missed so much.

"Nothing," I said, "I'm just glad I'm here too."

Epilogue

.D., please," said Varla before taking my Texas driver's license in her huge, hairy-knuckled fingers. Varla Rose was a sensationally messy drag queen known less for her stage shows and more for her nasty attitude, which was generally served out the side of her half-frozen face. Tonight at the Bonham Exchange I'd be seeing her ill-reviewed show, which I'd heard entailed less actual dancing and more drunken leaning: against poles, chairs, and walls. I'd told my friends that if we were lucky, things would get physical. We might get to see her verbally degrade someone or snap a nail off in another diva's wig.

"That's pretty sad when a drag queen has to check IDs for *her own show*," whispered Shelly through her long, kinky red bangs.

"Thanks, peaches," slurred Varla, letting out a belch. As her left eye wandered in a different direction from her right, I had a feeling we'd be in for a great show.

"It's barely eleven and she's already walleyed," I whispered as we walked into the club. Shelly tilted back her head and laughed like a maniac, showing off the wide gap between her two front teeth.

"You could park a car in there," I chuckled, pointing at her gaping maw.

She smacked the back of my head and looked back to our friends. "Hurry up, fuckers!"

Behind us was Jeff, a tall philosophy major with prematurely salt-and-pepper hair. I knew him through Kim, the petite blonde beside him whom I'd met in my still-life photography class. I'd met Shelly during my sophomore year in college as an art major. Tonight I was taking us all to the Bonham Exchange, which I was entering legally for the first time as a twenty-one-year-old.

"Wait up," yelled Kim, running up in her thrift-store heels and baby-doll dress. "I need to fix your hair, Crabb," she said, reaching up to finesse the bleach-blond spikes of my Mohawk. "It's like a haystack or some shit!"

"Where's the bathroom?" Jeff asked, fanning himself in the club's crowded main hall. He looked at himself in a mirror and gasped, "Oh, girl. I need to pull my face together."

"Actually, I need to powder my nose," added Kim with a wink.

"It's right over there," I screamed over the distant thump of house music. "Meet us on the dance floor!"

Shelly and I moved down the wide, eighty-foot-long hallway of the old synagogue, squeezing through a mix of young- to middle-aged gay San Antonians in their Friday-night best. They fanned themselves with flyers and free downtown papers in the mid-July heat.

"These guys are so hot!" yelled Shelly, passing a gaggle of lean Hispanic men with perfectly shaped beards in fitted black tops. "I feel like a hippie schlub, David!"

"Shut up! You look beautiful!" I screamed back, catching our reflections as we passed a mirrored wall. Shelly was in purple leggings and a blue velveteen dress, each arm covered in a dozen chunky vintage bracelets. She wore her favorite beaded lip ring and a floppy brimmed hat atop wild auburn curls. I wore my favorite Smashing Pumpkins shirt under a too-small vest that was covered in band pins for Hole, Garbage, and the Pixies. My torn blue jeans and Converse high-tops were stained from semesters' worth of painting classes and photo-chemical mishaps.

The grungy, alt-rock nineties were in full swing. Any attraction I'd had to clean lines and grayscale was long gone. I was queer. I was an art major. And I was twenty-one.

"This is amazing!" Shelly screamed, looking up at the massive disco ball hanging from the three-story vaulted ceiling.

It was as amazing as I'd remembered it being three years earlier, the last time I'd snuck in. It was nice to be back, and I was relieved that not much had changed. I ordered drink upon drink, proudly flashing the glow-in-the-dark stamp on my left hand. At midnight on the patio I grabbed Kim's hand and dragged her around the side of the building.

"Where are you fucking taking me, Crabb?" she demanded, covering her nose from the stench of the alley's dumpsters.

"It's still there!" I exclaimed, slurring a bit.

"Are you high?" she laughed as I pushed on the loose two-by-four. "It's a hole in a fence!"

"Yeah," I smiled, realizing I was far too drunk to explain what that hole meant to me.

Everywhere on the dance floor I noticed a certain type of boy: boys with badly copied stamps smeared on their hands; boys hanging on the darker edge of the dance floor for fear that the pulsing lights would reveal their peach fuzz and acne; boys on the arms of their loud, brassy girlfriends, hiding in plain sight with cohorts they call their brothers who they're actually dying to kiss; boys who owed the first genuinely dazzling night of their lives to a hole in a fence.

By 2 a.m. I'd lost Kim and Jeff to some other part of the club. Shelly had met a short, pixie-haired lesbian named Sky, whom she'd decided to flirt with in the basement. Although Shelly wasn't gay, she *was* a liberal-arts major who listened to a lot of Sarah McLachlan. Eventually Shelly and Sky started making out at the bar, violently flicking their tongue piercings together as a remix of Madonna's "Don't Cry for Me, Argentina" blared through the sound system.

I took my cue and left to walk around alone, drunkenly trying to recall the spots where I'd gotten sick from tequila or tipped my first stripper or felt the explosion of a thousand supernovas in my chest as a tab of acid kicked in.

In the small ground-floor bar I sat alone and thought about the only night I'd come here with Max. I remembered sitting in exactly the same spot, with Greg and Sylvia laughing on either side of me about nothing I could recall. I wasn't listening to them because I was staring at Max, twenty feet away, cornered by two older queens who were ogling him like a piece of meat, their eyes wandering up and down his figure. It was nice to be the one checking in on Max for a change, and charming to watch him suffer their questions so politely. As the two men cackled about something and gave each other a high five, Max looked at me with those squinty Buddha eyes and shrugged with the sweetest smile I'd ever seen, a giant sun patiently shining light on all the tiny moons drawn into his orbit. Max was simply too full of love not to give it to anyone who asked, if only for a moment; even to a couple of drunk queens three times his age trying to get into his pants. I remembered that moment as he looked at me and how I knew, in some ineffable way, that love as strong as this wasn't about reciprocity. The gift wasn't in having it returned, but in feeling it at all, if only for one incredible summer.

I got up from the bar and moved through the main hall, reaching the crowded grand staircase, an eight-foot-wide walkway that led to the upstairs ballroom. I squeezed myself onto the first step of the staircase, which was as dense as a New York City subway entrance at rush hour.

"Move it, girl!" a platinum-headed man in front of me yelled to a group of stationary boys on the landing above. "You can't stand there, assholes!"

I slowly moved up another two stairs as more bodies piled up at my back.

"Sorry," said a voice behind me as I tripped forward.

"Watch it," I began, prepared to tell off the asshole at my heels. Over my shoulder was a tall boy about my age with short, brown hair, wearing chunky black glasses and a red T-shirt.

"Oh," I stammered, taken aback by the fact that even on the stair behind me, he was still a bit taller. "It's okay."

"There's just so many people and—"

"Watch yourself, motherfucker!" someone ahead interrupted. I stood on my tiptoes to see a ponytailed twink being yelled at by a very inebriated Varla Rose, her left eye now fully disengaged from her right.

"You think you know glamour, bitch?!" Varla raged, teetering on her heels while brandishing a beer bottle over her head.

Two security guards rushed past me just as they began to fight. As they were dragged down the staircase, I looked over my shoulder.

"Looks like Varla's show probably won't . . ." but the boy in chunky glasses was gone.

On the landing, things got tighter as a horde of shirtless boys came down the stairs, their cluster too wide to accommodate for the traffic on the right side of the staircase.

"David!" I heard someone yell in the crowd. I turned as the voice yelled my name again from somewhere behind me. I looked down and saw him, four bodies away. He was shirtless and glistening, with a tribal tattoo across his six-pack abs. He was adorned with neon glow-stick necklaces and tiny silver hoops in each ear.

"Greg!" I screamed, trying to turn myself around on the staircase.

"David! Oh my God!" he beamed, his hair still perfectly coiffed even when doused in twenty remixes' worth of nightclub sweat.

"Greg, I'm stuck," I yelled as the flow of people moved me farther up the stairs.

"Come dance!" Greg screamed, pointing downstairs as a posse of boys nudged him away.

"I said I'm stuck!" I screamed as the crowd took me higher. "I'll find you in a bit!"

"What?" he yelled again. All I could do was laugh as a sudden upward thrust pushed me farther up the staircase. I was trapped in the current, like a salmon during spawning season.

"I miss you!" I shouted.

"What?" Greg yelled, smiling as he begin to dissolve into the flock.

"I'll find you!" I screamed, gripping the banister to maintain my balance. "Just go dance!"

"What are you saying?" he yelled, only a sliver of his face visible through the crowd.

"I love you! Now go . . ."

And then he was gone, absorbed into the throng of bodies and onto the dance floor, where I'd imagined him for years.

It took me another few minutes to get to the third floor, a process made easier by simply surrendering to the gravitational pull around me. Upstairs I chugged a pint of water at the near-empty bar, feeling the muffled beat of the dance floor below vibrating in my feet. Above that thudding bass I heard a new sound. A familiar song emanated from the speakers at the end of the bar. Digital flutes and wah-wah guitars built to a crescendo as a glittering harp opened the sonic doors to a new world. As the Pet Shop Boys' "Being Boring" played I remembered that night four years ago when the idea that happiness was an option still scared the hell out of me; when the possibility of living and loving fully was still bound to my fears of isolation, rejection, and death. I pictured myself alone in that little room feeling like I'd disappointed my family and lost all my friends. Quietly, I hummed along to the lyrics in the second half of the song.

> *I never dreamt that I would get to be*
> *The creature that I always meant to be*
> *But I thought in spite of dreams*
> *You'd be sitting somewhere here with me.*

I looked out the small, round attic window onto downtown San Antonio, a truly beautiful city at night. In the dark, its taco stands and pickup trucks and shopping malls all disappeared. It looked like a galaxy, a beautiful cosmos of planets, stars, and constellations thousands of miles away.

This could be any city, I thought, letting that feeling of anonymity wrap its arms around me like an old friend. And for a moment, the solitude was nice.

"We almost died on those stairs, huh?"

I turned from the window to see the red-shirted boy from the staircase standing above me.

"Um, yeah," I answered as he sat down. He leaned forward and smiled, his eyes twinkling with reflections of the city out the window behind me.

"I'm Jack," he said, extending his hand. I slipped my fingers around his, which somehow felt twenty degrees warmer than mine. A twinge of anxiety descended over me as we shook hands, holding on to each other a bit longer than two strangers really should. My brain was fumbling for the right words, and in that manic stillness I needed to escape. I wanted to become invisible, for just long enough to slip away from this handsome boy in black glasses. I wished, for just a moment, to shroud myself in my old uniform: a pair of pleated khakis and white sneakers with a simple button-down. But there I was in my moth-eaten T-shirt and torn jeans, smelling of patchouli, with studs in each ear, anything but invisible.

I took a deep breath and sighed, feeling the bass from the dance floor below in my bones.

As Jack held on to my hand, I was overcome with that feeling you get when you meet someone who seems familiar and you just know you're going to be good friends.

"Hi," I answered. "My name's David."

Thanks to:

andy Sharp, Brian Barnhart, Marc Palmieri, and everyone at Axis Theatre Company, where the solo show this book is based on was first produced. Your support and friendship made this possible. You're like a family to me and our adventures together are some of my favorite memories. The term "lifesaver" gets thrown around a lot, but when I say you saved my life, I literally mean it. Thank you so much.

My agent, Alex Glass, who opened a door I never even knew I wanted to step through. As often as you've made me feel proud of my work, it bears noting how constantly impressed I am by *you*. You are my literary superhero. Here is *not* where the story ends.

My editor, Laura Brown, who's encouraged and enriched my work with thoughtful feedback, kind words, and delicious cookies. Now that this is done, can we smear on black mascara and go dancing somewhere in a fog machine together?

The indispensable Michael Ferrante, whose constructive notes and advice-filled emails kept me trucking through parts of this process I wasn't sure I could finish. I'm so happy to call you my friend, free lunches or not.

My copy editor, Julie Hersh, who has come to love Erasure & the Pet Shop Boys entirely through my copyedit replies. Thanks for your thoughtful comments and much-needed LOLs.

Everyone at Harper Perennial, who have been so supportive and genuinely interested in this project. I'm a lucky guy to have you all in my corner.

To my friends who've taken the time to read my writing, especially Diana Spechler, Julia Weideman, and Kerri Doherty. I'm honored to have friends as talented as you, let alone ones that return my needy emails and phone calls with such thoughtful feedback.

Thanks to Britt Genelin, Kelly Cox, Lucas Longacre, and Jacob Cox, not only for your amazing friendship, but for all your assistance in helping me launch *Bad Kid The Show*. I am consistently amazed by your wit, vision, and ability to cope with my mood swings.

I'm fortunate to have been one-half of some pretty amazing duos in my time. So much love to the abundantly talented Abby Savage, Seth DeCroce, Margo Passalaqua, and Cammi Climaco. "I learned by watching YOU!"

Every storyteller I've ever heard, taught, booked, hosted, interviewed, or received pointers from. I'm lucky to be a part such an amazing community. Thanks for constantly reminding me what a better place the world could be if everyone shared their stories.

To all my wonderful teachers: Kevin Allison, Michelle Walson, Julie Brister, Sara Barron, Jeanie Massie, Carl Toth, and especially Eric Weller, who reminded me that there was another world out there, and then pushed me into it.

The Moth, who provide me and so many others a platform to tell our stories. The world would be a darker place without your work in it. Thanks for giving me and so many others a microphone and a stage. I doubt this book would exist without your support and kindness.

My Jackie, who's my best friend and favorite scene partner. You're my sunshine when there isn't any. I would be a paler, sadder, even *more* agitated version of myself without you. Thanks for loving me when I felt unlovable.

To Charlie, even though you can't read and have paws for hands, I want to thank you for laying in my lap during significant portions of this writing process. I think you'll enjoy laying on this book as well.

The Perry's, thanking you after a pet seems ridiculous. (Then again, you know more than anyone how insane we are about that dog.) I'm so lucky to be a part of your family. Thanks for all your love, warmth, and apple cake. Now forget you read *any* of this.

My step-siblings. A lot of kids wouldn't have been so cool with a sixteen-year-old weirdo suddenly living in their home. Thanks for gracefully accepting me into your lives and letting me blast spooky music at all hours.

To Josh Matthews. What can I say? Who knew when we started building a little solo show that it would connect with so many people? Without your direction I would've never had the drive and focus to make it happen. Thanks for fifteen years of laughter, insight, friendship, and dialect practice. Like, seriously? Do we EVER speak to each other in our actual voices? Halal, buddy.

Thanks to all the great musicians whose inspirational tunes have indelibly colored the prose in this book. The Smiths, Morrissey, The Cure, Depeche Mode, Joy Division, New Order, NIN, Erasure, Yaz, Siouxsie, The The, The Sundays, The Drums, and Pet Shop Boys. Thanks for holding the torch in the corner of my room and making sure I was never alone.

To "Greg" and all the other bad kids, especially Scott, Steve, Jim, and Molly. I love you even more than I did when we were sixteen. There aren't words to express how overjoyed it makes me to see you all so happy. Then again, to quote my father, "I'm just glad they're alive at all!"

To my father, mother, and stepfather: I'm sorry for putting you through all that mess, but so thankful you put the lockdown on me when the time came. I probably yelled a lot of stuff to the contrary at seventenn, but I only meant a small fraction of it. And yes, I should call more. I know. I love you and am thankful every day to have been raised by such incredibly funny, complex, thoughtful people.

About the Author

David Crabb is a writer, performer, teacher, and story-teller. He lives in Brooklyn with his partner and their Jack Russell/Chihuahua mix Charlie, the most Instagrammed dog in the tristate area. David is a *Moth* StorySLAM host and teaches storytelling across the country. His solo show *Bad Kid* was named a *New York Times Critics'* Pick. He probably loves Morrissey more than you do.